Commodity Culture in Dickens's
Household Words
The Social Life of Goods

CATHERINE WATERS
University of New England, Australia

LONDON AND NEW YORK

First published 2008 by Ashgate Publishing

2 Park Square, Milton Park, Abingdon, Oxfordshire OX14 4RN
52 Vanderbilt Avenue, New York, NY 10017

Routledge is an imprint of the Taylor & Francis Group, an informa business

First issued in paperback 2019

Copyright © Catherine Waters 2008

All rights reserved. No part of this book may be reprinted or reproduced or utilised in any form or by any electronic, mechanical, or other means, now known or hereafter invented, including photocopying and recording, or in any information storage or retrieval system, without permission in writing from the publishers.

Notice:
Product or corporate names may be trademarks or registered trademarks, and are used only for identification and explanation without intent to infringe.

Catherine Waters has asserted her moral right under the Copyright, Designs and Patents Act, 1988, to be identified as the author of this work.

British Library Cataloguing in Publication Data
Waters, Catherine
Commodity culture in Dickens's Household words : the social life of goods. – (The nineteenth century series)
　1. Household words 2. Commercial products – Great Britain – History – 19th century
　I. Title
　052

Library of Congress Cataloging-in-Publication Data
Waters, Catherine.
Commodity culture in Dickens's Household words : the social life of goods / by Catherine Waters.
　p. cm. — (The nineteenth century series)
Includes bibliographical references.
ISBN-13: 978-0-7546-5578-7 (hbk)
　1. Household words. 2. Commercial products—Great Britain—History—19th century.
I. Title.

PN5130.H6W66 2008
052—dc22
　　　　　　　　　　　　　　　　　　　　　　　　　　　　　　　2007052224

ISBN 978-0-7546-5578-7 (hbk)
ISBN 978-0-367-88791-9 (pbk)

COMMODITY CULTURE IN DICKENS'S
HOUSEHOLD WORDS

For Mary and in memory of Ron

Contents

General Editors' Preface		*vi*
Acknowledgements		*vii*
1	Introduction	1
2	Advertising Fictions	19
3	The Genuine Article, the Sham, and the Problem of Authenticity	39
4	'The Key of the Street'	65
5	'Men Made by Machinery'	83
6	Worldly Goods	101
7	'Trading in Death'	125
8	'Fashion in Undress'	141
Bibliography		*157*
Index		*175*

The Nineteenth Century Series
General Editors' Preface

The aim of the series is to reflect, develop and extend the great burgeoning of interest in the nineteenth century that has been an inevitable feature of recent years, as that former epoch has come more sharply into focus as a locus for our understanding not only of the past but of the contours of our modernity. It centres primarily upon major authors and subjects within Romantic and Victorian literature. It also includes studies of other British writers and issues, where these are matters of current debate: for example, biography and autobiography, journalism, periodical literature, travel writing, book production, gender, non-canonical writing. We are dedicated principally to publishing original monographs and symposia; our policy is to embrace a broad scope in chronology, approach and range of concern, and both to recognize and cut innovatively across such parameters as those suggested by the designations 'Romantic' and 'Victorian.' We welcome new ideas and theories, while valuing traditional scholarship. It is hoped that the world which predates yet so forcibly predicts and engages our own will emerge in parts, in the wider sweep, and in the lively streams of disputation and change that are so manifest an aspect of its intellectual, artistic and social landscape.

Vincent Newey
Joanne Shattock
University of Leicester

Acknowledgements

My deepest thanks go to Robert Dingley for his acute readings of drafts of almost all the chapters presented here. His wealth of knowledge about the Victorians has been a constant source of insight and inspiration for me. I am also grateful to other colleagues and friends who have provided assistance or encouragement at various stages throughout, particularly Margaret Harris, Dugald Williamson, Judy McKenzie, Fred D'Agostino and members of 'the walking-group.' Final thanks go as ever to my family for their loving support.

Earlier versions of Chapter 7 and Chapter 8 appeared in *Victorian Periodicals Review* and the *Journal of Victorian Culture* respectively; I wish to thank the editors for permission to reprint them here.

Chapter 1

Introduction

On 1 June 1850, two months after the appearance of its first number, *Household Words* published an article by its sub-editor, W.H. Wills, marvelling at the growing 'Appetite for News.'[1] Wills begins by describing the eagerness with which the 'city clerk emerging through folding doors from bed to sitting-room, though thirsting for tea, and hungering for toast, darts upon that morning's journal,' while '[e]xactly at the same hour, his master, the M.P., crosses the hall of his mansion,' enters the breakfast-parlour and 'fixes his eye on the fender, where he knows his favourite damp sheet will be hung up to dry.' Elsewhere, in like fashion, the 'oppressed farmer' cannot 'handle the massive spoon for his first sip out of his sèvres cup till he has read of ruin in the "Herald" or "Standard,"' and the 'financial reformer' cannot 'know breakfast-table happiness till he has digested the "Daily News," or skimmed the "Express."'[2] Wills's description of these avid journal readers captures the 'mass ceremony' of simultaneous consumption identified by Benedict Anderson as a key factor forming the imagined community, across a range of social classes, that is the hallmark of modern national identity.[3] The extent of the nation's immense appetite for news can be gauged, Wills writes, not only in the circulation figures suggested by the number of 'newspaper stamps which were issued in 1848 (the latest year of which a return has been made),' but in the 'printed surface' sent forth by the press, which amounted 'in twelve months to 349,308,000 superficial feet' in daily papers alone: 'If to these are added all the papers printed weekly and fortnightly in London and the provinces, the whole amounts to 1,446,150,000 square feet of printed surface, which was, in 1849, placed before the comprehensive vision of John Bull.'[4] Not content with the abstract economic measure provided by the stamp tax, Wills's mind-boggling statistics regarding the material substance of the periodical press emphasize its identity as a thing, as well as a commodity. They illustrate the peculiar focus upon matter, and its making into consumable objects, that characterizes *Household Words*'s engagement with mid-Victorian commodity culture.

Founded and 'Conducted' by Dickens from 1 March 1850 to 28 May 1859, *Household Words* was a weekly miscellany, costing twopence, which aimed to 'instruct' and 'entertain' its middle-class readers, as well as helping 'in the discussion

---

1 [W.H. Wills], 'The Appetite for News,' *Household Words*, 1 June 1850, 1: 238–40.
2 Ibid.: 238–9.
3 Benedict Anderson, *Imagined Communities: Reflections on the Origin and Spread of Nationalism*, Revised ed. (London: Verso, 1991), 35.
4 [Wills], 'The Appetite for News,' 239.

of the most important social questions of the time.'[5] The choice of the title 'Conductor' is singular. While the OED records two examples of its use for the management of a journal—in 1799 and 1843—both of these usages are plural, and Dickens's choice of this term when 'Editor' might more automatically suggest itself indicates not only his strong hand in the editorial selection process, but his influence upon the writing of his contributors, especially in relation to the journal's non-fiction prose. He plays upon the artistic role of a music conductor: 'the director of an orchestra or chorus, who indicates to the performers the rhythm, expression etc. of the music by motions of a baton or the hands' (OED 6.). According to Percy Fitzgerald, the youngest amongst the journal's established group of contributors, '"Conducting" was the fitting word, for, like the manager of a theatre, [Dickens] had to find and direct suitable men and characters, study his public, play upon their feelings, follow and divine their humours, amuse and divert by the agency of others, and, when that failed him, by his own.'[6] In keeping with mid-century periodical convention, contributions were generally unsigned; but no effort was made to keep authorship secret and, as a result of the invaluable work of Anne Lohrli on the *Household Words* Office Book (to which this study is enormously indebted), most contributors have been identified.

Dickens positioned his new venture in the periodical market carefully, employing a novel combination of cheapness of form and price with respectability of content. As he had written to Forster of his plans as early as 1846, 'it should be something with a marked and distinctive and obvious difference, in its design, from any other existing periodical.'[7] Distinguishing *Household Words* from the villainous fare of the penny bloods on the one hand, and such 'cast iron and utilitarian' competitors as *Chambers's Edinburgh Journal*[8] on the other, he aimed to raise the quality of the cheap press with his serialization of original fiction, poetry and informational articles on a wide range of topics. As Fitzgerald later observed, '[i]t is only when contrasting *Household Words* with its penny or three-halfpenny contemporaries that we see at once what a new and original thing it was'[9]; for as well as the high literary quality of its fiction—contributed by some of the most celebrated authors of the day—the journal was most significantly distinguished by its imaginative non-fiction prose, which blurred the boundary between journalism and literature with cultural effects that have yet to be properly recognized, as we shall see.

Published in the decade of the Great Exhibition of 1851, *Household Words* appeared at a key moment in the emergence of commodity culture in Victorian England. As Thomas Richards, Andrew Miller and others have argued, the Great

---

5   Quoted in Anne Lohrli, *'Household Words' A Weekly Journal 1850–1859 Conducted by Charles Dickens, Table of Contents, List of Contributors and Their Contributions Based on The "Household Words" Office Book* (Toronto: University of Toronto Press, 1973), 4.

6   Percy Fitzgerald, *Memories of Charles Dickens.* (Bristol: J.W. Arrowsmith, 1913), 105.

7   John Forster, *The Life of Charles Dickens*, ed. A.J. Hoppé, 2 vols. (1872–74; London: Dent, 1969), 1: 443n.

8   Letter to Mrs S.C. Hall, 23 April 1844, in Madeline House, Graham Storey, and Kathleen Tillotson, eds., *The Letters of Charles Dickens*, 12 vols. (Oxford: Clarendon Press, 1965–2002), 4: 110.

9   Fitzgerald, *Memories of Charles Dickens*, 127.

Exhibition marked a watershed in the development of a specifically capitalist form of representation centring upon the spectacle of the commodity.[10] It was, says Richards, 'the first outburst of the phantasmagoria of commodity culture. It inaugurated a way of seeing things that marked indelibly the cultural and commercial life of Victorian England.'[11] While the 'birth of consumer society' has been located by historians Neil McKendrick, John Brewer and J.H. Plumb in eighteenth-century Britain and its evidence of 'a convulsion of getting and spending,'[12] these processes were also part of an ongoing development to which new mass production techniques, and changes in retail practices and advertising, contributed as the capitalist economy matured. By the middle of the nineteenth century, ordinary men and women were experiencing the pleasures and pains of consumer choice on a scale hitherto unknown. The widening of this new class of potential purchasers of non-essential goods is one of the features that distinguishes commodity culture in mid-Victorian Britain from its eighteenth-century origins. As Thad Logan argues, the bourgeois home became crowded with newly mass-produced objects that were 'not primarily functional,' but rather participated 'in a decorative semiotic economy.'[13] What you owned said something not only about your disposable income, but about who you were, as the possibility of 'communicating status or other forms of social relationship through commodities was no longer restricted to the upper classes.'[14]

Dickens's fictional interest in the objectification and commodification of subjects, and his animation of objects which seem, in his novels, to take on a life of their own, have long been recognized by critics. In her influential analysis of the English novel's form and function in 1953, Dorothy Van Ghent identified Dickens's characteristic 'transposition of attributes'—between, for example, Mrs Joe and her apron stuck all over with pins, or Mr Jaggers and his huge forefinger—as symptomatic of a world in which 'the qualities of things and people were reversed': 'people were becoming things, and things ... were becoming more important than people.'[15] Critics since have often noted Dickens's use of clothing, appurtenances, gestures, or verbal tics to establish character, and his preoccupation with animism, anthropomorphism, and reification as part of this process. J. Hillis Miller, for example, argues that the 'metonymic reciprocity between a person and his surroundings, his clothes, furniture, house, and so on, is the basis for the metaphorical substitutions

---

10 Andrew Miller, *Novels Behind Glass: Commodity Culture and Victorian Narrative* (Cambridge: Cambridge University Press, 1995), Thomas Richards, *The Commodity Culture of Victorian England: Advertising and Spectacle 1851–1914* (Stanford: Stanford University Press, 1990). See also Louise Purbrick, ed., *The Great Exhibition of 1851: New Interdisciplinary Essays* (Manchester: Manchester University Press, 2001).

11 Richards, *The Commodity Culture of Victorian England*, 18.

12 Neil McKendrick, 'The Consumer Revolution of Eighteenth-Century England,' in *The Birth of a Consumer Society: The Commercialization of Eighteenth-Century England*, ed. Neil McKendrick, John Brewer, and J.H. Plumb (London: Europa, 1982), 9.

13 Thad Logan, *The Victorian Parlour: A Cultural Study* (Cambridge: Cambridge University Press, 2001), 26.

14 Ibid., 92.

15 Dorothy Van Ghent, *The English Novel: Form and Function* (New York: Harper and Row, 1961; reprint, 1953), 128–9.

so frequent in Dickens's fiction.'[16] Herbert Sussman and Gerhard Joseph argue for the widespread acceptance 'that an interchange between animate human subject and inanimate object characterizes his world view.'[17] But as Murray Roston has shown, the development of commodity culture at mid-century may provide a more specific context for examining the interest of Dickens and his contemporaries in the changing relationship between people and things.[18] In *Capital*, Marx famously describes the process of reification by which commodities become 'social things': the commodity's fetishization consists in the process of mystification by which the social character of men's labour appears to them as a relation between the products of their labour. Here we see an inversion in the 'natural' relation between people and things, as objects acquire a life of their own and come to dominate those who produce them. As Roston has argued, the principle of demonic animism in Dickens's fiction can be related to the inception of a commodity culture dependent upon the taste of the consumer rather than the producer: 'It is, I suggest, that new quality of the age which Dickens grasped so shrewdly and incorporated into his fiction as a distinctive literary mode, seeing within the proprietary selection of goods a method of differentiating character.'[19] Thus, Dickens employs the possessions, homes, and habiliments of his characters 'as animated external emblems of their inner being.'[20]

The critical recognition of Dickens's peculiar treatment of subject-object relations in his fiction has fed into a growing interest in Victorian material culture over the last decade or so.[21] These studies have focussed upon the nineteenth-century novel and the welter of consumer goods through which its effects of realism are generated. In the most recent of them, Elaine Freedgood presents a compelling argument for the existence of 'thing culture,' a form of object relations that preceded commodity culture and was not necessarily characterized by the processes of abstraction, alienation and spectacularization associated with the commodity form.[22] Freedgood distinguishes between metaphoric and metonymic modes of reading the things of the Victorian novel in order to restore attention to their materiality, and to uncover the fugitive meanings hidden within such hitherto unnoticed objects as calico curtains in *Mary Barton*, or 'Negro head' tobacco in *Great Expectations*. Arguing against the critical tendency to 'conflate things and commodities,'[23] she works to

---

16 J. Hillis Miller, 'The Fiction of Realism: *Sketches by Boz, Oliver Twist*, and Cruikshank's Illustrations,' in *Dickens Centennial Essays*, ed. Ada Nisbet and Blake Nevius (Berkeley: University of California Press, 1971), 97.

17 Herbert Sussman and Gerhard Joseph, 'Prefiguring the Posthuman: Dickens and Prosthesis,' *Victorian Literature and Culture* 32 (2004): 617.

18 Murray Roston, *Victorian Contexts: Literature and the Visual Arts* (New York: New York University Press, 1996).

19 Ibid., 77.

20 Ibid., 83.

21 See, in addition to Miller (cited above), Elaine Freedgood, *The Ideas in Things: Fugitive Meaning in the Victorian Novel* (Chicago: University of Chicago Press, 2006), Christoph Lindner, *Fictions of Commodity Culture: From the Victorian to the Postmodern* (Aldershot: Ashgate, 2003), Logan, *The Victorian Parlour*.

22 Freedgood, *The Ideas in Things*, 8.

23 Ibid., 140.

distinguish their 'objectness' from the abstractness of their exchange value, noting that 'although we are all commodity fetishists now, and our literary criticism often reflects this problem, our nineteenth-century forebears may well have maintained a more complex relationship to the goods by which they were surrounded and intrigued.'[24]

The materialist turn in study of the Victorian novel draws upon developments in 'thing theory.' A special issue of *Critical Inquiry* was devoted to the topic in 2001, where John Frow explains that

> [i]t makes sense to recognize both the heterogeneity of things in the world—complexly ordered along intersecting scales running from the material to the immaterial, the simple to the complex, the functional to the non-functional, the living to the inert, the relatively immediate to the highly mediated—and the fluidity of the relations between these categories. Thingness and the kinds of thingness are not inherent in things; they are effects of recognitions and uses performed within frames of understanding (which may be markets or ad hoc negotiations of action or desire or bodily skills as much as they may be intellectual formattings or sedimented codes). And persons, too, count or can count as things. This is the real strangeness: that persons and things are kin; the world is many, not double.[25]

Frow argues against the kind of binary thinking that opposes use-value to exchange-value, matter to representation, immediacy to mediation, or, as Freedgood's study sometimes insists, things to commodities. The strange kinship of persons and things—'a mixing in which things and persons exchange properties and partly resemble and partly don't resemble each other'[26]—is the disquieting perception of subject-object relations that emerges from *Household Words*'s engagement with commodity culture. To be sure, the Marxist concept of the commodity strictly refers not to things as such, but to the form they take when produced for exchange rather than immediate use—a form that subordinates use to exchange value, and creates a mystification in which the social character of the labour invested in production is converted into 'an objective character of the products themselves.'[27] But the concept of 'commodity culture'—a culture shaped by the production, exchange, and consumption of goods and services—is more capacious as an analytic category and remains open to the fluidity of relations between people and things remarked by Frow. Indeed, sociologists and cultural anthropologists have drawn attention to the wider range of meanings carried by goods. As Frow observes elsewhere, the narrow Marxist concept of the commodity has been destabilized by the anthropological models developed by Arjun Appadurai and others in *The Social Life of Things*, where the form is defined in terms of a *situation* of exchangeability.[28] Adapting my

---

24 Ibid., 142.

25 John Frow, 'A Pebble, a Camera, a Man Who Turns into a Telegraph Pole,' *Critical Inquiry* 28/1, 'Things' (2001): 285.

26 Ibid.: 278.

27 Karl Marx, *Capital: An Abridged Edition*, ed. David McLellan, World's Classics (1867; Oxford: Oxford University Press, 1995), 45.

28 John Frow, *Time and Commodity Culture: Essays in Cultural Theory and Postmodernity* (Oxford: Clarendon Press, 1997), 143.

subtitle from Appadurai's book, my critical focus has been shaped by the extent to which the writers in *Household Words* anticipate his injunction 'to follow the things themselves,' for it is only through 'the analysis of [their] trajectories that we can interpret the human transactions and calculations that enliven things.'[29] Appadurai's argument 'that commodities, like persons, have social lives,'[30] is amply demonstrated in the representation of commodity culture in *Household Words*.

At the same time that interest in Victorian material culture has grown, scholarly attention to that most prolific and ubiquitous of Victorian commodities, the periodical, has also expanded, with specialist studies of individual titles as well as more wide-ranging analyses of the press appearing with increasing frequency.[31] The conjunction is not entirely coincidental, for as Margaret Beetham observes, the 'material characteristics of the periodical (quality of paper, size of the pages and lack of hard cover) have consistently been central to its meaning.'[32] The explosion in the nineteenth-century periodical press is described in the *Household Words* essay with which I began, as Wills observes that while for 'half a century from the days of the Spectator, the number of British and Irish newspapers was few,' owing to the imposition of the so-called taxes on knowledge from 1712 onwards, by 1848, 'eighty-two millions of stamps,—more than thrice as many as were paid for in 1821,' were issued for English, Irish, and Scotch newspapers.[33] Critical recognition of the importance of the press in satisfying the Victorians' 'Appetite for News' regarding the complex and rapidly changing world that was unfolding around them is now widespread. Surprisingly, however, no book-length study has yet been devoted to either of Dickens's weekly periodicals. Notwithstanding John Drew's excellent study of *Dickens the Journalist* (2003), discussion of *Household Words* and *All the Year Round* remains tied to and, arguably, constrained by, the identity of their famous editor. As Brian Maidment lamented in 2000, '*Household Words* is still more read as something to do with Dickens than as an extremely complex assemblage of important journalism. Welcome as Michael Slater's Dent edition of Dickens's journalism is, nonetheless it continues to promote the line of thought which says that periodicals exist mainly as celebrations of their most distinguished contributors.'[34] To be sure, nineteenth-century journalism remains notoriously difficult to bring into critical focus. Its fractured, heterogeneous and multi-vocal form resists the protocols of traditional literary analysis (and while Dickens exercised tight editorial control and

---

29 Arjun Appadurai, 'Introduction: Commodities and the Politics of Value,' in *The Social Life of Things: Commodities in Cultural Perspective*, ed. Arjun Appadurai (New York: Cambridge University Press, 1986), 5.

30 Ibid., 3.

31 See, for example, Andrew King, *The London Journal 1845–1883: Periodicals, Production and Gender* (Aldershot: Ashgate, 2004), Peter Sinnema, *Dynamics of the Pictured Page: Representing the Nation in the 'Illustrated London News'* (Aldershot: Ashgate, 1998).

32 Margaret Beetham, 'Towards a Theory of the Periodical as a Publishing Genre,' in *Investigating Victorian Journalism*, ed. Laurel Brake, Aled Jones, and Lionel Madden (Basingstoke: Macmillan, 1990), 23.

33 [Wills], 'The Appetite for News,' 239.

34 Brian Maidment, 'Review of Peter W. Sinnema, *Dynamics of the Pictured Page—Representing the Nation in the 'Illustrated London News*,' *Journal of Victorian Culture* 5 (2000): 164.

even rewrote contributions to *Household Words*, the journal's form is nevertheless dialogic, with differing lights being cast on a given topic, and the individual voices of such writers as George Augustus Sala, Harriet Martineau, Wilkie Collins, and of course Dickens himself, readily distinguishable to the avid reader despite the policy of anonymity). While Dickens necessarily continues to be a central figure in my story, I analyze *Household Words* as 'an extremely complex assemblage of important journalism' around the subject of commodity culture, and thereby approach the question of the mediating power of this mid-nineteenth-century periodical from a direction suggested by the form and contents of the journal itself.

Dickens filled *Household Words* with articles addressing commodity culture in one way or another: biographies of raw materials; stories spun from advertisements; process articles describing visits to manufactories; tales of the flâneur; and narratives describing those residual or marginal economies in which waste is recycled. Some contributors, such as Charles Knight, famous as the publisher of the *Penny Magazine* on behalf of the Society for the Diffusion of Useful Knowledge, attempted to provide an explanatory theoretical framework for their descriptions of commodities. Some, like Sala, were fascinated by the life of goods on the city streets, in their shops and arcades. Some, like Harriet Martineau, sought to restore the history of the production of a commodity, as if to combat the process of its fetishization, seeing in the objects described the labour invested in their manufacture. Many articles raise wider questions as to how far society should go in permitting people to buy and sell goods and services, how far the *laissez-faire* market should extend. In both its mode and degree of responsiveness, *Household Words* reveals the ambivalence with which many mid-Victorians greeted the increasing presence of the commodity in their daily lives.

The periodical, as Hilary Fraser and Daniel Brown observe, was an urban form—sharing the scale, diversity, fragmentation, and anonymity of the metropolis—whose nineteenth-century development 'correlates with the demographic movement to the cities.'[35] A key factor in its growth was the way in which it helped members of the new mass reading public to acquire the cultural capital that might enable them to be upwardly mobile or to 'consolidate middle-class status.'[36] The flexible mode of the periodical essay lent itself to this task, fulfilling the demand 'for organized information delivered in a manageable length and pleasing variety.'[37] The form had its immediate antecedents in the early-nineteenth-century contributions to such journals as the *London Magazine, New Monthly Magazine,* and *Examiner,* of Hazlitt, Lamb, Hunt, and De Quincey, who themselves looked back to the writings of Addison and Steele. Characterized by a winning combination of metropolitanism, wit, and a humanitarian impulse, the *Spectator* became the most popular model for English prose composition. As Graham Smith argues, 'Dickens clearly adored its

---

35 Hilary Fraser and Daniel Brown, *English Prose of the Nineteenth Century* (London: Longman, 1997), 5.

36 Ibid., 9.

37 Lee Erickson, *The Economy of Literary Form: English Literature and the Industrialization of Publishing, 1800–1850* (Baltimore: Johns Hopkins University Press, 1996), 102.

miscellaneous character, the variety embodied in its range of material from grave to gay, from delight in popular amusements to social satire.'[38] Forster quotes Dickens, saying of his plans for what became *Household Words*, 'I strongly incline to the notion of a kind of *Spectator* (Addison's)—very cheap and pretty frequent.'[39]

Recommending his paper to 'the Fraternity of Spectators who live in the World without having any thing to do in it; and either by the Affluence of their Fortunes, or Laziness of their Dispositions, have no other business with the rest of Mankind, but to look upon them,' Addison presents himself in number 10 as an early flâneur.[40] As Dana Brand argues, Addison and Steele were not the 'first to deal with such staples of later urban spectatorial literature as the incongruity of London signs, the absurdity of London dress, the cacophony and human variety of London streets and marketplaces, and the fascination and profusion of London types,' but they changed 'the way in which London was being represented for literary consumption.'[41] Steele's essay 454 on the 'Hours of the Day and Night' in London, for example, revels in the social diversity of the city, and offers a vision of spatial and temporal mobility that continued to attract later writers on the metropolitan scene: the 'Hours,' writes Steele, 'are taken up in the Cities of *London* and *Westminster* by People as different from each other as those who are Born in different Centuries. Men of Six-a-Clock give way to those of Nine, they of Nine to the Generation of Twelve, and they of Twelve disappear, and make Room for the fashionable World, who have made Two-a-Clock the Noon of the Day.'[42] Similarly, Addison's essay 69 on the Royal Exchange seems to anticipate some of the characteristic strategies of *Household Words*'s writing on the city as commodity spectacle in its description of the 'Metropolis [as] a kind of *Emporium* for the whole earth':

> Almost every *Degree* produces something peculiar to it. The Food often grows in one Country, and the Sauce in another. The Fruits of *Portugal* are corrected by the Products of *Barbadoes*: The Infusion of a *China* Plant sweetned with the Pith of an *Indian* Cane. The *Philippick* Islands give a Flavour to our *European* Bowls. The single Dress of a Woman of Quality is often the Product of an Hundred Climates. The Muff and the Fan come together from the different Ends of the Earth. The Scarf is sent from the Torrid Zone, and the Tippet from beneath the Pole. The Brocade Petticoat rises out of the Mines of *Peru*, and the Diamond Necklace out of the Bowels of *Indostan*.[43]

The effect of a cornucopia created by the catalogue of worldly goods anticipates the breathless listing of commodities in *Household Words*. The animation attributed to the 'Muff and the Fan,' or the 'Brocade Petticoat,' prefigures the lively goods depicted in Dickens's journal. *Household Words*'s interest in rediscovering provenance may

---

38 Graham Smith, *Charles Dickens: A Literary Life* (Houndmills: Macmillan, 1996), 61.
39 Forster, *The Life of Charles Dickens*, 1: 443n.
40 [Addison], No. 10, 12 March 1711, *The Spectator*, ed. Gregory Smith, Everyman's Library (London: Dent, 1945) 1: 32.
41 Dana Brand, *The Spectator and the City in Nineteenth-Century American Literature* (New York: Cambridge University Press, 1991), 31–2.
42 [Steele], No. 454, 11 August 1712, *The Spectator*, 3: 402.
43 [Addison], No. 69, 19 May 1711, *The Spectator*, 1: 213.

also be glimpsed in Addison's global survey. However, there is a quality of urbanity about the detached stance of Mr Spectator, and a balance and patterning evident in the style of his inventorying—like the artful catalogue of the contents on Belinda's dressing-table in the *Rape of the Lock*—that contrast with the 'streetiness' of a flâneur like Sala and his lists of goods which imitate in their unruliness the teeming thoroughfares of the mid-nineteenth-century metropolis. As Brand argues, while the city depicted by Addison and Steele is fluid and discontinuous, they 'suggest the possibility of a spectator who is able to impose order, continuity, and coherence *in the act of watching* what appears to be chaotic.'[44] Such narrative control and reassurance contrast with the aesthetic of fragmentation and disconnection that so often characterizes *Household Words*'s visions of the metropolis.

Walter Benjamin's studies of the Paris of the Second Empire, together with Georg Simmel's essays on metropolitan modernity, provide important models for the theorization of nineteenth-century commodity culture and inform my study throughout. But their perspective upon the city had its antecedents in nineteenth-century commentary on the periodical press. In his 1855 essay on 'The First Edinburgh Reviewers,' for example, Walter Bagehot anticipates later accounts of metropolitan life in remarking 'the casual character of modern literature. Everything about it is temporary and fragmentary.'[45] Identifying the role of the review essay in facilitating the historical shift, he characterizes the 'difference between the books of this age, and those of a more laborious age,' as that which 'we feel between the lecture of a professor and the talk of the man of the world':

> – the former profound, systematic, suggesting all arguments, analysing all difficulties, discussing all doubts, ... —the latter, the talk of the manifold talker, glancing lightly from topic to topic, suggesting deep things in a jest, unfolding unanswerable arguments in an absurd illustration, expounding nothing, completing nothing, exhausting nothing, yet really suggesting the lessons of a wider experience. ... —fragmentary yet imparting what he says, allusive yet explaining what he intends, disconnected yet impressing what he maintains. This is the very model of our modern writing.[46]

As Fraser and Brown remark, Bagehot's 'man of the world' resembles the flâneur, that nineteenth-century connoisseur of the city streets: 'The flâneur and the historically self-conscious periodical essayist work in the economic marketplace, both studying and commenting upon this modern world and deriving their livelihood from it.'[47] The archetypal modern subject, the flâneur is the passive but passionate spectator open to all that is ephemeral, fugitive, and fragmented in the metropolis. In Benjamin's account, his perceptive style—physiognomic and impressionistic— is crucially linked to journalism. He captures modernity, not only as the poet and 'painter' of the city described by Baudelaire, but as the writer of the *feuilleton* section of the Parisian newspapers and as author of the 'modest-looking, paperbound,

---

44 Brand, *The Spectator and the City in Nineteenth-Century American Literature*, 33.
45 [Walter Bagehot], 'The First Edinburgh Reviewers,' *National Review*, October 1855, 1: 254.
46 Ibid : 256.
47 Fraser and Brown, *English Prose of the Nineteenth Century*, 15.

pocket-size volumes called "physiologies."'[48] 'The physiologies were the first booty taken from the marketplace by the flâneur—who, so to speak, went botanizing on the asphalt,'[49] writes Benjamin, and they helped shape the phantasmagoria of Parisian life by making the city legible, ordering its potentially disorienting diversity in the definition of visible types. Quoting Simmel, Benjamin remarks their function in assuaging the peculiar uneasiness felt by dwellers in big cities, where 'interpersonal relationships ... are distinguished by a marked preponderance of the activity of the eye over the activity of the ear.'[50] As Judith Wechsler explains in her study of physiognomy and caricature in nineteenth-century Paris, as well as social types, 'there were also physiologies of neighbourhoods and institutions, such as the press, the cafés, the balls.'[51] Selling half a million copies during its vogue in the 1840s, this popular literature, together with such physiognomic analyses as those found in Balzac's *La Comédie humaine*, made manageable the anxieties associated with a constantly growing and increasingly disorienting urban environment of strangers.

The desire to impose order, to codify urban types, and to derive inward character from the fixed forms of outward appearance was felt in London too, as the urban sketch writers of *Household Words* demonstrate.[52] Contributors like Dickens, Sala, William Blanchard Jerrold, Dudley Costello, and Andrew Wynter relish the urban crowd, with its sheer size, kaleidoscopic variety, and striking contrasts. A particularly piquant example of the city sketch is provided in 'Passing Faces,' published on 14 April 1855, where Eliza Lynn's cross-dressing as flâneur raises questions about the encoding of gender in the article's situation of address.[53] 'We have no need to go abroad to study ethnology,' Lynn begins. 'A walk through the streets of London will show us specimens of every human variety known.'[54] As Mary Cowling remarks in her brilliant study of type and character in Victorian art, it was 'a favourable pastime for those with a physiognomical interest to seek out in the streets for evidence to

---

48 Walter Benjamin, *Charles Baudelaire: A Lyric Poet in the Era of High Capitalism*, trans. Harry Zohn (London: Verso, 1983), 35.

49 Walter Benjamin, *The Arcades Project*, trans. Howard Eiland and Kevin McLaughlin (Cambridge, Mass.: Belknap Press of Harvard University Press, 1999), 372.

50 Benjamin, *Charles Baudelaire*, 38.

51 Judith Wechsler, *A Human Comedy: Physiognomy and Caricature in 19th Century Paris* (London: Thames and Hudson, 1982), 34.

52 On the genre of the urban sketch see, in addition to Brand, Carol L. Bernstein, *The Celebration of Scandal: Toward the Sublime in Victorian Urban Fiction* (University Park, Pennsylvania: Pennsylvania State University Press, 1991); Kristie Hamilton, *America's Sketchbook: The Cultural Life of a Nineteenth-Century Literary Genre* (Athens: Ohio University Press, 1998); Deborah Epstein Nord, *Walking the Victorian Streets: Women, Representation, and the City* (Ithaca: Cornell University Press, 1995).

53 Until her marriage to William James Linton in 1858, Eliza Lynn published under her maiden name. As Lynda Nead notes of this article, Lynn's voice as flâneur begins 'to reveal the tensions between official and private responses to the city and the range of behaviour and personae from which women drew in their occupation of the mid-nineteenth-century streets.' Lynda Nead, *Victorian Babylon: People, Streets and Images in Nineteenth-Century London* (New Haven: Yale University Press, 2000), 79.

54 [Eliza Lynn], 'Passing Faces,' *Household Words*, 14 April 1855, 11: 261.

support their physiognomical theories about the social classes; and to the expectant, not to say prejudiced, eye, the evidence was not difficult to find.'[55] Thus, Lynn is assured of being able to 'read' 'nature's evidence, printed in unmistakeable type' on the passing faces in the street.[56] The metaphor of printing gives way to the notion of 'type' as a species as Lynn develops an analogy between animal and human physiognomy in describing the variety of birds and beasts encountered, from the bull-dog in the brown suit with bandy legs and heavy shoulders to the 'cow-faced woman, generally of phlegmatic temperament and melancholy disposition, given to pious books and teetotalism.' Lynn's caricatures resemble the anthropomorphic fantasies of the French illustrator, Grandville, who, as Judith Wechsler argues, while drawing upon a long tradition of animal fables used to represent moral concerns, greatly extended the 'range of characterological traits associated with animals.'[57] Like other tales of the flâneur in *Household Words*, Lynn's sketch produces what Lyn Pykett has called a 'curiously fictive form of knowledge,'[58] involving as it does the construction of speculative narratives and histories about the 'passing faces' in order to make sense of the ever-changing urban scene:

> Look at that pale woman, with red eyes, sunken cheeks, and that painful thinness of the shabby genteel [writes Lynn]. She is the wife of a gambler, once an honourable and a wealthy man, now sunk to the lowest depths of moral depredation—fast sinking to the lowest depths of social poverty as well. He came home last night, half mad. The broad bruise on her shoulder beneath that flimsy shawl would tell its own tale, if you saw it.[59]

Lynn's fictive account of the shabby-genteel woman is typical of the imaginative handling of so-called non-fictional prose in the journal. Raising questions about the boundaries between the factual and fanciful, between journalism and literature, Lynn's testing of these generic borders is complicated further by the gender transgression involved in her guise as flâneur: a guise that is secured not only by the way in which her reading of the faces passed on the street is typical of the anthropological interest shown by other (male) urban sketchers in *Household Words*, but by the assumption—encouraged by the practice of anonymity—that articles by other contributors were written by Dickens himself.[60] She demonstrates the mid-Victorian ubiquity of the idea that different social types were physiognomically distinguishable, even as she defies such stereotyping herself in her guise as flâneur. The limits of physiognomic interpretability may be glimpsed as she turns finally to observe a beguilingly demure young woman in the street:

> The sweet-looking girl walking alone, and dressed all in dove-colour, is an authoress; and the man with bright eyes and black hair, who has just lifted his hat to her and walks on,

---

55 Mary Cowling, *The Artist as Anthropologist: The Representation of Type and Character in Victorian Art* (Cambridge: Cambridge University Press, 1989), 122.
56 [Lynn], 'Passing Faces,' 261–2.
57 Wechsler, *A Human Comedy*, 100.
58 Lyn Pykett, *Charles Dickens, Critical Issues* (Houndmills, Basingstoke: Palgrave, 2002), 34.
59 [Lynn], 'Passing Faces,' 264.
60 See the discussion in Chapter 2, p. 22.

with a certain slouch in his shoulders that belongs to a man of business, is an author, and an editor; a pope, a Jupiter, a czar in his own domain, against whose fiat there is neither redress nor appeal. No despotism is equal to the despotism of an editor.[61]

The hint of knowingness in this account is the only clue to the irony with which Lynn's modest yet flattering self-representation belies her identity as a rather emancipated Englishwoman, the first to draw a regular salary as a journalist, and showing a tendency, Dickens wrote to Wills, to get 'so near the sexual side of things as to be a little dangerous at times.'[62]

Representing and participating in mid-Victorian commodity culture themselves by rendering the city as a spectacle for consumption in *Household Words*, writers like Lynn build upon Boz's anthropological sketches of London from two decades earlier. To be sure, the flâneurs who record their metropolitan perambulations in Dickens's journal often show an aesthetic of engagement—as in Lynn's account of the shabby-genteel woman—that distinguishes their perspective from that of the detached consumer of urban novelty and spectacle critiqued by Benjamin. While the Parisian flâneur is a kind of aristocrat (in stance if not necessarily in class terms), midway chronologically between the dandies of the early nineteenth century and the Wildean aesthetes of the fin-de-siècle and standing apart from the crowd, the *Household Words* flâneur is much more of a participant-observer, an eyewitness reporter assiduously engaged in the accumulation of facts and impressions—the commodities in which he or she deals. The best of them infuse their physiognomical categorization of city types with a strong sense of individualized particularity.

Notwithstanding his difference from the Parisian type, the flâneur remains a handy figure for the journal's writers. Like him, and like Bagehot's modern periodical essayist—the 'man of the world' or 'manifold talker'—who was criticized by some for writing that is fragmentary, allusive, superficial and subjective,[63] the *Household Words* writer is typically a non-specialist. From this position, he broaches a range of disparate topics upon the basis of his wide general experience, and familiarizes his readers with contemporary debates in a conveniently digestible form. Eschewing the systematic study of the professor, a flâneur like Sala, for example, presents himself as one of nature's connoisseurs, one whose experience of the world has enabled him to pick up a lot of miscellaneous learning without ever falling into the pedantry of specialist knowledge.[64] He offers what Kate Campbell distinguishes as 'aesthetic cognition' in place of 'intellectual cognition' as a way of knowing the modern world.[65] He suggests a beguiling role-model for socially-aspirant readers who need reassurance that their own lack of expert information is not a handicap to

---

61 Ibid.
62 Quoted by Lohrli, *'Household Words' A Weekly Journal 1850–1859 Conducted by Charles Dickens*, 344.
63 Fraser and Brown, *English Prose of the Nineteenth Century*, 15.
64 My discussion of Sala here is deeply indebted to the insights shared by my colleague, Robert Dingley.
65 Kate Campbell, 'Journalistic Discourses and Constructions of Modern Knowledge,' in *Nineteenth-Century Media and the Construction of Identities*, ed. Laurel Brake, Bill Bell, and David Finkelstein (Houndmills, Basingstoke: Palgrave, 2000), 44.

their making the right consumer choices. Responding to the anxieties of those new, upwardly mobile middle-class readers with disposable income in this way, he points to the distinctive social conjunctures at mid-century that the journal was addressing in its representation of commodity culture.

Setting store by experience rather than hide-bound authority, by the university of life, rather than by the arid doctrines of the schools, Sala's eschewal of 'elite' values and knowledges earned the censure of cultural commentators like Matthew Arnold. In Letter XII from 'A YOUNG LION' (of the *Daily Telegraph*) dated 26 November 1870, Arnold satirizes Sala for having 'studied in the book of the world even more than in the world of books': 'But his career and genius have given him somehow the secret of a literary mixture novel and fascinating in the last degree: he blends the airy epicureanism of the *salons* of Augustus with the full-bodied gaiety of our English Cider-cellar.'[66] Acknowledging this popular 'mixture' as 'the very thing to go down,' Arnold derides its vulgar commercialism. But his criticism of Sala helps us to pinpoint a key feature of *Household Words*'s non-fiction prose. For Sala's journalese, developed as a contributor to *Household Words*, reveals the extent to which the journal's idiom is often indistinguishable from that of the commercial world it was attempting to critique. As a mass-circulation weekly, averaging sales of around 40,000 copies per week,[67] *Household Words* was itself a popular commodity. Dickens's requirement that articles for his journal must be 'imaginative' had marketability clearly in view.[68] While 'carelessness about facts' could be 'damaging,' Dickens wrote to Wills, 'dullness' was 'hideous.'[69] The journal's fanciful house style can be seen particularly vividly in its many 'biographies' of commodities—'What There Is in a Button,' 'All about Pigs,' 'Done to a Jelly' and so on—where goods seem to take on a life of their own.[70]

Such liveliness is sometimes achieved through the narrative of a thing, as in Sidney Laman Blanchard's 'Biography of a Bad Shilling,' which describes the career of a counterfeit coin. This peculiar treatment of subject-object relations has antecedents in the eighteenth-century narrative device of the speaking object, found in such works as Charles Gildon's *The Golden Spy* (1709) or Charles Johnstone's *Chrysal; or, The Adventures of a Guinea* (1760), as well as what might be called 'alien observer' satires, such as Montesquieu's Persian letters or Goldsmith's *Citizen of the World*. Both genres shared the strategy of defamiliarization that finds its way into much of *Household Words*'s reportage. Christopher Flint argues that the appearance and popularity of the eighteenth-century it-narratives was not just an

---

66 Matthew Arnold, *Culture and Anarchy, with Friendship's Garland and Some Literary Essays*, ed. R.H. Super, Complete Prose Works of Matthew Arnold (Ann Arbor: University of Michigan Press, 1965) 5: 350.

67 Richard D. Altick, *The English Common Reader: A Social History of the Mass Reading Public, 1800–1900*, Second ed. (Columbus: Ohio State University Press, 1998), 394.

68 Letter to W.H. Wills, 17 November 1853, in House, Storey, and Tillotson, eds., *The Letters of Charles Dickens*, 7: 200.

69 Quoted in Lohrli, *'Household Words,'* 11.

70 [George Dodd], 'All About Pigs,' *Household Words*, 31 July 1852, 5: 471–4; [George Dodd], 'Done to a Jelly,' *Household Words*, 24 June 1854, 9: 438–40; [Harriet Martineau], 'What There Is in a Button,' *Household Words*, 17 April 1852, 5: 106–12.

attempt to spark interest through the striking proposition of an inanimate narrator, but, more importantly, was linked to concerns about the alienation of authorship in a modern print economy, as text was transmuted from manuscript to book to commodity: 'As principal narrators that represent authorship, speaking objects symbolized the promiscuous movement of text, the commodification of stories, the international entanglements in the book trade, and the loss of narrative identity and authority that stem from circulation in the social sphere.'[71] The genre was revived by Douglas Jerrold in his first novel, *The Story of a Feather*, which was serialized in *Punch* during 1843. As Michael Slater notes, the novel was very popular and the 'bizarre device' of 'having the story narrated by an ostrich-feather' enabled Jerrold 'to make a link between the highest and the lowest echelons of society' in his vigorous attack upon social injustice and the plight of the poor.[72] Forster records that Dickens 'derived much enjoyment'[73] from reading *The Story of a Feather* in *Punch*, and when Jerrold sent him a copy of the revised volume publication in May 1844, he was equally enthusiastic in his response.[74] Slater observes that Dickens derived a repentant-prostitute scene from it for *The Chimes*;[75] but what has not been noted is the extent to which Jerrold's it-narrative anticipates the interchange between people and things so often involved in the journalism of *Household Words*. As the feather, finding itself amongst 'the cast-off finery which formed the stock in trade of Madame Spanneu,' warns the 'gentle reader':

> Never, ... so long as you have a stitch about your anatomy, believe yourself alone. If thoughtless people could only know what their left-off clothes say about them, sure I am, they would resolve upon one of two things: either to reform their lives, or to go naked. Let no man harbour a black spot in his breast, and believe that his waistcoat is wholly ignorant of the stain. Let no man drop an ill-gotten guinea into his pocket, and think the poke unconscious of the wrong. His very glove shall babble of the bribe that has burnt his hand. His cravat shall tighten about his throat, if that throat be seared with daily lies.[76]

As the feather proceeds to recount the biography of one of his companions—a scarlet-heeled shoe—the device anticipates the peculiar extrapolation of story from second-hand clothing by contributors like Sala in *Household Words*.

Like Jerrold's feather, and like the eighteenth-century speaking object, Blanchard's coin begins his picaresque narrative in *Household Words* with an account of his pedigree:

> My parents were respectable, notwithstanding that one belonged to the law—being the zinc door-plate of a solicitor. The other, was a pewter flagon residing at a very excellent hotel, and moving in distinguished society; for it assisted almost daily at convivial parties

---

71 Christopher Flint, 'Speaking Objects: The Circulation of Stories in Eighteenth-Century Prose Fiction,' *PMLA* 113 (1998): 224.

72 Michael Slater, *Douglas Jerrold 1803–1857* (London: Duckworth, 2002), 133.

73 Forster, *The Life of Charles Dickens*, 1: 329.

74 Slater, *Douglas Jerrold 1803–1857*, 137.

75 Ibid., 175.

76 Douglas Jerrold, *The Story of a Feather* (London: Bradbury, Evans and Co., 1867), 85–6.

Introduction 15

in the Temple. It fell victim at last to a person belonging to the lower orders, who seized it, one fine morning, while hanging upon some railings to dry, and conveyed it to a Jew, who—I blush to record the insult offered to a respected member of my family—melted it down.[77]

Also like its predecessors, the bad shilling's narrative is a hybrid combination of satire, allegory, biography, and moral tale. It exposes a venal world in which, says the shilling, 'habitual intercourse with the best society has relieved me from the embarrassing appendage of a conscience.... [A]nd, like the counterfeits of humanity, whose lead may be seen emulating silver at every turn, my only desire is—not to be worthy of passing, but simply—to pass.'[78] More common in *Household Words* than Blanchard's use of the eighteenth-century form, however, are object narratives devoted to detailing the processes of industrial manufacture or to recovering the provenance of imported raw materials, as Chapters 6 and 7 will show.

While some of the devices used by *Household Words* to enliven its non-fiction prose were more successful than others, critics have too readily dismissed its characteristic style as exaggerated or fanciful flourish—something superadded in accordance with Dickens's injunction, cited above, to keep the journal 'imaginative,' or what Mrs Gaskell, herself a contributor, disparaged as a requirement to be 'Dickensy.'[79] Reviewing Sala in 1859 as a representative of what it calls the 'mannerist school of prose' employed by *Household Words*, the *Saturday Review* sniffed: 'Nowhere else is to be found in such purity that style, cultivated by Mr Dickens and his followers, the leading characteristic of which is a subordination of matter to manner.'[80] Another regular *Household Words* contributor, John Hollingshead, later expressed embarrassment at the superficiality of some of the articles he wrote for the journal, blaming the Conductor: 'He wanted "readable" papers. "Let Hollingshead do it," he said, more than once. "He's the most ignorant man on the staff, but he'll cram up the facts, and won't give us an encyclopædical article."'[81] Even 'the driest subjects,' wrote Hollingshead, were to be infused with 'some degree of fancy and imagination.'[82] While the style of writing no doubt contributed to the imaginative effect, the specific techniques employed to achieve this I think themselves contribute to the cultural significance of the representation of commodities in the journal. The breathless listing of randomly juxtaposed goods is an important topos is this regard. Like a miniature Great Exhibition, these exuberant catalogues encapsulate a central point in my argument about the paradoxical nature of commodification, for they simultaneously enhance the exciting variety of the things listed, and seek to suppress

---

77 [Sidney Laman Blanchard], 'A Biography of a Bad Shilling,' *Household Words*, 25 January 1851, 2: 420.

78 Ibid.: 421.

79 Quoted by, *'Household Words' A Weekly Journal 1850–1859 Conducted by Charles Dickens*, 10.

80 'Mr Sala on Life in London,' *Saturday Review*, 3 December 1859: 677.

81 John Hollingshead, *My Lifetime*, 2nd ed., 2 vols. (London: Sampson Low, Marston and Co, 1895), 1: 190.

82 John Hollingshead, 'Preface,' in *Under Bow Bells: A City Book for All Readers* (London: Groombridge and Sons, 1860), v.

it by implying their interchangeability or exchangeability. Another significant device used is the animation of commodities. For example, in giving an account of the process of paper-making told from the perspective of the raw materials used in 'A Paper Mill,' or describing the way in which advertisements turn London into a city of streets that speak as pavements are 'made eloquent by lamp-black lithograph' in 'Bill-Sticking,' or personifying the cast-off clothes to be found in Mrs Brummus's shop in 'Fashion,'[83] *Household Words* reveals a fascination with changing relationships between people and things that distinguishes its attempt to come to terms with the mid-nineteenth-century development of commodity culture.

Arguably, it is the fluidity of the boundary between informational and imaginative writing that makes *Household Words*'s non-fictional prose its most distinctive and significant feature. Certainly, Wills seemed to think so. Comparing it with 'other publications of its class,' he wrote to Dickens in 1851, it is 'universally acknowledged that subjects of an uninviting nature are treated—as a rule—in *Household Words* in a more playful, ingenious, and readable manner than similar subjects have been hitherto presented in other weekly periodicals.'[84] While there has been much discussion of the fiction published in its pages, including studies considering the ways in which the instalments of a serialized novel, like *Hard Times*, relate to what is going on around them in the same issue,[85] scant critical attention has been given to the journalism of contributors other than Dickens himself. This neglect impels my focus on *Household Words*'s non-fiction prose in the chapters that follow, which are organized around some recurring themes in the journal's engagement with commodity culture. Contextualizing my discussion with reference to other contemporary miscellanies, I attempt to address the extent of the journal's distinctiveness in responding to the increasingly ubiquitous presence of the commodity in daily life. I begin, in Chapter 2, with *Household Words*'s keen interest in advertising. While not carrying any advertisements beyond the few referring to its own publications and those appearing inside the wrappers of the monthly reissues, a number of articles use newspaper advertisements to 'reconstruct' the biographies of those whom they solicit. Although critical of puffery's omnipresence, these narratives never quite manage to obtain the critical purchase on it that they seek because of the journal's simultaneous complicity with the discourse of advertising. Chapter 3 moves from the impostures of puffery and publicity to the more general problem of authenticity in an age of mechanical reproduction and mass consumption. It considers the fraudulent goods and services associated with spiritualism, adulteration, and quackery, together with the anxieties about authenticity found in the journal's treatment of travel and tourism. The figure of the flâneur reappears in Chapter 4, as I examine the ways in which *Household Words* renders the city as commodity spectacle. The metropolitan travel writing of

---

83 [Charles Dickens and Mark Lemon], 'A Paper-Mill,' *Household Words*, 31 August 1850, 1: 529–31; [Charles Dickens], 'Bill-Sticking,' *Household Words*, 22 March 1851, 2: 601–6; [George A. Sala], 'Fashion,' *Household Words*, 29 October 1853, 8: 193–6.

84 R.C. Lehmann, ed., *Charles Dickens as Editor, Being Letters Written by Him to William Henry Wills His Sub-Editor* (New York: Haskell House, 1972), 74.

85 See, for example, Joseph Butwin, '*Hard Times*: The News and the Novel,' *Nineteenth-Century Fiction*, 32 (1977), 166–87.

contributors like Dickens, Sala, Lynn, Hollingshead, and Henry Morley shows a level of social engagement that links it with the rise of investigative journalism. At the same time, however, together with the journal's attention to the commodification of urban leisure found in the shows of London, and its descriptions of window-shopping, these tales of urban rambling turn visual experience into commodity forms. Chapter 5 examines the 'process article,' a form of industrial tourist tale which held the promise of demystifying the commodity and restoring awareness of the labour involved in its production. While some contributors, like Harriet Martineau, extol the virtues of industrialism and political economy, others like Dickens and Morley register unease about the material confusions of worker and machine in factory production. Raw materials for Britain's factories came from all corners of the empire, and Chapter 6 surveys the journal's representation of foreign goods, its interest in the trajectories of objects within a global market. Chapters 7 and 8 focus upon two areas of trade in which the journal showed a recurring interest: death and second-hand clothing. Dickens filled *Household Words* with articles about the paraphernalia of mortality, many of which show instances of conflict about the commodity status of the object described and an ambivalent response to the idea of 'trading in death.' 'Fashion in Undress' explores the journal's fascination with cast-off clothes and considers what happens when goods are recycled, when the cultural meaning of their selection by consumers is complicated by second-hand purchase. As the many writers in *Household Words* who republished their contributions later in book form clearly knew, goods have a use and an exchange value that extends beyond the first cycle of consumption. Second-hand goods complicate the journal's efforts to ensure that commodities continue to speak about their origins, and about the social relations invested in their production, to those who buy them. They question the privilege accorded to production within accounts of commodity-chains, as Nicky Gregson and Louise Crewe argue.[86] And as their biographies extend indefinitely in time and space, and as the vestiges of the labour that originally produced them are overlaid by the imagined histories of their subsequent owners, they provide the potential for new understandings of the relationship between people and things.

---

86 Nicky Gregson and Louise Crewe, *Second-Hand Cultures* (Oxford: Berg, 2003), 5.

Chapter 2

Advertising Fictions

Issued without wrappers, the weekly numbers of *Household Words* did not carry the array of advertisements that were included with its successor, *All the Year Round*, from the mid-1860s. The few that it printed referred to its own supplementary publications (such as the *Household Narrative of Current Events* or the *Household Words Almanac*), forthcoming serialized novels, the semi-annual indexed volumes of the journal, or Dickens's public readings. These occupied a small space following the last item in the number. Nevertheless, the journal shows a recurring engagement with advertising—thematically, as a topical issue; and formally, as a kindred discursive practice sharing its narrative interest in the social life of goods. As Jennifer Wicke observes in her groundbreaking study of the relationship between the discourses of the nineteenth-century advertisement and the novel (from which I take my chapter title), 'Dickens' texts are both a reading of advertisement and a harbinger of it.'[1] Dickens's childhood employment labelling jars at Warren's Blacking marked the moment when 'product was beginning to be conjoined to text,' she argues, and his own later foray into advertising as a composer of comic verses for the firm indicates the extent to which the 'boundaries sharply delineating newspaper writer, advertising writer, and aspiring "author" were still shifting' at this time.[2] Wicke is concerned to uncover the shared history and mutual influence of advertising and the novel as both discourses emerged from the mass culture of industrial production, and others, like Gerard Curtis, Daniel Hack, and Emily Steinlight, have built upon her work.[3] But it was of course the nineteenth-century periodical, rather than the novel, which most visibly embodied the commodity form. As Lucy Brown argues, newspapers and advertising 'had grown up together during the eighteenth century—the names *General Advertiser*, *Daily Advertiser*, *Hull Advertiser*, proclaim the fact,'[4] and while editorial policy gradually came to draw distinctions within newspaper content between news, comment or advertisement, the generic ambiguities of advertising remain evident in the mid-nineteenth-century periodical press. *Household Words* shares with nineteenth-century advertising its structure of evanescence, multi-authorship (subsumed in the branding of a corporate voice), design to create a

---

1   Jennifer Wicke, *Advertising Fictions: Literature, Advertisement and Social Reading* (New York: Columbia University Press, 1988), 20.
2   Ibid., 25–6.
3   Gerard Curtis, *Visual Words: Art and the Material Book in Victorian England* (Aldershot: Ashgate, 2002); Daniel Hack, *The Material Interests of the Victorian Novel* (Charlottesville: University of Virginia Press, 2005); Emily Steinlight, '"Anti-Bleak House": Advertising and the Victorian Novel,' *Narrative* 14 (2006), 132–62.
4   Lucy Brown, *Victorian News and Newspapers* (Oxford: Clarendon Press, 1985), 15.

regular demand for the product from consumers, and employment of a wide range of genres. As a 'cheap' miscellany, designed to appeal to a broadly middle-class target audience and eschewing the high cultural ground of the quality monthlies or quarterlies, the journal's efforts to establish a critical purchase upon advertising simultaneously betray its complicity with it.

Walter Bagehot's oft-quoted assessment of Dickens's powers of urban perception as a novelist captures the affinity between advertising and the periodical form:

> London is like a newspaper. Everything is there and everything is disconnected. There is every kind of person in some houses; but there is not more connection between the houses than between the neighbours in the lists of 'births, marriages, and deaths.' As we change from the broad leader to the squalid police report, we pass a corner and we are in a changed world. This is advantageous to Mr Dickens's genius. His memory is full of instances of old buildings and curious people, and he does not care to piece them together.... He describes London like a special correspondent for posterity.[5]

Understood as a proliferating text composed of miscellaneous fragments, the city shares its multitudinous and ever-changing form not just with Dickens's fiction, but with the periodical and its advertising columns announcing 'births, marriages, and deaths.' The emphasis upon 'reading' the city emerges from an earlier nineteenth-century genre of journalistic sketches detailing the various classes and types of people to be encountered in the new urban environment—exemplified by Boz's *Sketches* and the popular French *Physiologies*.[6] But as Wicke notes, the *Sketches* delineated 'a London without the palpable advertising evidence that would pervade it as little as a decade later.'[7] The serial instalments of Dickens's novels carried copious and varied advertisements for a host of commodities, ranging from Morison's Pills through Mappin and Webb's electro silver plate and cutlery to Edmiston's pocket siphonia.[8] These appeared in supplements, named after the serial novel (such as the 'Bleak House Advertiser'), inside the green paper wrappers that became a familiar distinguishing feature of the monthly shilling parts—a form of branding that is still employed by modern journals devoted to Dickens studies, such as the *Dickensian* and the *Dickens Quarterly*.[9]

Household Words, however, eschewed such advertising supplements and the new forms of visual appeal associated with their development, although the paper

---

5 [Walter Bagehot], 'Charles Dickens,' in *Dickens: The Critical Heritage*, ed. Philip Collins (London: Routledge, 1971), 394.

6 For an excellent account of the *Physiologies* see Judith Wechsler, *A Human Comedy: Physiognomy and Caricature in 19th Century Paris* (London: Thames and Hudson, 1982).

7 Wicke, *Advertising Fictions*, 27.

8 Curtis observes that while advertisements for books dominated the early serials, with patent medicines following closely behind, there was a notable rise in the advertising of domestic products by mid-century, reinforcing the view 'that in the middle to late nineteenth century there was a broadening out of the middle-class domestic market for luxury goods.' Curtis, *Visual Words*, 138n35.

9 Curtis notes that this is also true of the original issues of the *Dickens Studies Annual* and the Garland Dickens Bibliographies. Ibid., 138n33.

covers of the monthly reissue carried printed advertisements on the insides.[10] In a brilliant analysis of the connection between *Household Words*'s material form and its construction of a new middle-class readership for itself, Lorna Huett argues that advertising in the journal 'was conspicuous by its absence.' She suggests this was a deliberate ploy on Dickens's part designed to differentiate his magazine from his part-issued fiction,[11] just as he was simultaneously seeking to distinguish it, as he avowed in 'A Preliminary Word,' from those 'Bastards of the Mountain, draggled fringe on the Red Cap, Panders to the basest passions of the lowest natures'[12]—in short, the penny press—so as to situate *Household Words* distinctively within the cheap periodical market. The formal proximity of *Household Words* to the cheap press and the penny blood was reflected not only through twopenny weekly publication, but paper size and quality, and the percentage of blank or wasted space appearing in each number.[13] Closely printed in double-columns using a small, eye-straining font, *Household Words* shows Dickens 'adopting the publishing and printing practices of the cheap educational magazines' while 'at the same time producing a journal which outwardly resembled the highbrow reviews' in its duodecimo format and lack of illustration.[14] The material form is certainly not attractive. But eye-catching graphic devices were employed in the typography of the first page banner, with the largest and boldest capitals used for the title, smaller italics for its Shakespearean source[15]—'*Familiar in their Mouths as HOUSEHOLD WORDS*'—and boldface capitals linking the title to the concluding announcement that the 'weekly journal' is 'CONDUCTED BY CHARLES DICKENS.' The announcement of the 'Conductor' appears across the top of every pair of facing pages in the journal: a form of branding that capitalized on Dickens's reputation and resembles the rhetoric of authenticity established through stamps and seals used to verify patent-protected products in advertisement. Branding serves to differentiate a standardized product within a mass market, helping to endow it with particular meanings and associations in order to direct consumer choice, and it was well underway by mid-century: as John Fisher Murray declared in surveying *The World of London* in 1843, 'Tea is no tea, if not Twining's; turtle merely the scrapings of a broth-pot, if not Birch's, or the London Tavern; twin turbots will not taste alike unless Grove purveys them; who will sit on a saddle if not of Laurie? Or handle a whip, if not by Swaine?'[16] Combined with the journal's policy of anonymity, such branding with the Conductor's name

---

10 Lorna Huett, 'Among the Unknown Public: *Household Words, All the Year Round* and the Mass-Market Weekly Periodical in the Mid-Nineteenth Century,' *Victorian Periodicals Review* 38 (2005): 76.
11 Ibid.
12 [Charles Dickens], 'A Preliminary Word,' *Household Words*, 30 March 1850, 1: 2.
13 Huett, 'Among the Unknown Public,' 77.
14 Ibid.: 78–9.
15 Percy Fitzgerald notes the alteration of the pronoun in the quotation from its source in *Henry V*, but acknowledges the appropriateness of the line: 'Nothing could be more entirely familiar to the community—the author himself a Household Word, his writings Household Words, and the paper to become as "familiar."' Percy Fitzgerald, *Memories of Charles Dickens*. (Bristol: J.W. Arrowsmith, 1913), 122.
16 John Fisher Murray, *The World of London*, 2 vols. (London: Blackwood, 1843), 1: 192.

led to the assumption that articles or stories by other contributors were written by Dickens himself. As Douglas Jerrold is reported to have quipped when he saw that *Household Words* was to carry its 'Conductor's' name at the head of every page, 'Ah, *mono*nymous throughout, I see!'[17] John Hollingshead noted later in the century that all Dickens's '"young men" were supposed to be imitators of the master, and the master was always credited with their best productions,'[18] while Sala complained that Dickens was unconsciously 'putting a bushel over the lights of his staff' and 'keeping them in that obscurity which inevitably meant indigence, while he was attaining, and properly attaining, every year greater fame and greater fortune.'[19] But as Fitzgerald argues, the branding paid off. Entering what by mid-century was a highly competitive periodicals market, *Household Words* needed to distinguish itself and did so by means of its conductor's '*personal* inspiration':[20]

> He was a force, a power, a romantic figure. Anything by Dickens, a letter, a paper, an opinion, was sought out, talked over and devoured, and people were eager to know what he thought on any and every subject. *Household Words*, a mere twopenny journal, was to be found on every table and in every room, in the palace and the cottage.[21]

In addition to the distinction associated with the name of its famous conductor, the branding of *Household Words* was secured by its peculiar house style, including its preference for punning or witty titles. Hollingshead noted that '[w]e were always very tricky with our *Household Words* titles, and many of them, very smart in themselves, served the purpose of raising curiosity in the mind of the reader, and concealing the subject which the writer was embroidering.'[22] Oxymoronic titles such as 'Dirty Cleanliness,' and punning titles such as 'India Pickle' or 'Ground in the Mill,' employ the sort of word-play or epigrammatic wit found in advertising copy. As the 'King of the Bill-Stickers' advises Dickens regarding the ingredients of a successful poster in an 1851 leader, 'what you wanted, was, two or three good catch-lines for the eye to rest on—then, leave it alone—and there you were!'[23] While the absence of an advertising supplement meant that *Household Words* did not evoke the kind of textual interchange that Wicke and Curtis describe as having occurred between a serial novel and its framing advertisements, the journal was not averse to introducing brand names, and the names of well-known tradesmen, into its pages. Reminiscing about the loss of Cranbourn Alley in 'Things Departed,' Sala recalls

---

17   Michael Slater, *Douglas Jerrold 1803–1857* (London: Duckworth, 2002), 174.

18   John Hollingshead, *My Lifetime*, 2nd ed., 2 vols. (London: Sampson Low, Marston and Co, 1895), 1: 96.

19   George Augustus Sala, *Things I Have Seen and People I Have Known*, 2 vols. (London: Cassell and Company, 1894), 1: 81–2. Despite his complaints in later life, Sala seemed, on the evidence of his letters to Edmund Yates, to have few qualms himself about using his mentor's 'name to gain sales, promote his work or enhance his public image.' Judy McKenzie, 'An Edition of the Letters of George Augustus Sala to Edmund Yates, in the Edmund Yates Papers, University of Queensland' (Diss. University of Queensland, 1994), 20.

20   Fitzgerald, *Memories of Charles Dickens*, 111.

21   Ibid., 135.

22   Hollingshead, *My Lifetime*, 1: 104.

23   [Charles Dickens], 'Bill-Sticking,' *Household Words*, 22 March 1851, 2: 605.

the splendour of Hamlet's—'not Hamlet the Dane, but Hamlet, the silversmith! How many times have I stood, wondering, by those dirty windows'[24]—as well as the blacking used to clean Hessian boots: 'The mirror-polished, gracefully outlined, silken tasselled Hessians exist no more—those famous boots, the soles of which Mr Brummell caused to be blacked, and in the refulgent lustre of which the gentleman of fashion immortalised by Mr Warren was wont to shave himself.'[25] In 'Houses to Let,' he wonders whether the 'infinitesimal subdivisions' of houses evident in the advertising pages of the *Times* are 'merely intended as ingenious devices to charm the house-hirer by variety, in the manner of Mr Nicholl, with regard to his overcoats, and Messrs. Swan and Edgar with reference to ladies' cloaks and shawls'[26]; and he imagines the inhabitant of a 'Bachelor's Residence' at ease 'consuming the grateful beer of Bass, and gently whiffing the cutty-pipe of Milo, or the meerschaum.'[27] In the first instalment of his two-part report on 'The Amusements of the People,' Dickens's description of the opening scene of the melodrama staged at one of Mr Whelks's favourite theatres invokes the famous patent medicine manufacturer, James Morison: 'Sir George Elmore, a melancholy Baronet with every appearance of being in that advanced stage of indigestion in which Mr Morison's patients usually are, when they happen to hear through Mr Moat, of the surprising effects of his Vegetable Pills, was found to be living in a very large castle.'[28] In a leader on 'Epsom,' Dickens marvels at the ubiquity of Fortnum and Mason's hampers: 'If I were on the turf, and had a horse to enter for the Derby, I would call that horse Fortnum and Mason, convinced that with that name he would beat the field. Public opinion would bring him in somehow. Look where I will—in some connexion with the carriages—made fast upon the top, or occupying the box, or tied up behind, or dangling below, or peeping out of window—I see Fortnum and Mason.'[29] Robert Gunter, the fashionable confectioner and caterer of No. 7 Berkeley Square, reaps publicity in articles by both Dickens and Sala,[30] and Moses and Son also get repeated mention. Such allusions to consumer goods and services are a window onto the particularized commercial geography of London at mid-century and reflect the status of these brand names as, precisely, household words. They bind the *Household Words* writer and reader to a larger social world of needs and desires, confirming through their recognition a shared commodity culture.

It is thus with some irony that the journal marvels at the ubiquity of advertising in London, as Dickens comically imagines the cruellest form of revenge that could be taken upon an enemy as consisting of the introduction of 'something that sat heavy on his conscience' into 'a Posting-Bill':

---

24 [George A. Sala], 'Things Departed,' *Household Words*, 17 January 1852, 4: 399.
25 Ibid.: 400.
26 [George A. Sala], 'Houses to Let,' *Household Words*, 20 March 1852, 5: 6.
27 Ibid.: 8.
28 [Charles Dickens], 'The Amusements of the People,' *Household Words*, 30 March 1850, 1: 14.
29 [Charles Dickens], 'Epsom,' *Household Words*, 7 June 1851, 3: 245.
30 See for example [Charles Dickens], 'New Year's Day,' *Household Words*, 1 January 1859, 19: 100; [George A. Sala], 'Want Places,' *Household Words*, 27 August 1853, 7: 605.

Thus, if my enemy passed an uninhabited house, he would see his conscience glaring down on him from the parapets, and peeping up at him from the cellars. If he took a dead wall in his walk, it would be alive with reproaches. If he sought refuge in an omnibus, the panels thereof would become Belshazzar's palace to him. If he took boat, in a wild endeavour to escape, he would see the fatal words lurking under the arches of the bridges over the Thames. If he walked the streets with downcast eyes, he would recoil from the very stones of the pavement, made eloquent by lamp-black lithograph. If he drove or rode, his way would be blocked up, by enormous vans, each proclaiming the same words over and over again from its whole extent of surface.[31]

Dickens's imaginative vision of being haunted by posting-bills is characteristic of *Household Words*'s handling of non-fiction prose. But the journal was hardly unique in recognizing the omnipresence of advertising in the 1850s. As Charles Manby Smith writes of the 'persecutions of Puff in its myriad shapes and disguises' in 1853, advertising is everywhere:

If you walk abroad, it is between walls swathed in puffs; if you are lucky enough to drive your gig, you have to 'cut in and out' between square vans of crawling puffs; if, alighting, you cast your eyes upon the ground, the pavement is stencilled with puffs; if in an evening stroll you turn your eye towards the sky, from a paper balloon the clouds drop puffs. You get into an omnibus, out of the shower, and find yourself among half a score of others, buried alive in puffs; you give the conductor sixpence, and he gives you three pennies in change, and you are forced to pocket a puff, or perhaps two, stamped indelibly on the copper coin of the realm.... Puff, in short, is the monster megatherium of modern society.[32]

The inescapability of advertising is similarly remarked by *Chambers's Edinburgh Journal* in 'Advertising Considered as an Art'[33] and derided by *Fraser's Magazine* in 'The Age of Veneer: The Science of Puffing.'[34] Nevertheless, *Household Words*'s inventive treatment of commodities and their promotion in its non-fictional articles is distinctive, marking the journal's kinship with the modern discourse of advertising. Offering an irresistible compound of entertainment with instruction, *Household Words* shares its winning formula with the nineteenth-century advertisement, which also attempts to combine the rhetorical and the informative. Advertising employs a

---

31 [Dickens], 'Bill-Sticking,' 601. The pervasive presence of advertising described here bears an ironic resemblance to the omnipresence of Dickens himself, recounted later by Sala in his memorial notice for the *Daily Telegraph* in 1870: 'Charles Dickens, when in town, was ubiquitous. He was to be met, by those who knew him, everywhere—and who did not know him? Who had not heard him read, and who had not seen his photographs in the shop-windows? The omnibus conductors knew him, the street-boys knew him; and perhaps the locality where his recognition would have been least frequent—for all that he was a member of the Athenaeum Club—was Pall Mall.' G.A. Sala, 'Charles Dickens,' in *Lives of Victorian Literary Figures I: Charles Dickens*, ed. Corinna Russell (London: Pickering and Chatto, 2003), 130–31.

32 Charles Manby Smith, *Curiosities of London Life* (London: 1853), 277–8.

33 'Advertising Considered as an Art,' *Chambers's Edinburgh Journal*, 28 December 1844, 2: 401.

34 'The Age of Veneer: The Science of Puffing,' *Fraser's Magazine*, January 1852, 45: 91.

range of genres and forms of persuasive appeal that are also apparent in the effects of the journal's efforts to enliven its accounts of things. As Judith Williamson explains, as well as the obvious function of selling things to us, advertising creates structures of meaning which are 'capable of transforming the language of objects to that of people and vice versa.'[35] Williamson decodes examples of modern advertisements to show how images, ideas, and feelings become transferred from other sign systems and attached to certain products in such a way that the products themselves become signs, developing 'such an aura of significance that they tell something about their buyers and actually become adjectival in relation to them,' helping to form them as subjects.[36] In its connection of people and things, its study of the social life of goods, *Household Words* partakes of the discourse of advertising that it is, nevertheless, simultaneously seeking to critique.

The richness of advertisement as a site for the reading of aspects of contemporary culture was widely recognized by the periodical press at mid century. As *Chambers's Edinburgh Journal* remarked of the advertisements in the *Times* as early as 1845, '[f]rom those ponderous pages the future historian will be able to glean ample and correct information relative to the social habits, wants and peculiarities of this empire. How we travel, by land or sea—how we live, and move, and have our being—is fully set forth in the different announcements which appear in a single copy of that journal.'[37] Similarly, Andrew Wynter remarks of 'The "Times" Advertising Sheet,' '[e]very ingredient of life seems mixed in this ever-open book: we laugh, we cry, we pardon, pity or condemn, as morning after morning it brings before us the swiftly-shifting scenes of this mortal life'[38]; and the anonymous author of *The Language of the Walls* describes advertising more generally as presenting 'us with an *epitome* of the history of civilisation—the progress of commerce—a chronicle of passing events—and a *multum in parvo* of all things.'[39] *Household Words* makes the same point in 'German Advertisements':

> Had he lived till now, [Voltaire] would have found the advertisements of a people a better index to their social tastes and habits. One Supplement of the Times, a file of the *Constitutionnel*, or a few numbers of the most extensively circulated of the German papers would be more suggestive of the wants and manners, locomotive, literary, and commercial habits of their various readers, than all the best treatises ever penned.[40]

---

35 Judith Williamson, *Decoding Advertisements: Ideology and Meaning in Advertising* (London: Marion Boyars, 1978), 12.

36 Ibid., 45.

37 'Advertisements of the Times,' *Chambers's Edinburgh Journal* 1845, 3: 199.

38 Andrew Wynter, *Our Social Bees: Pictures of Town and Country Life* (London: David Bogue, 1866), 235. The book collects items originally published in periodicals such as *Once a Week*.

39 [James Dawson Burn], *The Language of the Walls: And a Voice from the Shop Windows. Or, the Mirror of Commercial Roguery* (Manchester: Abel Heywood, 1855), 11. Thomas Richards identifies the anonymous author as Burn. Thomas Richards, *The Commodity Culture of Victorian England: Advertising and Spectacle 1851–1914* (Stanford: Stanford University Press, 1990), 47.

40 [W.H. Wills, Grenville Murray, and Thomas Walker], 'German Advertisements,' *Household Words*, 5 October 1850, 2: 35.

In 'A Golden Newspaper,' John Keene and W.H. Wills describe the advertisements appearing in the *Sydney Morning Herald* immediately after the discovery of gold near Bathurst—'"Tents for the Gold Regions;" "Boots for the Gold Regions;" "Biscuits for the Gold Regions;" "Bottled Beer for the Gold Regions;" "Razors for the Diggings;" "Trousers for the Mines;" "Hats for the New Dorado;" "Bedsteads for the Placers;"—as providing 'a distinct and suggestive sign of the times in Australia,'[41] while Dudley Costello studies a file of South American newspapers 'to describe the wants and wishes, the habits of life, and something of the pervading tone of society, in certain parts of that hemisphere, as shown in the advertisements of the periodical journals.'[42]

Interest in curiosities from the advertisements of the *Times* was widespread at mid-century, with many writers remarking the allusiveness and piquancy of the personal columns in particular. Andrew Wynter describes the 'lost and found' advertisements as 'exceedingly suggestive and rich,'[43] while *Chambers's* finds those devoted to 'romance' 'mysterious as melodramas, and puzzling as rebuses': '[o]ut of such an advertisement, a novelist of ordinary tact might construct a whole plot.'[44] Of course the 'Agony column' of the *Times* generally *was* coded, thus providing a simultaneous puzzle and 'real life' drama. Addressing that 'class of advertisements which follow us to our homes—sit beside us in our easy chairs—whisper to us at the breakfast-table—are regular and cherished visitants,' Charles Knight declares:

> Newspaper advertisements are to newspaper news what autobiography is to the narrative of a man's life told by another. The paragraphs tell us about men's sayings and doings: the advertisements *are* their sayings and doings. There is a dramatic interest about the advertising columns which belongs to no other department of a newspaper. They tell us what men are busy about, how they feel, what they think, what they want.[45]

Knight values the immediacy and the multi-vocality of the newspaper advertisement. But while he observes 'how easily might a practised story-composer manufacture a domestic tale' out of the material of the *Times* advertisements, *Household Words* shows the cultural significance of advertising in the 1850s to extend beyond the mere evidence of 'men's sayings and doings' to explore questions of modern urban subjectivity. An essay by Sala entitled 'Where Are They?', for example, uses the advertisements of the *Times* to speculate about the people who place them there, fashioning from their perusal an account of metropolitan identity. While *Chambers's* had earlier shown how easily a rudimentary story might be composed from the fragments of a personal advertisement,[46] Sala constructs a

---

41 [John Keene and W.H. Wills], 'A Golden Newspaper,' *Household Words*, 22 November 1851, 4: 208.

42 [Dudley Costello], 'Picture Advertising in South America,' *Household Words*, 14 February 1852, 4: 494.

43 Wynter, *Our Social Bees*, 239.

44 'Advertisements of the Times,' 199.

45 Charles Knight, *London* (London: Henry G. Bohn, 1851).

46 The essay-writer composes a story about 'Jemima' eloping from the 'bun-shop' with 'Charles' from the following advertisement: 'To CHARLES.– Be at the pastry-cook's at the corner of S—— Street, at two. Jemima is well.– Alice.' 'Advertisements of the Times,' 199.

vertiginous account of the alienation involved in modern urban social life by asking, where 'are the vast majority of the advertisers and the people that are advertised for? and, more than that, what sort of people can they be?'[47] Considered collectively, these advertisements bespeak the anonymity and atomization of a world teeming with 'people who do and are doing the most extraordinary things around us daily and hourly' and who yet remain completely unknown to us:

> They must be somewhere, these people, yet we never saw them, never shall see them perhaps; we may have sate next them at dinner yesterday, ridden in the same omnibus, occupied the next seat in the pit, sat in the same pew at church, jostled against them in the city, five minutes ago, yet we are no wiser . . .[48]

The 'imagined community' represented by the newspaper advertisements read by Sala remains a society of strangers.[49] Rather than experiencing the unifying engagement with a wider public that W.H. Wills captures in his 1850 account of the 'mass ceremony' of reading the daily newspaper in the nineteenth century,[50] Sala registers an uneasy awareness of simultaneous proximity and disconnection. As he finds an imaginary form of flânerie in perusing the advertising columns of the newspaper, his essay gives dramatic form to the connections Benjamin would later draw between the advertisement, the commodity, and the flâneur. The uncanny effect of the anonymous urban encounters Sala describes is compounded by the mounting list of his rhetorical questions that capture, in their proliferation, the crowded, kaleidoscopic life of the metropolis:

> Where is the gentleman for whom the silk-lined overcoat, or the patent leather boots were made, but whom they did not fit; which is the sole reason of their being offered to us at so reduced a rate? Where is that unflinching friend of the auctioneer, a gentleman, who has such a number and such a variety of articles of property—from ready-furnished freehold shooting boxes, to copies of Luther's Bible—and who is always going abroad, or is lately deceased? Where is the lady who is always relinquishing housekeeping, and is so strenuously anxious to recommend her late cook or housekeeper? Whereabouts, I wonder, are the two pounds per week which can with facility be realised by painting on papier mâche, or by ornamental leather work? Where is the fortune that is so liberally offered for five shillings? Where are the smart young men that want a hat? Where are all the bad writers whom the professors of penmanship in six lessons are so anxious to improve? Where are the fifty thousand cures warranted to have been effected by De Pompadour's Flour of Haricoes? Where are all the wonderfully afflicted people who suffered such excruciating agonies for several years, and were at last relieved and cured by two boxes of the pills, or two bottles of the mixture; and who order, in a postscript, four dozen of each to be sent to them immediately, for which they enclose postage stamps?[51]

---

47 [George A. Sala], 'Where Are They?' *Household Words*, 1 April 1854, 9: 153.
48 Ibid.: 152.
49 Benedict Anderson, *Imagined Communities: Reflections on the Origin and Spread of Nationalism*, Revised ed. (London: Verso, 1991).
50 See the discussion in Chapter 1.
51 [Sala], 'Where Are They?,' 157–8.

The dishonesty of advertising was a common target amongst periodical commentators. Murray declares that 'advertising will do anything': 'No imposition is so glaring, no quackery so apparent, no humbug so gross and palpable, which may not be turned to account, by an enterprising fellow, through the medium of the newspapers.'[52] In 'The Age of Veneer,' *Fraser's* ironically laments the loss of the 'genuine marks of fabrication or exaggeration' that were apparent in the advertisements penned a couple of decades earlier by the prince of auctioneers, George Robins: 'Everybody knew that he dealt in fiction and that his surcharged promises were intended to tickle the public curiosity and were not deliberately framed to deceive.' This 'merry mode of hoodwinking the public' has been succeeded by 'a more subtle system' in which the 'modern advertiser vouches for the touching interest he feels in the fate of his customer.'[53] William Blanchard Jerrold makes a similar point in 'Why People Let Lodgings.' Disclaiming the 'contrivances and struggles of what the vulgar call "gentility,"' he finds ample evidence of the 'universal system of hypocrisy on the subject of riches' in the newspaper columns 'where people who let lodgings advertise the attractions of their respective households.'[54] Scorning any pecuniary interest, they let lodgings because '[t]heir house is too large for them; they are anxious to add "a few companions to their social circle;"—or they let their apartments, "not for the sake of emolument, but to meet with a respectable tenant."' The shades of Mrs Bardell, whose advertisement for 'a single gentleman' to take a room was so naively answered by Mr Pickwick, may be seen in the 'lodging-letting widows, whose only wish is to lift the responsibility of housekeeping off the shoulders of "a respectable bachelor or widower," and with a touching self-sacrifice to place the burden upon their own back.'[55] The lodging-letters provide '"all the comforts of home without its cares,"' 'a serene establishment "where there are no children, or any other nuisances,"' and 'they are, without exception, in the most fashionable locality.' In short, '[t]hey are Utopias of elegance, comfort, learning, morality, and respectability,' and 'offer splendour, the highest respectability, morality, music, French, and natural solicitude, at the lowest possible figure; for "money is no object."'[56]

Jerrold's ridicule of the disingenuous newspaper advertisers of lodgings to let is echoed in Henry Morley's satiric account of scholastic advertisements in the *Times*. His narrator, Mr Green, remarks to his wife that '[s]chool life is now so happy,' as evidenced by the advertisements, that it would be harsh in a parent to send a child anywhere that gives holidays.[57] Marvels of cheapness, offering '"Diet unlimited, and of the best description"' and 'freedom from all that is vulgar,' the advertised schools 'monopolise all the most incontestably salubrious sites in the country' and their prospectuses contain '[t]estimonials equal to anything in the repertoire of Mr

---

52 Murray, *The World of London*, 200.
53 'The Age of Veneer,' 89.
54 [William Blanchard Jerrold], 'Why People Let Lodgings,' *Household Words*, 9 November 1850, 2: 167.
55 Ibid.: 168.
56 Ibid.
57 [Henry Morley], 'Scholastic,' *Household Words*, 15 January 1853, 6: 409.

Holloway or Mr Rowland.'[58] Morley quotes the advertisement of a schoolmaster in Ireland whose proclamation is 'a piece of ornamental penmanship, which begins with a Psalm in short hand, two quotations from Shakespeare, and some other matter; and then runs thus:'

> EDUCATION.—To show the age the very fashion of the time, its form and pressure, THADY MURPHY, Mercantile, MATHEMATICAL and Scientific Scholiast, Plain, occult, *fashionable*, ornamental Penman and general Amanuensis, will open *SCHOOL* in Shannon Street on Monday. He avers that his best exertions shall be used in order to elucidate the Branches he professes which he deems will more incontestably authenticate his abilities than the most pompous prospectus, his terms will be moderate, and attention most assiduous…[59]

While the absurdity of this advertisement derives from its bombast and the clumsiness with which it attempts to solicit prospective pupils by connecting the educational services of Thady Murphy with the cultural capital of Shakespeare and the Bible, it nevertheless displays the strategic correlation between a product and other values that Williamson identifies with modern advertising technique. As Sala wryly observes of advertising in 1852, '[w]here our benighted grandfathers had boys' and girls' schools, we have seminaries, academies, lyceums, and colleges, for young ladies.'[60] Much of Morley's satire depends upon appearing to take the advertisers at their word: thus Mr Green remarks of another ludicrously pretentious advertisement, the 'high privilege' it would be 'to have a daughter to send (and fifty pounds that can be paid over) to a lady more than eminently "qualified by her sphere in which she has moved to convey by example a high-toned accomplishments [sic], so necessary for a young lady moving in good society."' As he also notes, however, teachers are ill paid, and in 'their advertisements and their prospectuses they often seek to trick us of our favour by the use of baits which we demand to swallow, and which they very often—if they would not starve—are forced to throw to us.'[61] The extent to which the persuasive powers of advertising are elicited by consumers themselves is also remarked by *Fraser's*, which regards 'the heterogeneous phases of puffery as important, chiefly because they betoken and shadow forth the public mind to which

---

58 Ibid.: 410–11. Comparison with the advertisement for 'an able assistant' at Dotheboys Hall is irresistible: '"EDUCATION.—At Mr Wackford Squeers's Academy, Dotheboys Hall, at the delightful village of Dotheboys, near Greta Bridge in Yorkshire, Youth are boarded, clothed, booked, furnished with pocket-money, provided with all necessaries, instructed in all languages living and dead, mathematics, orthography, geometry, astronomy, trigonometry, the use of the globes, algebra, single stick (if required), writing, arithmetic, fortification, and every other branch of classical literature. Terms, twenty guineas per annum. No extras, no vacations, and diet unparalleled. Mr Squeers is in town, and attends daily, from one till four, at the Saracen's Head, Snow Hill. N.B. An able assistant wanted. Annual Salary £5. A Master of Arts would be preferred."' Charles Dickens, *Nicholas Nickleby*, ed. Paul Schlicke (1838–39; Oxford: Oxford University Press, 1990), 26.

59 Ibid.: 410.
60 [Sala], 'Houses to Let,' 6.
61 [Morley], 'Scholastic,' 412.

they are addressed.'[62] This mutually constitutive relation anticipates the methods of modern advertisements, which, as Williamson argues, sell us something else besides consumer goods: 'in providing us with a structure in which we, and those goods, are interchangeable, they are selling us ourselves.'[63] Such an interchange is not merely remarked, but enacted in *Household Words*'s use of advertisements to reconstruct the lives of the commodities they announce, or of the people who buy and sell them.

Thus Sala declares, with characteristically self-conscious verbosity, that the subject of 'Houses to Let' is 'fraught with speculative interest' for those who 'can find sufficient food for philosophy in the odds and ends, the sweeping of the house of life—who can read homilies in bricks and mortar, sermons in stones, the story of a life, its hopes and fears, its joys and woes, in the timbers of a dilapidated pigstye, in the desolation of a choked-up fountain, or the ruins of a springless pump.'[64] Sala's redundant epithets resemble the flourishes of Sheridan's Puff, who, as a literary advertising man, cries up the virtues of new plays, and claims to have first taught the auctioneers '"to crowd their advertisements with panegyrical superlatives, each epithet rising above the other, like bidders in their own auction-rooms! From me they learned to inlay their phraseology with variegated chips of exotic metaphor: ... by me they were instructed to clothe ideal walls with gratuitous fruits—to insinuate obsequious rivulets into visionary groves—to teach courteous shrubs to nod their approbation of the grateful soil."'[65] Sala's verbal pyrotechnics establish the affinity of his linguistic style with the practices of contemporary advertisement that he goes on to critique. While unable to resist the impulse to 'drop into Latin' himself, he contrasts the primitive simplicity of advertising in the eighteenth century—the 'announcement *pur et simple*' regarding a house to let in the *Daily Courant*, the *Public Ledger* or the *Evening Intelligencer* [66]—with the florid descriptiveness of current methods: 'A spade isn't a spade in 1852, but something else; and with our house agents, a house is not only a house, but a great many things besides':

> A House to Let may be a mansion, a noble mansion, a family mansion, a residence, a desirable residence, a genteel residence, a family residence, a bachelor's residence, a distinguished residence, an elegant house, a substantial house, a detached house, a desirable villa, a semi-detached villa, a villa standing in its own grounds, an Italian villa, a villa-residence, a small villa, a compact detached cottage, a *cottage ornée*, and so on, almost *ad infinitum*.

While satirizing the techniques of the advertisers in the comic catalogue of varying epithets, Sala clearly relishes their linguistic exuberance and invention. He declares

---

62 'The Age of Veneer,' 92.
63 Williamson, *Decoding Advertisements*, 13.
64 [Sala], 'Houses to Let,' 5–6.
65 Richard Brinsley Sheridan, 'The Critic; or, a Tragedy Rehearsed,' in *Plays*, ed. Ernest Rhys (London: Dent, 1906), 325–6.
66 The first successful daily paper, the *Daily Courant* was launched in March 1702; the *Public Ledger* was a daily founded in 1760. I have not been able to identify the *Evening Intelligencer*. See Jeremy Black, *The English Press in the Eighteenth Century* (London: Croom Helm, 1987).

that 'the immense variety of Houses to Let has always been to me a mystery, the subtle distinctions in their nomenclature sources of perplexed speculation,' and taking each classification in turn, he proceeds to construct an entire sociology of London's housing from the language of the advertisements, describing the buildings and the lives of those who have come to occupy them. To be sure, other contemporary periodical writers also noted the creative power of the language of advertising copy. As an essayist on 'The Philosophy of Advertising' in *Once a Week* in 1863 notes, the 'advertisement pure and simple has been driven out of the field by the puff genus. This class has before it a far higher ideal than that of supplying wants: it aims to create wants, to call consumers into being'[67]; and *Fraser's* had made the same point about the role of advertising in discovering 'new wants' earlier in 1852: 'Necessity is no longer the mother of invention; she is her daughter.'[68] Sala exploits this perception about the power of advertising to create its own subjects by reconstructing the biographies of those who have inhabited the 'Houses to Let.' His narratives anticipate later understandings of advertisement as a semiotic system in which the product becomes a 'personality' so as to help consumers make an individual choice that will articulate fine gradations of identity or status. Whether we are talking about the appeal of the 'noble mansion' or the 'Italian villa,' as Baudrillard argues, the 'pattern of "personal" value' is the same ... for all of us beating a path through the "personalized" jungle of "optional" merchandise, desperately seeking the foundation cream that will reveal the naturalness of our face, the little touch that will show up our deep individual bent, the difference which will make us ourselves.'[69]

Rather than denouncing the rhetorical ploys with which advertising solicits consumers by selling them their selves, Sala exposes this process by fictionalizing the inhabitants of the houses to let. From the advertisement for the 'mansion,' for example, he imagines it to be 'situate at Kew, possibly Chiswick, peradventure at Putney,' and sketches the figures of the 'Misses Gimp,' who once ran 'Minerva House Finishing Academy for Young Ladies' there:

> The Misses Gimp devoted themselves to the task of tuition with a high sense of its onerous duties, and strenuously endeavoured to combine careful maternal supervision with the advantages of a finished system of polite education (*vide* Times). But the neighbourhood was prejudiced against the scholastic profession, and the Misses Gimp found few scholars, and fewer friends. Subsequently, their crack scholar, Miss Mango, the heiress, eloped with Mr DeLypey, professor of dancing, deportment, and callisthenics. The resident Parisienne married Mr Tragacanth, assistant to Mr Poppyed, the chemist, and the Misses Gimp went to ruin or Boulogne.[70]

Such narratives parody social stereotyping even as they assume that these advertised 'Houses to Let' give form to the individualized subjects who inhabit them. Extrapolating the identity of the consumer from the commodity advertised, Sala's

---

67 'The Philosophy of Advertising,' *Once a Week*, 1 August 1863, 9: 163.
68 'The Age of Veneer,' 92.
69 Jean Baudrillard, *The Consumer Society: Myths and Structures*, ed. Mike Featherstone, trans. Chris Turner (London: Sage, 1998), 87.
70 [Sala], 'Houses to Let,' 7.

reliance upon social types again anticipates Baudrillard's analysis of the illusion of personalization in advertising. According to Baudrillard, although they employ the logic of personalization, the significations of advertising 'are never *personal*: they are all differential' and 'to differentiate oneself is precisely to affiliate to a model, to label oneself by reference to an abstract model.'[71] Sala's sketches show something of this paradox of personalization and abstraction in their tension between the particularized biographies of the Misses Gimp, the Reverend Doctor Brushback, or Captain Vere de Vere Delamere and his family, and the codes and generic classifications involved in caricature. But they are also distinguished by their combination of comic entertainment with social critique. While laughing at the ignominious fate of the heir who inherits the 'noble mansion' once inhabited by the 'Earl of Elbowsout' or mocking the notice of 'An Italian Villa to Let' because it is 'only Italian in so far *as it possesses Venetian blinds*,'[72] Sala also observes 'other cottages, dreadful cottages, squalid cottages, cottages in Church Lane, Saint Giles's, where frowsy women in tattered shawls crouch stolidly on the door-step; where ragged, filthy children wallow with fowls and pigs amidst the dirt and squalor.'[73]

Sala employs a similar technique, combining the comic character sketch with sober social comment, in two more articles devoted to the advertising columns of the *Times*: 'Want Places' and 'More Places Wanted.'[74] This time extrapolating the biographies of the advertisers from their advertisements (and focusing only upon women), he uses the stock phrases and epithets they employ to identify the various social types distinguishable amongst the housekeepers, nurses, lady's maids, cooks, and housemaids who announce their want of a place in the *Times*. 'More Places Wanted' begins with the following announcement:

> AS LADY'S-MAID, a young person who has lived in the first families, and can have four years' good character. Fully understands dressmaking, hair-dressing, and getting up fine linen. Address Miss T., Bunty's Library, Crest Terrace, Pimlico.[75]

Sala attributes this advertisement to Miss Fanny Tarlatan, who does not reside at Bunty's library, but 'is an old colleague of Mrs Bunty's (once Miss Thorneytwig, my Lady Crocus's waiting woman,) and calls her Matilda, and is by her called "Fanny, and a dear girl;" and therefore she gives Bunty's library as an address; it being considered more aristocratic than Tidlers' Gardens' (where she actually lives). Fanny's skilful versatility elicits Sala's 'great respect,' as well as a wry perception of the elegant economies she helps to sustain: 'Some ladies make a merit of their Tarlatanism, stating with pride, that their maids "do everything for them;" others endeavour uneasily to defend their economy by reference to the hardness of the times, to their large families, to the failure of revenue from my lord's Irish estates, to the extravagance of such and such a son or heir, or to Sir John having lost enormously

---

71 Baudrillard, *The Consumer Society*, 88.
72 [Sala], 'Houses to Let,' 10.
73 Ibid.; 11.
74 [George A. Sala], 'More Places Wanted,' *Household Words*, 15 October 1853, 8: 156–62; [Sala], 'Want Places.'
75 [Sala], 'More Places Wanted,' 156.

in railways or by electioneering.'[76] Far surpassing Miss Tarlatan in dress-making skill, however, is Mademoiselle Batiste, 'warranted from Paris,' who has 'a pedigree of former engagements of such magnitude and grandeur, that rank and fashion are fain to bow to her caprices.'[77] She is 'not only apt but erudite in all the cunning of her craft' as a fine lady's maid, and even the celebrated 'M. Anatole, of Regent Street, might take lessons in hair-dressing from her.'

In 'Country News,' Henry Morley's perusal of the advertisements appearing in the 'Brocksop, Garringham, and Washby Standard' leads him, like Sala, to speculate about the lives of those 'for whose information they were issued.'[78] In this case, however, the comic effect depends upon the ingenuity with which he can incorporate the miscellaneous advertisements—for 'The Great Lincolnshire Medicine' or 'Wind Pills,' 'Luxuriant Whiskers,' a 'Mourning and Funeral Warehouse' and so on—into a single biography:

> I could not refrain from picturing to myself a native of those parts in luxuriant whiskers, riding forth after a light breakfast of Wind Pills, on a steed watered with British Remedy, or well rubbed down with Synovitic Lotion. He would be going out to buy a windmill, or to engage a governess who did not want remuneration, and he would meet by the road, perhaps, a neighbour with magnificent legs who would talk over with him the news supplied by their gratuitous paper, and speculate upon the chance of the odd hundred pounds that might be paid them for the job of reading it. The women coming out of the show-rooms, weeping in Bayadere robes for those husbands or children who had omitted to use any Pill, Drops, Elixir, Wafers, Lotion, or ointment, for the sustenance of existence, would also form some interesting groups illustrative of life in those comparatively unknown regions.[79]

Morley's comic sketch of 'the ways and wants' of the inhabitants of Brocksop, Garringham, and Washby from the advertisements appearing in their local newspaper establishes a correspondence between people, and the commodities they buy and sell through advertisement, to construct biographies that give social lives to these goods.

Such extrapolation from advertisements is employed for ironic social comment in William Blanchard Jerrold and W.H. Wills's satire on charity subscriptions. They expose the function of 'The Subscription List,' published in circulars and newspapers, as an 'expedient for spreading a small amount of charity over a large surface of publicity,' and offer the following example of subscribers to a hospital fund:

The Right Honourable Lady Bittern	10s.	0d.
The Honourable Blanch Bittern	7	6
The Honourable Fanny Bittern	5	0
The Honourable Alicia Bittern	2	6
The Honourable Jemima Bittern	2	6
The Honourable Chas. De Brandenburgh Bittern	2	6

---

76   Ibid.: 157.
77   Ibid.: 158.
78   [Henry Morley], 'Country News,' *Household Words*, 2 July 1853, 7: 427.
79   Ibid.

Lady Bittern is an economist. No one knows better than her ladyship how to lay out thirty shillings in charity with profit to the reputation of her numerous family.[80]

Similarly, quoting the subscription of 'Miss Letitia Latterday, of Latterborough Hall ... £10,' Jerrold and Wills remark that 'the conspicuous advertisement of Miss Latterday's name and euphonious address at full length, betrays an anxiety that her benevolent desires, together with the fact of her being the possessor of Latterborough Hall, should be extensively known to the public at large.' What these charity subscribers clearly buy with their advertised donation is social capital.

Household Words explores the growing importance of self-promotion and celebrity elsewhere in its discussion of the photography 'mania.' In an 1857 leader, 'Your Life or Your Likeness,' the Rev. James White protests against the current craze for biography and photography and the invasion of privacy it entails. The title plays with the form of a threatening ultimatum, capturing the persecutions comically denounced in the article. While White concedes that it is largely possible to escape the clutches of the biographers who endlessly solicit material for their prospective volumes, the 'portrait-mongers,' armed with their portable photographic apparatus, are more difficult to evade:

> [they] snap you up at your most unguarded moments, in your most unbecoming deshabille, and stamp you for ever with such insolent resemblance of attitude and feature, that it is impossible to deny the identity[,] and yet, so altered in the process, so harshened in the expression, so vulgarised in the apparel, that you might safely indite the performance as a libel; being calculated to bring you into hatred and contempt.[81]

White's objection to the unflattering likeness captured by the photographic portrait-mongers echoes the observations made by Morley and Wills earlier in the decade, as they record a visit to the photographic portrait studio of Mr Mayall in Regent Street: amidst a 'thousand images of human creatures of each sex and of every age—such as no painter ever has produced,' they remark '[y]oung chevaliers regard[ing] us with faces tied and fastened down so that, as it seemed, they could by no struggle get their features loose out of the very twist and smirk they chanced to wear when they were captured and fixed. Here a grave man was reading on for ever, with his eyes upon the same line of his book; and there a soldier frowned with brow inanely fierce over a rampart of moustachios.'[82] The language of entrapment suggests their ambivalence about the new technology, even though Morley and Wills anticipate the many

---

80 [William Blanchard Jerrold and W.H. Wills], 'The Subscription List,' *Household Words*, 28 September 1850, 2: 11.

81 [Rev. James White], 'Your Life or Your Likeness,' *Household Words* 25 July 1857, 16: 75.

82 [Henry Morley and W.H. Wills], 'Photography,' *Household Words*, 19 March 1853, 7: 54–5. Regina B. Oost notes that the May 1853 instalment of *Bleak House* included a brochure for Mayall's Daguerreotype Portrait Galleries and that Dickens had sat for his portrait there earlier in December 1852. Regina B. Oost, '"More Like Than Life": Painting, Photography, and Dickens's *Bleak House*,' in *Dickens Studies Annual*, ed. Stanley Friedman, Edward Guiliano, and Michael Timko (New York: AMS Press, 2001), 143–4.

benefits likely to flow from it in the future.[83] However by 1857, as White suggests, the photography mania has given birth to the first paparazzi. These 'biographic and photographic enthusiasts' exemplify not only the 'inquisitive propensities of the present age,' but the commodification of personality. 'If you are somebody,' White complains, 'they insist on your insertion among the great ones of the earth. You join the Wellingtons, Napoleons, Caesars, and Alexanders, and are content with your fellow-immortals, for haven't you invented a new cheese-press, or in some other way been of use to your country and species?' And it is such 'immortals' whose celebrity is conjoined to commodities by wily entrepreneurs as a marketing ploy. In 'A Pill-Box,' George Dodd describes the 'psychological study' involved in the design of boxes for packaging goods and the importance of celebrity portraits as cover illustrations, for a 'box is often a lure, a bribe, a coaxing machine. Its contents may be pretty or valuable, or both. But the box frequently entices to the purchase of that which would not be purchased if the box were not.'[84] The Duke of Wellington is recognized as having been a particularly profitable image although now surpassed by Uncle Tom:

> The Australian diggings, Jenny Lind, the Bloomers, the Duke of Wellington, Uncle Tom's Cabin—all are fish that comes to [the illustrator's] net; he keeps an eye upon what is passing in the world around him, seizes on any matter of public interest, and fixes it down on paper directly, or rather on stone, for the pictures are lithographed. Our manufacturer has by him drawers full and portfolios full of sheets of pictures, some newly springing into popularity, others passing into oblivion: the maker and the artist taking especial care that new beauties shall be ready to attract the eye before passed beauties have waned too much. The Duke was a capital subject; he sold many scores of grosses of boxes. At present Uncle Tom is the reigning favourite.[85]

As well as employing topical subjects like the gold diggings, the box-makers capitalize on the commercial value of celebrity, employing the same principle as the advertisers in annexing the image to an unrelated commodity. This is more than a matter of mere decoration, as Dodd suggests. The box-makers are keenly attuned to fluctuations in popular interest and adjust their products accordingly. As John Plunkett notes of the power given to individual consumers by the rise of the *carte-de-visite*, it 'was through their choices that celebrities were formed.'[86]

Indeed, the powerlessness of the reluctant celebrity to evade the commodification and circulation of his or her image is satirically outlined in 'A Counterfeit Presentment.' John Hollingshead's sketch is narrated by 'the celebrated Sweetwort,' who 'was a happy man' while his identity as author of 'those powerful letters which appear occasionally under the signature of Hydrophobius' remained a secret.[87] But

---

83 [Morley and Wills], 'Photography,' 61.
84 [George Dodd], 'A Pill-Box,' *Household Words*, 12 February 1853, 6: 517.
85 Ibid.: 519.
86 John Plunkett, 'Celebrity and Community: The Poetics of the *Carte-De-Visite*,' *Journal of Victorian Culture* 8 (2003): 70.
87 [John Hollingshead], 'A Counterfeit Presentment,' *Household Words*, 3 July 1858, 18: 71.

'in a moment of weakness [he] allowed the veil to be torn asunder' and became 'a literary lion.' It was then 'suddenly found by photographic artists that a public demand existed for my portrait' and the persecutions began, first with an attack of letters, followed by unwanted personal visits:

> My excited imagination saw the detestable lens pointed at me in the street, levelled at my dressing-room curtain as I went through the task of shaving; lurking for me in bye-lanes, and under cover of the trees in the open meadows; stationed even in the very centre of the green-coated German band who played their operatic selection before my breakfast-room window.

Sweetwort manages to elude them all, until he is finally confronted by one enterprising photographer who draws from his pocket a picture of 'a beetle-browed man, with the Sunday complexion of a master chimney-sweep, the lineaments of a church-warden mixed with those of the professional burglar.' It is a portrait of '"Bill Tippets—the Lambeth Phenomenon."'

> 'Now,' continued my visitor, 'I'm a practical man. I've got an order for two thousand copies of your portrait, for home consumption, and fifteen hundred for exportation. I don't want to do anything offensive; but, knowing your objection to sit for a photograph, I have been compelled to look amongst my stock for something like you, and I can find nothing so near the mark as Bill Tippets.'[88]

The supposed resemblance is particularly unflattering for a literary lion like Sweetwort, given that the heads of pugilists were typically used to exemplify the phrenological and physiognomic expression of animal propensities or passions, in contrast to the higher moral and intellectual faculties expressed by a straight profile and refined features.[89] Faced with the stranger's threat to supply the demand for his portrait with a 'counterfeit presentment,' the celebrated Sweetwort succumbs, and is finally discovered 'sitting helplessly, under a broiling sun, in a glass cage upon the tiles of an elevated house near the Haymarket, W., composing [his] countenance according to the imperious instructions of the relentless photographer.'

Hollingshead's comic sketch attests to the increasingly commercial character of photography in the 1850s and the commodification of personality in celebrity images. Curtis notes that by mid-century, portraits had 'become a necessary promotional mechanism for products as well as for public figures,' with *Punch* in 1846 decrying the development of the 'Puff Pictorial.'[90] Not only is Sweetwort's celebrity as an author alienated by being reduced to the exchange-value of his photograph, his very likeness is subject to fabrication by the portrait-mongers if he refuses to cooperate. While Curtis argues that '[s]ignatures and portraits were coming, at this time, to be trademark features for certain products, acting, in an echo of portraits on coinage, as stamps or seals to protect against fraudulent imitators,'[91] 'A Counterfeit

---

88 Ibid.: 72.
89 Mary Cowling, *The Artist as Anthropologist: The Representation of Type and Character in Victorian Art* (Cambridge: Cambridge University Press, 1989), 74.
90 Curtis, *Visual Words*, 126–9.
91 Ibid., 132.

Presentment' calls the authenticating power of the image into question.[92] Ten years after the appearance of Hollingshead's sketch, on his reading-tour of America in 1867, Dickens sought to control the copyright of his portrait image by posing for an exclusive photographic sitting, and was attacked by the *New York Herald* for attempting to profit from his trademark image:

> Since the dust of the Pharoahs was sold as a nostrum and mummy became merchandise there has been nothing so precious and wonderful in the market as the face of Charles Dickens. Hence it is natural there should be danger from counterfeits, and that the happy merchant who possesses a monopoly of the real article should take all pains to prevent deceptions. Even in commodities of a viler stamp such precautions are necessary.[93]

As Andrew J. Kappel argues, the *Herald*'s efforts to discredit Dickens as a money-hungry self-publicist were largely motivated by revenge for his caricature of 'Hamerica' in *American Notes* and *Martin Chuzzlewit*.[94] But the editor's lampoon also demonstrates the way in which the marketing of celebrity and the practices of advertising are inextricably entwined with problems of assuring the authenticity of the 'genuine article'—problems of assurance that pertain not just to the quality of the commodity itself, but to the knowledge, or lack thereof, possessed by the would-be-discerning consumer. Such anxieties about authenticity and their significance for *Household Words's* engagement with commodity culture form the subject of the next chapter.

---

[92] The suspect value of the photographic portrait as a verification of the real is suggested elsewhere in *Household Words* as Morley and Wills describe 'a belted soldier with a red coat, a large cocked hat, and a heavy sword' posing for his photograph, who turns out to be 'an army doctor, by whose side, if army regulations suffered it, there should have hung a scalpel, not a sword,' [Morley and Wills], 'Photography,' 55. And in 'Photographees,' James Payn outlines the ludicrous props and poses associated with the stock genres of family photographic portraiture, including the 'domestic' grouping, the 'classical' and the 'romantic. [James Payn], 'Photographees,' *Household Words*, 10 October 1857, 16: 394.

[93] Quoted in Andrew J. Kappel, 'The Gurney Photograph Controversy,' *Dickensian* 74 (1978): 170.

[94] Ibid.: 167.

Chapter 3

The Genuine Article, the Sham, and the Problem of Authenticity

In a leader published on 20 February 1858, entitled 'Well-Authenticated Rappings,' Dickens mocks two species of imposture satirized in *Household Words* throughout the 1850s: the practice of food adulteration and the craze for spiritualism. Recounting 'three spiritual experiences' of the writer, the article begins by establishing its ironic claim to authenticity through the exaggerated provision of details concerning the exact circumstances of the events described, with an elaborate account of the provenance and location of the watch used to ascertain the time of the first visitation as 'twenty minutes before ten' on the 'twenty-sixth of December last': 'On that memorable morning, at about two hours after daylight, the writer, starting up in bed with his hand to his forehead, distinctly felt seventeen heavy throbs or beats in that region.'[1] Convinced that these 'rappings' are 'of spiritual origin,' given the amount of alcohol consumed at Christmas dinner the previous day, the writer summons the spirits to disclose themselves. He is alarmed to learn from his first spiritual experience that the 'Port' he had consumed was mixed with 'Sloe-Juice, Logwood, Blackberry,' and from his second, that the Pork Pie was contaminated with 'Lead.'[2] These adulterants are the source of the rappings whose 'authenticity' is comically warranted by the pain in his head. The third spiritual experience is described as 'an exquisite case of Tipping,' in which an 'obnoxious young man,' enamoured of 'Miss L.B.,' fumbles his attempt to pass her a billet-doux beneath the family dinner table. The letter is mistakenly put into the hand of her father, causing consternation among the assembled family and guests which her brother, 'Young B.,' tries to cover by blaming the spirits, claiming to be a medium and warning that '"There'll be a Tipping presently, father. Look out for the table!"'[3] Young B.'s diversionary tactic is apparently appreciated and rewarded by the obnoxious young man, for after the overturned table and agitated family group are eventually restored to order, the writer observes in Young B. 'a noticeable attraction (I might almost term it fascination) of his left hand, in the direction of his heart or waist-coat pocket.'

While fraud is as old as human society itself, adulteration and spiritualism were forms of imposture that had assumed peculiar prevalence by the middle of the nineteenth century when they were subject to vigorous debate in the periodical press as part of a more general concern about the 'low state of trading morality.' In

---

1 [Charles Dickens], 'Well-Authenticated Rappings,' *Household Words*, 20 February 1858, 17: 217.
2 Ibid.: 219.
3 Ibid.: 220.

a series on 'Shops, Shopkeepers, Shopmen, and Shop Morality' published in 1850, *Chambers's Edinburgh Journal* identified 'the transactions of the market [as] a series of attempts to cheat on both sides' that is driven by the 'universal spread of the bargaining spirit':

> Counterfeit wares in every possible branch of manufacture, possessing little more than the semblance of the things they represent, fill our shops and warehouses. Things real are kept in the background, for the demands of the sensible few who are uninfected with the bargain fever. In the departments of art, literature, and science, it is the same. Rubbish for bargainers is the principle staple, while the genuine picture, the sterling book, the efficient instrument, find but few admirers and purchasers.[4]

For Carlyle, fraudulent goods sold by the retailer were symptomatic of the more widespread social problems of Mammonism and materialism and the acceptance of 'temporary Semblances' in lieu of the 'eternal Substance': 'We are governed, very infallibly, by the "sham-hero,"—whose name is Quack, whose work and governance is Plausibility, and also is Falsity and Fatuity; to which Nature says, and must say when it comes to her to speak, eternally No!'[5] Debunking the spurious solution of a 'Morison's Pill for curing the maladies of Society,' Carlyle's fierce diatribe against shamming reflects the importance of 'authenticity' as a key concept in Victorian culture more generally, ranging from ideas of the legible body involved in the so-called science of physiognomy, through debates over international copyright and patent law, to the exploration of anxieties about mistaken or fraudulent identity in sensation fiction.

The pursuit of authenticity is a peculiarly modern problem whose development Lionel Trilling traces from the writings of Diderot, Hegel, and Rousseau, showing its relation to historical changes in the understanding of selfhood. From Rousseau, he argues, 'we learned that what destroys our authenticity is [metropolitan] society,' where our 'sentiment of being depends upon the opinion of other people,' making impersonation a condition of social existence.[6] For Victorian moralists, such as Carlyle, Ruskin, and Arnold, the great enemy of authentic being was having—the increasingly dominant principle of capitalist accumulation diminishing the experience of selfhood.[7] The diagnosis of such modern self-alienation is what leads sociologist Dean MacCannell to identify the tourist as 'one of the best models available for modern-man-in-general,'[8] because for 'moderns, reality and authenticity are thought to be elsewhere: in other historical periods and other cultures, in purer, simpler life-styles.'[9] A reflex of the anxiety about the idea of the autonomous self that developed

---

4 'Shops, Shopkeepers, Shopmen, and Shop Morality: Concluding Article,' *Chambers's Edinburgh Journal* 14 (1850): 245.

5 Thomas Carlyle, *Past and Present*, ed. Ernest Rhys, Everyman's Library (1843; London: Dent, 1912), 25.

6 Lionel Trilling, *Sincerity and Authenticity* (London: Oxford University Press, 1972), 93.

7 Ibid., 124.

8 Dean MacCannell, *The Tourist: A New Theory of the Leisure Class*, Revised ed. (New York: Schocken Books, 1989), 1.

9 Ibid., 3.

with modern capitalist society, tourism is a quest for an authentic realm of being. In the context of a developing commodity culture, the dilemma regarding existential authenticity and the moral life posed by modern self-alienation is compounded by the question of object authenticity, as goods become expressive of—indeed the repository for—perdurable selfhood. Analysing the power of the souvenir, Susan Stewart argues that

> [w]ithin the development of culture under an exchange economy, the search for authentic experience and, correlatively, the search for the authentic object become critical. As experience is increasingly mediated and abstracted, the lived relation of the body to the phenomenological world is replaced by a nostalgic myth of contact and presence. 'Authentic' experience becomes both elusive and allusive as it is placed beyond the horizon of present lived experience, the beyond in which the antique, the pastoral, the exotic, and other fictive domains are articulated.[10]

Whether understood in idealist terms as a quality of selfhood or in empirical terms as the 'genuine article,' the idea of authenticity raises questions about the relationship between people and things in a culture organized around the exchange of material goods.

Household Words was no different from other mid-nineteenth-century miscellanies in addressing the problem of authenticity in relation to a range of goods and services: food adulteration, the spirit trade, quack medicine, cheap shopkeeping, and the investment in foreign travel and tourism as a quest for 'authentic' cultural experience. But the peculiar imaginative treatment of these issues in the journal is distinctive. The specific contours of mid-Victorian commodity culture become apparent in the distinctive social conjunctures to which the journal responds. The impact of commodity culture on identity and agency is a key focus. While the age of mechanical reproduction raised questions for critics, like Ruskin, about the debasement of aesthetic values and the threats to historical understanding posed by the loss of originality, concerns about discrimination and identity were also reflected in the increasing emphasis placed upon 'taste' in the discussions surrounding the Great Exhibition—memorably satirized by Henry Morley in 'A House Full of Horrors,' which tells the unfortunate tale of Mr Crumpet, who has acquired some 'Correct Principles of Taste' from a visit to the Department of Practical Art exhibition mounted by Henry Cole at Marlborough House, and is thereafter haunted by the discovery that he has been living among 'horrors' in his home.[11] Morley's comic tale speaks to the concerns of those middle-class readers of *Household Words* enjoying the new opportunities offered by affordable, mass-produced consumer goods to create a tasteful setting for themselves through the furnishing and decoration of their homes. The successful exercise of consumer choice depended upon knowledge and discernment. But the new culture of the copy made it increasingly difficult to distinguish authenticity, and the preoccupation with the provenance of goods shown

---

10 Susan Stewart, *On Longing: Narratives of the Miniature, the Gigantic, the Souvenir, the Collection* (Durham: Duke University Press, 1993), 133.

11 [Henry Morley], 'A House Full of Horrors,' *Household Words*, 4 December 1852, 6: 265.

in the genre of the 'process article,' discussed in Chapter 5, is one response to concern about the difficulty of assuring the quality of goods in an era of mass-production.

The processes of industrialization and urbanization created a large, anonymous class of consumers whose relationship to producers and sellers was increasingly impersonal and gave rise to new anxieties about the genuineness of goods and services and how to discern this. In the absence of product standardization (even of textiles)[12] and of any knowledge of the provenance of goods, how could the consumer be sure of their quality? As noted in Chapter 2, *Household Words* attempted to address a new sort of middle-class audience, one with an increasing disposable income for the purchase of non-essential goods, but without, in many cases, the necessary education and social assurance to distinguish the real from the fake. The problem was made all the more acute by the uncertain status of expert opinion in the period while the professions were yet to be institutionalized. How, for example, can one know when a medicine touted by a 'doctor' is fraudulent if the qualifications for medical practice are not uniformly accredited? How can one tell whether the reputed work of an old master is genuine or not when there is no agreement about the procedures for establishing a painting's authenticity? The *Household Words* writer—the non-specialist 'man of the world' already described in Chapter 1—could serve as something of a guide in this regard for the journal's audience. The knowingness of a writer like Sala—effected through his classical tags, flamboyant neologisms, and throwaway allusions, combined with serious street cred—seems designed to establish his own powers of discernment as a reassurance to readers that lack of expert knowledge is no handicap to making the right consumer choices. He can tell if a Titian is likely to be fake, being up to the tricks of the trade, and in a world in which the conspicuous consumption of commodities was increasingly a constituent of selfhood, whether or not one bought or sold the 'real thing' had significant implications for identity.

As Trilling argues, one of the 'chief intentions' of the work of art throughout the nineteenth century was to provide its audience with the authenticity of which the object itself was the model. 'The authentic work of art instructs us in our inauthenticity and adjures us to overcome it,' he writes.[13] For Benjamin, the authenticity of the work of art is not reproducible, but is paradoxically an effect of the copies subsequently made of it—the 'presence of the original is the prerequisite to the concept of authenticity'[14]—and the development of differentiations between original and copy 'was an important function of the trade in works of art.'[15] The commercial effects of aura and their manipulation are satirically exposed in Sala's essay on his 'Travels in Cawdor Street.' A street ethnography, like those discussed in Chapter 4, Sala's article offers a more complex study of the practice of shamming than that found in *Chambers's* account of 'Shops, Shopkeepers, Shopmen and Shop Morality.' He begins by contrasting his own sharp-eyed, physiognomic sight-seeing with the behaviour of the 'unobservant peripatetic,' the 'ordinary street lounger,' who takes Cawdor Street for granted, and observes no more than a 'few musty shops, filled

---

12 Dorothy Davis, *A History of Shopping* (London: Routledge and Kegan Paul, 1966), 256.

13 Trilling, *Sincerity and Authenticity*, 100.

14 Walter Benjamin, 'The Work of Art in the Age of Mechanical Reproduction,' in *Illuminations*, ed. Hannah Arendt (New York: Schocken Books, 1968), 220.

15 Ibid., 243n2.

with ancient furniture[,] half-a-dozen dingy book-stalls, some brokers' shops, and a score or more receptacles for cloudy-looking oil pictures in tarnished frames.'[16] His allusion to *Macbeth* plays upon the idea of 'Wardour Street English' to identify the original street that had become renowned for its imitation-antique trade, and is thus the first in a series of false identities unmasked in the course of the essay. No different from any other London thoroughfare on the surface, behind the scenes in Cawdor Street 'dwell the great tribe of manufacturers of spurious antiques, of sham *moyen-age* furniture, of fictitious Dresden china, of delusive Stradivarius violins. In Cawdor Street abide the mighty nation of picture-dealers, picture-forgers, picture "clobberers," picture-pawners, and other picture traffickers, whose name is legion.'[17] Speculating about the astonishment with which Raphael, Rembrandt, or Michaelangelo would view the 'multitudinous pictures which bear their names' in this 'thoroughfare of deceptions and shams,' Sala moves on to inspect the stock of Messrs. Melchior Saltabadil and Co., retailers of 'ancient furniture, armour, old china, cameos, and other curiosities and articles of *vertu*,' every one of which has 'its appropriate legend':

> That china monster belonged to the Empress Maria Louisa; that battered helmet was picked up on the field of Naseby; that rusted iron box was the muniment chest of the Abbey of Glastonbury; that ivory-hafted dagger once hung at the side of David Rizzio; and that long broadsword was erst clasped by one of Cromwell's Ironsides.

As Stewart explains, the antique seems to make contact with the past, linking it to the souvenir in its offer to authenticate an experience remote in time and space;[18] and part of this value derives from the imagined histories and geographies inhering in the antique—the commodity biographies which for Benjamin define the authenticity of a thing.[19] The manufactures of Cawdor Street derive much of their value from the fictitious narratives of origin produced as they are situated within the processes of second-hand exchange. But the spuriousness of these antiques is known to 'an old traveller in Cawdor Street,' like Sala, who has seen the art-manufactures that are carried on in 'garrets, in frowsy little courts, and mysterious back slums adjoining thereon.' He cites the example of Mr Turps, who 'deals only in dead masters,' and boasts among his treasures an 'almost priceless picture—a little, old shabby panel, on which you can discover something dimly, representing a man's head, blinking through a dark brown fog. This is THE Rembrandt "Three-quarter Portrait of the Burgomaster Six," painted in 1630.' In reality, Turps 'had it painted himself on a panel taken from a mahogany chest of drawers he picked up cheap at a sale,' paying 'Young M'Gilp (attached to a portrait club, and not too proud to paint a

---

16 [George A. Sala], 'Travels in Cawdor Street,' *Household Words*, 21 February 1852, 4: 517.
17 Ibid.: 518.
18 Stewart, *On Longing*, 140.
19 'The authenticity of a thing is the essence of all that is transmissible from its beginning, ranging from its substantive duration to its testimony to the history which it has experienced.' Benjamin, 'The Work of Art in the Age of Mechanical Reproduction,' 221.

sign occasionally) just fifteen shillings for it.'[20] Sala describes in some detail the processes by which the effects of age and the aura of originality are manufactured in two large attics at the top of Mr Turps's house. While uncovering such deceptions, however, he shows little sympathy for the victims of Turps: they are 'mostly recruited from the ranks of the vulgar with money, who purchase fine pictures as a necessary luxury, just as they buy fine clothes and carriages and horses,' and who buy 'against each other; Brown becoming frantic if Jones possess more Titians than he does; Robinson running neck and neck with Tomkins in Claudes, and beating him cleverly sometimes with a Canaletto.' Turps's sham pictures are purchased by humbugs to express their social pretension, so that it becomes a moot point as to who is doing the cheating here. In such trading, the aesthetic value of the artwork is completely displaced by its value as a positional good, conferring a spurious social distinction that ironically bespeaks the inauthenticity of the pseudonymous buyers, Brown, Robinson, and Tomkins. As Trilling notes, the names given by the nineteenth-century novelists to the abandonment of an original class position, 'to the indication of diminished authenticity, were snobbery and vulgarity.'[21] The role of such commodity consumption in the formation of false social identities contrasts with the plight of the producers, forced into 'grinding-work for the picture-dealers.' Having experienced poverty as an artist of sorts in his youth, Sala imagines 'that not a few painters, who have had R.A. appended (and worthily) to their names, and have dined at the tables of live Dukes and Duchesses, may have thought of their old Cawdor Street days with a sort of tremor.' The trade in fakes is thus symptomatic of a more pervasive problem concerning the morality of the market:

> Cawdor Street, standing, as it does, in the midst of that land, and of that city, so bursting, so running over, with commercial competition, that, panting to do business at any price, it cannot refrain from vending counterfeit limbs, spurious garments, sham victuals and drink even. The worst of it is, that, knowing how many of the curiosities and rarities in these seeming shops are cunning deceits, a man is apt to get sceptical as regards them all.[22]

The encouragement of scepticism regarding the genuineness of commodities reflects a more widespread social concern about identity and authenticity within an increasingly commercial culture that is also shown in the journal's attack upon false mendicancy. In 'Departed Beggars,' an unidentified contributor laments the passing of those London beggars who were 'strictly professional,' and contrasts their openness with the 'covert mendicancy' of the current day in which begging is conducted under the guise of a sham market exchange:

> Aged and infirm people go from door to door with small stocks of lucifer-match boxes, or stay and boot laces, or memorandum-books or almanacks, and under shelter of this array of small traffic, they—beg. The children, little girls especially, beg under the odour of violets, 'only a penny a bunch,' even in winter. They profess no mendicancy; but their dress, their look, their tone, their straggling hair and protruding toes, are all mendicants' pleas, and they sometimes beg directly.[23]

---

20 [Sala], 'Travels in Cawdor Street,' 520.
21 Trilling, *Sincerity and Authenticity*, 115.
22 [Sala], 'Travels in Cawdor Street,' 519.
23 [Wood], 'Departed Beggars,' *Household Words*, 29 May 1852, 5: 245.

In a leader published on 18 May 1850, Dickens castigates 'The Begging-Letter Writer' as 'one of the most shameless frauds and impositions of this time' whose most grievous effect is 'the immeasurable harm he does to the deserving,—dirtying the stream of true benevolence, and muddling the brains of foolish justices, with inability to distinguish between the base coin of distress, and the true currency we have always among us.'[24] Dickens deplores his swindling as a 'trade,' passed on to sons and daughters, that exploits the difficulty of distinguishing genuine from counterfeit distress. But as Geoffrey Hemstedt astutely notes, Dickens's indignation is complicated by the repressed recognition of the begging-letter writer as an uncanny double who rivals his own facility with language and modes of utterance.[25] Dickens invokes 'the results of the real experience of a real person … with a personal knowledge of the extent to which the Begging-Letter Trade has been carried on for some time'[26] to authenticate his call for a public resolution to 'crush the trade.'[27] But the effort to distinguish his personal voice from the ingenious proposals of the begging-letter writer is compromised by the form of comic ventriloquism adopted in the sketch. While condemning the deception, the article also suggests how difficult it is to get at the 'real self' in a world where identity is mediated by fictions of commodity culture.

The figure of Doctor Dulcamara, the loquacious charlatan from Donizetti's *L'Elisir d'Amore*, is repeatedly invoked in *Household Words* to satirize the rhetorical performances of commercial imposture. In 'Down Whitechapel, Far Away,' Sala describes the booth of Messrs. Misture and Fitt who 'have gone into the quack line of business, in a Bohemian or travelling manner,' erecting their monster marquee in Liverpool's Whitechapel to display 'a bountiful spread of nasty-looking preparations, pills, pots of ointment, bottles of sarsaparilla, cases of herbs, blisters, plaisters and boluses.'[28] Fitt's style of eloquence in cajoling his customers is described as falling somewhere between the broadness of 'Cheap Jack' and the 'loftiness' of Dulcamara. The accents of Doctor Dulcamara are also invoked by Henry Morley in relation to the spiritualist press, as he reports the 'Latest Intelligence from Spirits' in a New England newspaper advertising 'Purifying Syrup, Nerve-Soothing Elixir, and Healing Ointment,' commodities which 'have the additional recommendation that they are prepared from Spirit directions—heaven-sent potions.'[29] Morley derides the ways in which the *Spiritualist*'s correspondence 'is made up in support of the gentlemen and ladies who have advertised' and the advertisements themselves are masked as leading articles, representing an early form of 'advertorial.'[30]

---

24 [Charles Dickens], 'The Begging-Letter Writer,' *Household Words*, 18 May 1850, 1: 169.

25 Geoffrey Hemstedt, 'Dickens's Later Journalism,' in *Journalism, Literature and Modernity*, ed. Kate Campbell (Edinburgh: Edinburgh University Press, 2000), 47.

26 [Dickens], 'The Begging-Letter Writer,' 171.

27 Ibid.: 172.

28 [George A. Sala], 'Down Whitechapel, Far Away,' *Household Words*, 13 August 1853, 7: 571.

29 [Henry Morley], 'Latest Intelligence from Spirits,' *Household Words*, 30 June 1855, 11: 513.

30 In a co-authored leader entitled 'Doctor Dulcamara, M.D.,' Wilkie Collins and Dickens remark, amongst the many impersonations of 'our eloquent, our far-famed, our magnificent

The spirit trade was a frequent satiric target in *Household Words*. In an 1853 article satirizing the reports on séances published in *The Spiritual Telegraph*, Dickens mocks the commercialism of the trade in its use of the new term, 'Tippings':

> We did at first suppose this excessive word to be of English growth, and to refer to the preliminary 'tipping' of the medium, which is found to be indispensable to the entertainments on this side of the Atlantic. We have discovered, however, that it denotes the spiritual movement of the tables and chairs, and of a mysterious piece of furniture called a 'stand,' which appears to be in every apartment.[31]

In 'Spirits Over the Water,' James Payn examines a prospectus for the *Spiritual Age*, 'published every Saturday at number fourteen, Bromfield Street (up-stairs), Boston, Massachusets, at the small charge of two dollars per annum, Invariably in Advance.'[32] Such 'extreme distinctness as to money matters' is also found elsewhere in the newspaper: 'Mrs E.T. French, for instance, clairvoyant physician, New York, advertises in good bold type (miraculous as her powers are, and yearning as her heart continuously is to effect the permanent cure of the whole suffering human family) that it is useless sending "a lock of your hair, and at least one of the prominent symptoms" of your complaint to her, without an accompaniment of five dollars.'[33] While these satiric accounts of the spiritualist press expose the pecuniary interests that underlie the vaunted humanitarianism of the practitioners, Morley takes the critique further in 'The Ghost of the Cock Lane Ghost' when he puts the advertised services of 'Mrs M.B. Hayden', 'just returned from the United States,' to the test for the fee of a guinea. Although giving a comical account of the rapping session in which the spirits get every question that is put to them wrong, Morley's earnest condemnation of the fraud goes beyond ridicule of its commercial dishonesty to express concern about the commodification of personhood involved in the trade:

> If that which is the holiest ground within the human heart be through such exhibitions dug into for gold by coarse impostures—if the simple questioner ... be played upon by cheats who laugh under their sleeves at her credulity and turn her money in their pockets,— then such cheating is no matter for amusement. That is an impiety and wickedness far exceeding the measure of ordinary fraud, which trades upon our solemn love towards the dead.[34]

For Morley, at stake in the spirit trade is a good embodied in the person—'our solemn love towards the dead'—that should remain beyond the scope of the market.

---

impostor,' one particular 'presentation of himself, on the twenty-eighth of October last (in the character of the Right Honourable Mr Sidney Herbert)' commending Charlotte Yonge's Puseyite novel—*The Heir of Redclyffe*—as 'the type and pattern of all English domestic novels.' Opponents of Puseyism's dogma, they object even more strenuously to the unreality of Yonge's characters. [Wilkie Collins and Charles Dickens], 'Doctor Dulcamara, M.P.,' *Household Words*, 18 December 1858, 19: 50.

   31 [Charles Dickens], 'The Spirit Business,' *Household Words*, 7 May 1853, 7: 218.
   32 [James Payn], 'Spirits over the Water,' *Household Words*, 5 June 1858, 17: 581.
   33 Ibid.
   34 [Henry Morley], 'The Ghost of the Cock Lane Ghost,' *Household Words*, 20 November 1852, 6: 217.

Threats to identity of a more material kind are examined in the recurrent discussion of the adulteration of food and drink in *Household Words*. In the eighteenth chapter of *Hard Times*, published as the leader on 3 June 1854, Mr Bounderby continues the fraudulent tale of his rise from the gutter by boasting of the 'hap'orth of stewed eels he had purchased in the streets at eight years old' and 'the calculation that he (Bounderby) had eaten in his youth at least three horses under the guise of polonies and saveloys.'[35] The dubious contents of such sausages had been disclosed four years earlier, in the fourteenth issue of the journal, where Richard H. Horne describes the scandalous co-location in Sharp's Alley of London's largest horse-slaughter-house with its largest sausage manufactory, explaining that the 'best of the diseased bullocks or "choppers," are taken to the sausage machine, to be advantageously mixed with the choppings of horse-flesh (to which latter ingredient the angry redness of so many "cured" sausages, *saveloy*, and all the class of *polonies* is attributable.'[36] Although adulteration pre-dates the Victorians, according to John Burnett it 'prevailed in the first half of the nineteenth century to an unprecedented and unsupposed extent,' arising from the greater opportunities for commercial fraud associated with the emergence of a consuming public 'distinct and separated from the producers of food' and the increasingly impersonal nature of retailing.[37] The temptation for traders to exploit the geographical gap between consumers and producers of food and to use untaxed adulterants to reduce the cost of such heavily excised items as tea, coffee, sugar, wine, and pepper, was driven largely by the 'excessive degree' of competition in the food trades.[38] A symptom of the strength of the ideology of economic liberalism, as well as the new conditions of mass production and consumption, adulteration reached its peak in the 1850s when revelations about its prevalence, published in the *Lancet* and disseminated more widely in the popular periodical press, effected a decisive shift in public attitudes towards the problem.

Henry Morley offers a summary of the latest examples of food adulteration afflicting the British consumer in 'Constitutional Trials,' published on 17 July 1852:

> From one side he is shouted at to mind his milk, and from another to beware of his bread; a sepulchral voice informs him when he lifts a cup of coffee to his lips that it contains chicory and coffins. In his tea, he is told to look for black-lead, Prussian blue and gypsum; in his wine, he is warned that there are drugs past reckoning; and in his cakes, he is kindly admonished; in his custards, prussic acid lies in waiting to destroy. Whatever the British consumer may feel inclination to devour, let him devour it at his peril; he will himself be thereby preyed upon, devoured, consumed.[39]

Household Words joined other contemporary periodicals in covering the issue of adulteration, and helping to popularize awareness of the findings of the 'Analytical Sanitary Commission' that were published by the *Lancet* in a series of articles from

---

35   Charles Dickens, 'Hard Times,' *Household Words*, 3 June 1854, 9: 359.

36   [Richard H. Horne], 'The Cattle-Road to Ruin,' *Household Words*, 29 June 1850, 1: 327.

37   John Burnett, *Plenty and Want: A Social History of Food in England from 1815 to the Present Day*, Third ed. (London: Routledge, 1989), 86.

38   Ibid., 95.

39   [Henry Morley], 'Constitutional Trials,' *Household Words*, 17 July 1852, 5: 423.

1851 to 1854. Arthur Hassall, physician and lecturer on medicine at the Royal Free Hospital, was appointed by the *Lancet*'s editor, Thomas Wakley, to conduct the investigation with the assistance of Henry Letheby, Professor of Chemistry and Toxicology in the Medical College of the London Hospital.[40] The inquiry was distinguished by the advanced scientific methods of its chemical analysis, including extensive use of the microscope to aid in detection, and the resolve to publish, after due warning, the names and addresses of manufacturers and traders whose products were found to be impure. Hassall investigated 30 of the commonest foods and drinks, taking his samples from hundreds of shops randomly selected throughout London, and found that adulteration occurred in almost every case, often in ways that were damaging to the health of consumers.

Between December 1850 and January 1851, *Household Words* published three 'Chips' by W.H. Wills and Charles Strange describing three of the most deleterious forms of adulteration: 'Death in the Teapot,' 'Death in the Bread-Basket' and 'Death in the Sugar Plum.'[41] These follow earlier accounts of the dilution of metropolitan milk with water, described by Richard H. Horne in 'The Cow with the Iron Tail,' and of the accidental adulterations associated with the unregulated sale of poison, deplored by Henry Morley in 'Poison Sold Here!'[42] James Hannay's account of 'The Great Coffee Question,' using the *Lancet* reports, appeared on 12 May 1851. It identifies the 'arch corruptor' of coffee as chicory, in itself harmless, but notes that 'even that must be villainously compounded; the adulteration itself must be adulterated. Chicory begins, but worse—that is to say, beans, corn, potato-flour, horse-chesnuts, acorns, dog-biscuit, rope-yarn, Russian glue, brick-dust, mahogany saw-dust, rotten coffin-wood, soot, and "other manures"—remain behind.'[43] Not surprisingly, given his medical background, Morley was the most vocal contributor to condemn the threat to public health posed by adulteration, detailing the poisonous components of sweetmeats, bread, and tea in 'Constitutional Trials' and providing a step-by-step guide for readers who might wish to test for themselves the purity of these and other comestibles, like coffee and sugar. But there is a noticeable shift in the tone of the journal's engagement with this topic throughout the decade, so that by 1855, after the conclusion of the 'Analytical Sanitary Commission,' Morley treats the subject comically in a sketch on the 'Starvation of an Alderman,' and of course Dickens's satire on 'Well-Authenticated Rappings' follows later in 1858.

Morley's sketch is couched as the desperate appeal of the alderman's daughter on behalf of her papa, Mr Alderman Crumpet, who had figured in the earlier satiric tale,

---

40 William F. Long, 'Dickens and the Adulteration of Food,' *Dickensian* 84 (1988): 160.

41 [Charles Strange and W.H. Wills], 'Death in the Teapot,' *Household Words*, 14 December 1850, 2: 277; [W.H. Wills and Charles Strange], 'Death in the Bread-Basket,' *Household Words*, 28 December 1850, 2: 323; [W.H. Wills], 'Death in the Sugar Plum,' *Household Words*, 25 January 1851, 2: 426–7.

42 [Richard H. Horne], 'The Cow with the Iron Tail,' *Household Words*, 9 November 1850, 2: 145–51; [Henry Morley], 'Poison Sold Here!,' *Household Words*, 9 November 1850, 2: 155–7. In addition to the articles discussed below, see also [William Blanchard Jerrold], 'The Milky and Watery Way,' *Household Words*, 20 June 1857, 15: 593–6, and [Henry Morley], 'Justice to Chicory,' *Household Words*, 13 November 1852, 6: 208–10.

43 [James Hannay], 'The Great Coffee Question,' *Household Words*, 12 April 1851, 3: 52.

'A House Full of Horrors,' and whose family now faces imminent starvation because they can find nothing safe to eat. As Dickens's earlier satiric sketch of Alderman Snoady and his appetite for turtle soup suggests,[44] members of the Court of Common Council, which governed the City of London, were renowned for their gormandizing and gluttony, thus adding point to Morley's joke. The alderman's daughter begins by describing her consternation at receiving a copy of Hassall's revised and collected reports (published as *Food and its Adulterations* in 1855) after requesting 'the latest scientific work upon the mysteries connected with the preparation of food' from the local bookseller in order to learn how to cook for the occasion of her forthcoming twentieth birthday. Determined to 'apply the torch of science to the fire of genius already laid within [her] soul,' Marie Crumpet reads Dr Hassall's book deep into the night 'until I grew haggard,' and regales her parents with the fruits of her study at breakfast the next morning.[45] Handing the alderman his customary cup of tea, she details, with mounting 'hysteria,' its contents: '"[e]xhausted tea leaves, leaves other than those of tea, beech, elm, sycamore, horse chesnut, plane, plum, fancy oak, willow, poplar, hawthorn, and sloe, lie tea, paddy hush, Dutch pink, rose pink, indigo, Prussian blue, mineral green, turmeric, logwood, Chinese yellow, verdigris, arsenite of copper, chromate and bichromate of potash, gypsum, mica, magnesia–."'[46] Discomforted by these revelations and asking for coffee instead, her father is assailed with a lengthy list of the adulterated coffees identified by Dr Hassall, including a 'sample purchased at a shop in one of the great thoroughfares of London,' warranted as the 'GOOD and GENUINE article' in a large advertisement disparaging those grocers who adulterate their coffee with 'Roasted Beans, Dog-biscuit, Chicory, and tan.' The advertisement is reproduced typographically in the narrative and employs the sloganeering that Burnett notes became common in the 1850s among traders who sought to cash in on the newly awakened public anxiety about adulteration.[47] Marie's list of inedibles grows with each attempt by her parents to find something safe to eat and drink, until the family decides 'that it was impossible to go on taking our meals.'[48]

In its comic characterization of the Crumpets, Morley's whimsical tale transforms the reportage of the *Lancet* findings found elsewhere, for example, in *Chambers's Edinburgh Journal* or the *Cornhill Magazine*,[49] to bring the threat home, situating it dramatically, albeit humorously, at the heart of the Victorian middle-class family. The Crumpet breakfast table, with its tea, coffee, cocoa, bread, anchovies, and sauce, illustrates the growing importance of the industrialization of food in the nineteenth century, with changes in the processes of preserving, mechanization, transport,

---

44 [Charles Dickens], 'Lively Turtle,' *Household Words*, 26 October 1850, 2: 97–9.
45 [Henry Morley], 'Starvation of an Alderman,' *Household Words*, 31 March 1855, 11: 214.
46 Ibid.: 215.
47 Burnett, *Plenty and Want*, 224.
48 [Morley], 'Starvation of an Alderman,' 216.
49 [A.H. Hassall], 'Adulteration, and Its Remedy,' *Cornhill Magazine* 2 (1860); 'The English Thugs,' *Chambers's Edinburgh Journal* 23/70 (1855).

wholesaling, and retailing shaping the Victorian middle-class diet.[50] Morley's sketch shows how commodities in the home express the conflicts inherent in larger social formations like urbanization and capitalism. It demonstrates the extent to which the practice of adulteration had, by the middle of the decade, become widely recognized as a prevalent social problem that could no longer be rationalized as a means of lowering the cost of food for the poor.[51]

Thomas Wakley, the editor who initiated the *Lancet*'s campaign against food adulteration, also spearheaded the attack on another sector of fraudulent retail affecting public health: patent medicines. According to the anonymous author of *The Language of the Walls: and a Voice from the Shop Windows. Or, The Mirror of Commercial Roguery*, 'one of the leading characteristics of the age is Quackery,'[52] and its 'principal handmaiden' is 'the newspaper press of Great Britain'[53] which '"circulate[s] the manifestoes of charlatans"' in advertisements and puffs.[54] Roy Porter notes that the eighteenth-century advent of newspaper advertising marked 'an epoch in quack medicine promotion' by vastly expanding the pool of potential buyers accessible to a vendor.[55] Dickens's publishers were as culpable as other sections of the nineteenth-century press in continuing the promotion, including the advertisements of inventive entrepreneurs, such as James Morison and Thomas Holloway, in the monthly numbers of his novels amongst notices for other vendors of universal medicines. Bernard Darwin describes a certain 'Ali Ahmed,' who touted his celebrated cough tablets, composed from a secret family receipt, in the fourteenth number of *Bleak House* in an advertisement headed by Arabic script and proclaiming the noble Persian descent of the pill-maker.[56] Such an effort to authenticate the nostrum through the fabrication of an oriental genealogy that is then circulated by the press is satirized in William Blanchard Jerrold's account of 'The

---

50   Jack Goody, *Cooking, Cuisine and Class: A Study in Comparative Sociology* (Cambridge: Cambridge University Press, 1982), 154.

51   Such recognition is also evident in Dickens's imaginative reworking of the terms of the debate to hit two satiric targets in 'Our Commission,' published as the leader on 11 August 1855, which uses 'the disclosures in reference to the adulteration of Food, Drinks, and Drugs' as inspiration for 'the idea of originating a Commission to inquire into the extensive adulteration of certain other articles which it is of the last importance that the country should possess in a genuine state.' Imitating the analytical procedures and language of Hassall's report, Dickens attacks government corruption and incompetence through the metaphor of adulteration, finding all samples of Public Office to be composed 'from seventy-five to ninety-eight per cent of Noodledom' and a 'specimen of Representative Chamber' brought from 'Westminster Market' to be 'fearfully adulterated with Talk, stained with Job, and diluted with large quantities of coloring matter of a false and deceptive nature.' [Charles Dickens], 'Our Commission,' *Household Words*, 11 August 1855, 12: 27.

52   [James Dawson Burn], *The Language of the Walls: And a Voice from the Shop Windows. Or, the Mirror of Commercial Roguery* (Manchester: Abel Heywood, 1855), vi.

53   Ibid., 84.

54   Ibid., 91–2.

55   Roy Porter, *Quacks: Fakers and Charlatans in English Medicine* (Stroud, Gloucestershire: Tempus, 2000), 111.

56   Bernard Darwin, *The Dickens Advertiser: A Collection of the Advertisements in the Original Parts of the Novels by Charles Dickens* (New York: Haskell House, 1930), 195.

Methusaleh Pill' in *Household Words*. The pill is the invention of an enterprising printer named Prattles, who bribes his cousin (a chemist at Bath) with a third share in the profits of the speculation to mix it. The printer then frames a learned history for the receipt, tracing its descent from Methusaleh to Prattles: 'It is well known to most people that the venerable Methusaleh lived to the good old age of NINE HUNDRED AND SIXTY NINE YEARS. The secret of so long a life has for ages remained an IMPENETRABLE MYSTERY. [But] about two years ago two gentlemen were travelling in THE ARID DESERTS OF ASIA MINOR....'[57] By a series of extraordinarily fortuitous circumstances detailed in the prospectus, they were entrusted with the secret by an old Arab who kept it on an ancient parchment hidden in his turban, and on their return to England 'the travellers entered into a negotiation with the present proprietor of the recipe, who offers his METHUSALEH PILLS to the British public at thirteenpence-halfpenny per box.' The pill is presumably based upon Parr's Life Pill, which featured in the Dickens Advertiser with an illustration of 'Old Parr Gathering Herbs' and was claimed to enable the consumer to live as long as he did, the oldest man in the world.[58] According to the biographical sketch published later in *Household Words*, Thomas Parr was touched for the king's evil as a child and died in 1635 at the astounding age of 153.[59] The (spurious) authenticity effect of Prattles's prospectus is achieved through the exotic, circumstantial detail of its narrative, together with the evidence of false testimonials; and the 'efficacy and wonderful properties of the Methusaleh Pill' are finally said to be 'proven' by the fact that 'Her Majesty's Government have granted to the proprietors, to the exclusion of all pretenders, the use of a splendid RED AND BLACK STAMP.'[60] As Jerrold's scorn makes clear, anyone could patent a medicine so long as its formula was novel, and quacks exhibited the seal or stamp as though it were a personal royal endorsement. In the absence of uniform accreditation for doctors, the distinction between the regular and the quack practitioner was in any case ambiguous, making the detection of a fraudulent medicine that much more difficult. Indeed, Mr Prattles was initially inspired by the success of an entrepreneur named Mr Smith, who 'conferred upon himself a diploma, and inducted himself into the chair in a college which he endowed, for that single purpose, somewhere,' after which his 'Universal Pill was found in every respectable house in the three kingdoms, as the special and particular pill of Professor Smith, M.D., without whose signature all others were spurious.'[61] As well as the obfuscation associated with fraudulent qualifications, the difficulty of determining authenticity was exacerbated by the peculiar economies of quack and regular medicine. As Porter explains, in contrast with the personal knowledge and face-to-face contact associated with the private practice of regular doctors, quacks 'were those seeking custom from the anonymous consumer—the faceless crowd,

---

57 [William Blanchard Jerrold], 'The Methusaleh Pill,' *Household Words*, 5 October 1850, 2: 37.

58 Darwin, *The Dickens Advertiser*, 193-4.

59 [Rev. James White], 'Long Life under Difficulties,' *Household Words*, 4 April 1857, 15: 328.

60 [Jerrold], 'The Methusaleh Pill,' 38.

61 Ibid.: 37.

the nameless reader—through the media of advertising, publicity, and the sale of standardized commodities.'[62] Quackery emerged in the gaps in knowledge between producers and consumers as an example of medical entrepreneurship in an expanding consumer society. 'Prattles's Pills sold prodigiously,' writes Jerrold,[63] and their success is further evidence of the fetishism that developed with commodity culture—the reification of healing in the pill exemplifying the tendency to endow material objects with agency. It also affirms the commercial myth of purchaser power—that health was something money could buy.[64] As Porter argues, '[q]uackery was the capitalist mode of production in its medical face,'[65] and it flourished in a climate of competition characterized by price wars, undercutting, and client-poaching.

Food adulteration and quackery were, however, only part of a larger concern about the morality of the market at mid-century. The practice of 'cheap shopkeeping' was a recurring topic of debate in the periodical press, *Chambers's Edinburgh Journal*, for example, decrying the 'low morality' displayed in the preparation of cheap goods. Driven by 'the insane rage of the public for bargains,' its writer argues, 'the cheapening practice is greatly deteriorating our manufactures,' resulting in the production of shoddy goods, the employment of 'inferior hands,' and the tradesman's abolition of his workshop and use of the sweating system instead.[66] While the *Chambers's* writer describes a number of the sharp 'manoeuvres'—such as the use of 'draw-boys,' the 'counter dodge,' or 'tingering'—typically employed by shopkeepers to trap the unwary consumer, *Household Words* uses the form of the satiric sketch in 'Twenty Shillings in the Pound,' where John Hollingshead attempts to put his 'finger upon some of the moral blots in commerce' in an account of the 'firm of Petty, Larceny and Co., the great haberdashers.' A 'monument of remarkable trading skill,' 'the first stone' of this firm's 'prosperity was laid by the purchase of job-lots, or goods sold at a sacrifice':

> They got a double reputation: one for always being ready with cash for goods to any extent, the other for always selling goods thirty per cent under the market-price. They always paid twenty shillings in the pound, but it was for forty shillings' worth of goods, and that, my simple friend, is a very different thing from buying forty shillings' worth of goods, and paying twenty shillings for them.[67]

The practice of underselling is attacked by Hollingshead again in 'Buying in the Cheapest Market,' but here the consumer is the culprit. Narrated by one 'born and nourished under the wing of political economy: not the theory, but the practice,'[68]

---

62 Porter, *Quacks*, 30.
63 [Jerrold], 'The Methusaleh Pill,' 38.
64 Porter, *Quacks*, 50.
65 Ibid., 52.
66 'Shops, Shopkeepers, Shopmen, and Shop Morality: Second Article,' *Chambers's Edinburgh Journal* 14 (1850): 218.
67 [John Hollingshead], 'Twenty Shillings in the Pound,' *Household Words*, 7 November 1857, 16: 444.
68 [John Hollingshead], 'Buying in the Cheapest Market,' *Household Words*, 28 August 1858, 18: 256.

it tells the tale of a bargain hunter who takes advantage of traders in commercial distress to force the cheapest deals and who thereby manages to furnish 'a large house from top to bottom in a style above the average, and at less than one-fourth of the usual cost.'[69] Surveying the tradesmen listed with the Bankrupt and Insolvent Registry Office who are 'embarrassed with writs, judges' orders, bills of sale, and county court judgements; and exposed to all the temptations which such a state of things must necessarily produce,' he selects a cabinet-maker in 'Great Carcass Street' who is subject to a 'Judges' Order for 22*l*,' and finding the proprietor of this 'small, unpretending shop' to be an 'easily-managed, impressible man,' he writes, 'I proceeded to manage him accordingly.'[70] He shrewdly offers the precise sum of the judges' order, 22 pounds, to buy a marble-topped sideboard on sale for 60 guineas. The unfortunate proprietor protests that this '"would not pay the cost of the raw material,"' but is compelled by his commercial distress to accept the paltry sum offered. Encouraged by his success with the embarrassed cabinet-maker, the narrator next experiments upon a pianoforte merchant 'suffering from a County Court judgement for fifteen pounds, eighteen shillings.'[71] The merchant ends up accepting 20 pounds for a pianoforte on sale for seventy, goes bankrupt, and receives a rebuke from the Commissioner 'about reckless trading and making away with stock; which I, of course, [says the narrator,] could not help, as I was only carrying out the law of supply and demand, and acting upon the maxim of buying in the cheapest market.' The tale gives dramatic form to the observation reported by the *Chambers's* writer that a bargain 'may be fairly defined as a fraudulent exchange, by which somebody must suffer.'[72] Together with 'Twenty Shillings in the Pound,' it forms part of the debate about cheap shops that reached a peak at mid-century. As Tammy C. Whitlock notes, the term 'cheap shop' was applied to 'innovative discount houses as well as small fraudulent shops' and thus became 'something of a catchall term to describe suspicious new methods in retail.'[73] Thus the cabinet-maker complains to the bargain-hunter in 'Buying in the Cheapest Market' that his '"trade is cut up by the cheap, advertising, rubbish shops in other parts of the town."'[74] Advertising, display, and bargain sales distinguished these new methods of retail that were criticized as the marketing of style over substance and as encouraging a retail culture of fraud.[75]

The problem of authenticity involved in concern about the elevation of style over substance, appearances over realities, in the new world of democratized consumer goods and innovative retail practices, can also be seen in the commodity culture of tourism that grew throughout the nineteenth century. The development of mass tourism was assisted by the press, whose coverage of foreign travel helped

---

69   Ibid.: 257.
70   Ibid.
71   Ibid.: 258.
72   'Shops, Shopkeepers, Shopmen, and Shop Morality: Concluding Article,' 245.
73   Tammy C. Whitlock, *Crime, Gender and Consumer Culture in Nineteenth-Century England* (Aldershot: Ashgate, 2005), 75.
74   [Hollingshead], 'Buying in the Cheapest Market,' 257.
75   Whitlock, *Crime, Gender and Consumer Culture in Nineteenth-Century England*, 72.

to normalize it as 'a "taken-for-granted" feature of middle-class life.'[76] John Frow argues that a sense of estrangement, of 'ontological homelessness,' is 'one of the central conditions of tourism,'[77] a loss of origin that, ironically, the tourist attempts to assuage with a product that is 'in its most general form,... a commodified relation to the Other.'[78] Also central to the development of modern tourism is the emergence of the 'tourist gaze': a particular form of looking directed towards features of landscape or townscape which separates them off from everyday life and in which they are consumed as visual experiences.[79] As James Buzard has argued, this form of gaze emerged from the nineteenth century's 'ambivalent confrontation with a democratizing and institutionalizing tourism'[80] evident in the transition from 'Grand Tourism to mass tourism'[81] that was enabled by steam locomotion and rising middle-class incomes. While *Household Words*'s contributors generally welcomed and exploited the extension of opportunities for foreign travel brought about by technological and commercial improvements, their narratives also satirize the inauthenticity of the tourist gaze and the commodification of foreign sites as part of the development of mass tourism in the nineteenth century. Indeed, they often find as much journalistic copy in the tourists themselves—in complaints about coping with currency exchange, for example, in 'The Modern Robbers of the Rhine'[82] or about the obstacles involved in taking the Marseille route to Italy in 'The Roving Englishman: The Great Do'[83]—as in descriptions of the life, customs or sights to be seen in the places visited.

In 'Cities in Plain Clothes,' Sala describes several key Continental destinations of the mid-Victorian tourist, but 'in their apparel of homespun, very different from the gala suit they wear on high days and holidays, and in books of travel.'[84] With a mock apology to the 'sentimental tourists, and writers of stanzas, and imaginative painters,'[85] Sala uses the clothing metaphor to expose the constructedness of the 'cities that poets sing, that painters limn, that rapturous tourists describe,'[86] presenting what James Buzard calls the '"prosaicist" reaction'[87] to the picturesque.

---

76   Jill Steward, '"How and Where to Go": The Role of Travel Journalism in Britain and the Evolution of Foreign Tourism, 1840–1914,' in *Histories of Tourism: Representation, Identity and Conflict*, ed. John K. Walton (Clevedon: Channel View Publications, 2005), 40.

77   John Frow, 'Tourism and the Semiotics of Nostalgia,' *October* 57 (1991): 135.

78   Ibid.: 150.

79   John Urry, *The Tourist Gaze: Leisure and Travel in Contemporary Societies*, ed. Mike Featherstone, Theory, Culture and Society (London: Sage, 1990), 2, 7.

80   James Buzard, *The Beaten Track: European Tourism, Literature, and the Ways to 'Culture' 1800–1918* (Oxford: Clarendon Press, 1993), 5.

81   John Pemble, *The Mediterranean Passion: Victorians and Edwardians in the South* (Oxford: Clarendon Press, 1987), 3.

82   [Frederick Knight Hunt], 'The Modern Robbers of the Rhine,' *Household Words*, 19 October 1850, 2: 90–93.

83   [Grenville Murray], 'The Roving Englishman: The Great Do,' *Household Words*, 19 March 1853, 7: 67–72.

84   [George A. Sala], 'Cities in Plain Clothes,' *Household Words*, 17 July 1852, 5: 418.

85   [Sala], 'Cities in Plain Clothes,' 422.

86   Ibid.: 419.

87   James Buzard, *The Beaten Track: European Tourism, Literature, and the Ways to 'Culture' 1800–1918* (Oxford: Clarendon Press, 1993), 211.

Let me take a city [he says].—Constantinople. What a holiday dress she wears in Mr Thomas Allom's pictures, in the pages of Byron and Hope, in Mr Lewis's lithographs, in the eyes even of the expectant tourist on board the Peninsular and Oriental Company's steamer, who, disappointed with Naples, Malta, and Athens, opens wide his eyes with wonder, admiration and delight, when he first surveys the City of the Sultan from the Golden Horn.[88]

That tourist 'is a native, we will say, of Clapham; Stockwell was his alma mater,' and he 'is the hope and joy of a wholesale house in the Manchester line, and in Bread Street, Cheapside. We will call him Moole.' Sala's characterization of Mr Moole picks up on contemporary changes in the social profile of the British tourist. Mr Moole is a 'gent,' a distinctive lower-middle-class urban type, whose geographical mobility here hints at his 'growing social mobility.'[89] Satirized by *Punch*, by Cruikshank in *The Progress of Mr. Lambkin (Gent)* (1844) and by Albert Smith in one of his *Natural Histories* (1847), the gent 'was to be found everywhere' and was immediately recognizable: 'The cheap ready-to-wear shops catered for his tastes with fashions called after aristocrats and dandies: the "Chesterfield" great-coat, the "Byron" tie and "Patent Albert" boots.'[90] Mr Moole's preconceptions about Constantinople compose an orientalist fantasy, liberally sprinkled with exotic terms that are comically derived from his reading of travellers' tales:

I shall listen to the dulcet tones of the mandolin, hear the pattering fall of perfumed waters, catch heavenly glimpses of dark-eyed beauties behind lattices, puffing lazily at the aromatic chibouque, or perchance become an unwilling witness of some dark and terrible tragedy,—the impalement of a grand vizier, or the sacking and salt-waterising of some inconstant houri of the Padisha.... And now, oh! Joy of joys, I catch a pair of black eyes circled with henna, fixed on me with a glance of tender meaning, through the folds of a silken veil. I see a little fairy foot peeping from loose Turkish trowsers: the vision disappears—but an old woman (the universal messenger of love in the East) accosts me with a bouquet ... [which plainly says] 'Meet me at eight this evening at the secret gate opposite the third kiosque past Seraglio point.'[91]

Mr Moole, however, will be disappointed—as of course all tourists are who, taught by the guidebook, seek access to the '*type* of the beautiful.'[92] Instead of odalisques, janissaries, and fret-worked mosques, he finds a 'dirty, swarming, break-neck city' in place of 'Stamboul the romantic, the beautiful, the glorious.'[93]

Turning next to Venice, Sala is confronted by 'fourscore poets, twelve score sentimental tourists, a bevy of blooming young ladies, far too numerous for me to count, and the editors of six defunct landscape annuals' who combine to paint a

---

88 [Sala], 'Cities in Plain Clothes,' 419.
89 Steward, "How and Where to Go': The Role of Travel Journalism in Britain and the Evolution of Foreign Tourism, 1840–1914,' 42.
90 Raymund Fitzsimons, *The Baron of Piccadilly: The Travels and Entertainments of Albert Smith 1816–1860* (London: Geoffrey Bles, 1967), 63.
91 [Sala], 'Cities in Plain Clothes,' 419.
92 Frow, 'Tourism and the Semiotics of Nostalgia,' 125.
93 [Sala], 'Cities in Plain Clothes,' 420.

vision of 'marble halls,' 'water-scapes with crimson, green and gold skies,' 'the Doge [as] a venerable old man, with a white beard and a high cap, constantly occupied in dandling the lion of St Mark,' and all the canals 'studded with gondolas, painted with fanciful arabesques, hung with splendid tapestry, filled with purple velvet lovers and white satin angels (see Lake Price), making love and eating ices beneath a moon certainly twice as large as any French, German, or English one.'[94] Similarly, Naples is falsified by the gaze of tourists and travel writers:

> Imagination incorrigible, in three vols. 8vo, just out (see Evening paper) persists in seeing only Naples the sunny, the romantic, the beautiful '*Vedi Napoli e poi morire*.' 'See Naples and die,' says Imagination. 'See Naples,' says Reality sternly in the shape of Mr Gladstone, 'see St Januarius's sham blood, and Poerio's fetters, and Ferdinand's Shrapnel shells, and then die with shame and horror.'[95]

Sala's allusion to Gladstone's letters on the State Prosecutions of the Neapolitan Government and the plight of imprisoned patriots like Carlo Poerio is in keeping with *Household Words*'s support for the Risorgimento throughout the 1850s,[96] and draws a sharp distinction between idealized, touristic representation and underlying social and political realities.

The desire for an authentic experience of cultural difference in Continental travel is expressed by Percy Fitzgerald in the first essay of his series, 'Down Among the Dutchmen,' where he laments the 'uniform Internationality' that 'the wandering man, the Voyageur, with taste for colouring and bits of picturesque, of all others, feels most acutely':

> His occupation is, in a manner, beginning to go; for the world he fancies he has left behind, travels abroad with him, and reappears at odd corners and unexpected places; so that he drags after him that lengthening chain, of which such piteous complaint was long since made—with a savour of flatness and staleness and utter insipidity. Most especially does this strike him in matters of costume and local colouring; and he must admit to himself with a sigh, that the hour is drawing on, when the habiliments of all the tribes will have subsided into the sober working dress of black broadcloth.[97]

For Fitzgerald, the uniformity of cosmopolitan dress is emblematic of a more general levelling influence that diminishes local particularity and robs continental travel of its colour and interest. Such a quest for cultural difference, for an authentic foreign encounter, propels many of the travellers who contribute to *Household Words*. Like Fitzgerald, Dickens seeks distance and difference from the familiar and conventional in Continental travel in 'Our French Watering-Place,' published as the leader on 4 November 1854. He delights in the unfashionableness of Boulogne as a

---

94 Ibid.

95 Ibid.: 421.

96 Following the release of the Neapolitan prisoners in 1859, Dickens offered to publish a 'narrative of their ten years trial' in his 'new successor to "Household Words."' Denis V. Reidy, 'Panizzi, Gladstone, Garibaldi and the Neapolitan Prisoners,' *eBLJ* Article 6 (2005): 14.

97 [Percy Fitzgerald], 'Down among the Dutchmen,' *Household Words*, 24 October 1857, 16: 398.

summer holiday resort for the English, and as the collective possessive pronoun of the title suggests, he positions himself as a participant observer and lays claim to a paradoxical holiday 'at-home-ness' in Boulogne, based upon a residence of 'two or three seasons,' that distinguishes him from the mindless guidebook follower:

> It is more picturesque and quaint than half the innocent places which tourists, following their leader like sheep, have made impostors of.... [T]here is an ancient belfry in it that would have been in all the Annuals and Albums, going and gone, these hundred years, if it had but been more expensive to get at. Happily it has escaped so well, being only in our French watering-place, that you may like it of your own accord in a natural manner, without being required to go into convulsions about it. We regard it as one of the later blessings of our life, that BILKINS, the only authority on Taste, never took any notice that we can find out, of our French watering-place.[98]

Similarly, William Owen appreciates the undiscovered quietness of 'our table d'hôte' at the Rhenish guesthouse in which he is staying.[99] It 'does not form part of the outworks of any of the large and fashionable Rhenish cities,' its does not advertise its name 'for the behoof of tourists,' and the company gathered in its 'dining and coffee-room' includes '[c]omparatively few English, armed to the teeth with Murray's hand-books, Panoramas of the Rhine, Sketch and Conversation Books, uglies, and—by the fair much loved—mushroom hats of portentous dimensions.'[100] Such desire to avoid the English tourist crowd is also expressed in 'Yourself at Turin,' in which William Howard Russell describes the 'confusion of a crowded *table d'hôte* breakfast' where 'a strong detachment of our own countrymen, women and children, [may be seen] regarding each other with that aversion which a true Briton always exhibits to a fellow-subject when on foreign travel.'[101]

A symptom of the ubiquity of English tourists on the Continent was the increasing provision of English amenities in the form of meals and accommodation, and in his first essay of a series on 'The Great Hotel Question,' published as the leader on 16 February 1856, Sala shares the 'true Briton's' spirit in deploring the 'purely English hotel abroad': the 'worst features of the continental system are grafted upon the worst features of the English,' he complains, although '[y]ou have, to be sure, the consolation of being swindled in your own language by your own countrymen, and of being bitten into frenzy by vermin that may, haply, have crossed the Channel in British blankets.'[102] Prompted by Albert Smith's diatribe against *The English Hotel Nuisance*, Sala's series takes a satiric look at the current state of French, Italian, Swiss and German hotels. To illustrate Italian hotels, he selects 'the great Caravanserai of travelling milords: say in Rome, Milan, or Florence, the Casa Borbonica. This was,

---

98 [Charles Dickens], 'Our French Watering-Place,' *Household Words*, 4 November 1854, 10: 266.

99 [William Owen], 'A German Table d'Hôte,' *Household Words*, 15 December 1855, 12: 478.

100 Ibid.: 479.

101 [William Howard Russell], 'Yourself at Turin,' *Household Words*, 6 November 1852, 6: 190.

102 [George A. Sala], 'The Great Hotel Question. In Three Chapters.—Chapter I.,' *Household Words*, 16 February 1856, 13: 101.

in old times, the palazzo of the princely Cinquantapercento family.'[103] Its good points are its splendour and cheapness: 'the rent of the malachite and gold, or of the ivory and black velvet suite, lags far behind the jocundly extortionate price which you have to pay for a first-floor in the Rue de la Paix, or a garret in Pall Mall.' But the landlord is a humbug, charging for sugar never eaten and wax candles never burnt, 'the rooms are awfully damp,' and 'after every shower of rain, the grand frescoed saloons are pervaded by sundry unwelcome visitants from the gardens.'[104]

The Swiss hotel is typically 'spacious, well-aired and cheerful,' but outrageously expensive:

> Few men have the courage to read a Swiss hotel bill straight through, or even to look at it in its entirety. The best way to take it is by instalments; folding it into slips, like a large newspaper in a railway carriage. Read a few items, then take a breath. Read again, and grumble. Read again, and swear. Then, make a sudden dive at the sum total, as at a hot chestnut from a fire bar. Reel, turn pale, shut your eyes, clench your teeth. Pay, and go thy ways; but to the Belvedere no more.[105]

As he goes on to explain, however, the Alps can be toured without having to pay such extortionate hotel prices—indeed, without even having to leave London at all. At the Egyptian Hall in Piccadilly, Albert Smith's multi-media show of his 'Ascent of Mont Blanc' played to sell-out crowds for six years from January 1852. Appearing before a set of stationary scenes depicting the route from Geneva to Chamonix during the first act, and a vertically-moving panorama of the ascent in the second, Smith offered his audiences a vicarious ascent, combining anecdote, impersonation, song, and, for the third season, ten St Bernard dogs and four chamois in his performance.[106] One of the biggest box-office hits of the age, the 'Ascent' earned 'gross receipts of over £17,000' in performances before nearly 200,000 people and realized a fortune from associated merchandising, 'including colouring books, fans, games, and miniature Mont Blancs.'[107] Dickens remarked the authenticity effect of the show in his toast to Smith as guest of honour at the Annual Dinner to celebrate the Anniversary of the Foundation of Commercial Travellers' School on 30 December 1854:

> So many travellers having been going up Mont Blanc lately, both in fiction and in fact, that I have recently heard of a Company to employ Sir Joseph Paxton to take it down. Only one of those travellers, however, has been enabled to bring Mont Blanc to Piccadilly, and, by his own ability and good humour, to thaw its eternal ice and snow, so that the most timid ladies may ascend it twice a day 'during the holidays' without the smallest danger or fatigue.[108]

---

103 [George A. Sala], 'The Great Hotel Question. In Three Chapters.—Chapter the Third.,' *Household Words*, 1 March 1856, 13: 148.

104 Ibid.: 149.

105 [Sala], 'The Great Hotel Question. In Three Chapters.—Chapter I.,' 102.

106 Richard D. Altick, *The Shows of London* (Cambridge, Mass.: Harvard University Press, 1978), 477.

107 Peter H. Hansen, 'Albert Smith, the Alpine Club, and the Invention of Mountaineering in Mid-Victorian Britain,' *Journal of British Studies* 34 (1995): 305.

108 Quoted in Fitzsimons, *The Baron of Piccadilly*, 135.

Sala captures this suggestion of a mutually constitutive relation between the Mont Blanc show and the place it purports to represent, identifying the range of entrepreneurs capitalizing upon Smith's success and throwing the difference between the Swiss original and its commodity-forms into question:

> [The Swiss] are visited occasionally by their friend and patron, Mr Albert Smith, who teaches them how to make toys in carved wood, and brings them prints of sham Swiss costumes from Paris, against the summer masquerading time. When the tourist season is about to commence, Mr Beverly and Mr Danson, from the Surrey Zoological Gardens, send over a staff of scene-painters and carpenters; and, the Switzerland of travellers, of dioramas, and of landscape annuals, is built up. The toy châlets are put together like huts for the Crimea, or houses for Australia; valleys are excavated by Messrs. Fox and Henderson; the mountains are 'flats,' the rocks 'set pieces,' the cataracts canvas on rollers. Mr Murray's Guidebook-maker is in the secret and writes the bill of the performance; and Mr Gunter does Mont Blanc by contract.... There is a grand dress-rehearsal of 'Switzerland as it isn't' just before the prorogation of Parliament; and then the thirteen cantons are ready for the avalanche of lords, invalids, Cambridge tutors, Oxford undergraduates, French countesses, German barons, travelling physicians, landscape-painters, fashionable clergymen, old maids, and cosmopolitan swindlers.[109]

Sala anticipates here the modern tourist phenomenon Dean MacCannell has referred to as 'staged authenticity.' According to MacCannell, 'the variety of understanding held out before tourists as an ideal is an *authentic* and *demystified* experience of an aspect of some society or other.'[110] But it is always possible that what is taken to be entry into the secluded and thus more authentic 'back region' of a foreign culture or place 'is really entry into a front region that has been totally set up in advance for touristic visitation.'[111] The disappearance of the distinction between front and back regions in the constitution of the tourist sight leads, as Sala recognizes, to a regime of simulation in which the difference between original and copy begins to disappear.[112] Indeed the very existence of an 'original' becomes a function of the copy. Sala's parody of Smith's exploitation of the public appetite for travel panoramas in his 'Ascent of Mont Blanc,' together with the publicity mania surrounding it, shows the performances constructing the attractions that will be sought out by hordes of tourists when the season commences.[113] Murray's guidebook, that unique and indispensable authority on foreign travel at mid-century, is seen as complicit in the process of dismantling the distinction between the staged authenticity of Smith's show and the reality it seeks to represent.[114] Mr Gunter, London's famous caterer and

---

109 [Sala], 'The Great Hotel Question. In Three Chapters.—Chapter I.,' 102.
110 MacCannell, *The Tourist*, 94.
111 Ibid., 101.
112 Frow, 'Tourism and the Semiotics of Nostalgia,' 128.
113 Raymund Fitzsimons claims that Smith's entertainments contributed towards the 'corruption' of the Chamoniards, as the pastoral life they 'had enjoyed for centuries yielded to a mercenary interest in the tourist trade, and soon every peasant in the valley catered, in one way or another, for the visitors.' Fitzsimons, *The Baron of Piccadilly*, 14.
114 Peter H. Hansen quotes the 1852 edition of the *Handbook for Travellers in Switzerland* acknowledging that the ascent 'of Albert Smith, in 1851, has effectually popularized the

confectioner, shows similar enterprise in having presumably created a Mont Blanc cake or pudding to capitalize on the success of the show.

Two years later, in a leader published on 27 February 1858, Smith provides something of a rejoinder in 'Nearly Lost on the Alps,' which describes a dangerous climb up the pass of the Great St Bernard during wild weather. Unsigned, of course, the article makes no explicit reference that would identify its author as the showman who had brought Mont Blanc to London, but instead presents a thrilling account of an alpine trip that is emphatically proffered as the 'real thing.' Elaine Freedgood has described the function of the Alps in helping mid-century middle-class Britons to forge new masculine identities, with mountaineering tourists, who take fewer risks and travel along established routes in trains and coaches, providing the foil against which alpine travellers could define their experience as authentic.[115] Smith's narrator presents himself as a well-seasoned traveller anxious to avoid the beaten track, and the authenticity and immediacy of his mountaineering experience are enhanced by the provision of local details. He describes setting out on 'the tenth of September last, with two chance fellow-travellers, and Venance Favret, a Chamouni guide,' and choosing a difficult road up the St Bernard pass, a route that 'is not in Murray,' in order to avoid going through 'the dull bourg of Martigny.'[116] Leaving his worn-out companions half way up the pass, he went on, 'knowing the road perfectly well,' although observing that 'the weather was still very sullen and threatening; and I heard that peculiar moaning noise amongst the mountains, which makes an Alpine traveller get on as fast as he can.'[117] Emphasizing the danger of the enterprise, Smith recalls observing 'some men putting up a little wooden cross on the edge of the precipice' just above Orsières 'to mark the scene of a terrible accident which had happened the week before.'[118] The weather worsens until it is no longer safe to ride, and he describes being forced to wait alone with the mule while a guide seeks help. He vividly recalls the terror of this interval and the relief of his rescue, and the authenticity effect of his narrative is finally underlined as he reaches beyond the frame of the article to remark that the 'ladies and gentlemen who were at the St Bernard on the tenth of September last year, may remember how I was put into a hot-air room to dry; how I was unable to touch the supper the good monks provided, from re-action and exhaustion; and yet how many questions I had to answer.'[119]

By the time of Smith's dangerous adventure along the St Bernard pass in 1857, his London show had evolved to a point where 'the ascent was relegated to an entr'acte' and the second half of the performance was devoted to another mountain capturing popular attention, Vesuvius, which as Altick dryly observes, 'had the

---

enterprise,' and the 1858 edition thanking Smith 'for his help with the text.' Hansen, 'Albert Smith, the Alpine Club, and the Invention of Mountaineering in Mid-Victorian Britain,' 300.

115 Elaine Freedgood, *Victorian Writing About Risk: Imagining a Safe England in a Dangerous World* (Cambridge: Cambridge University Press, 2000), 124.

116 [Albert Richard Smith], 'Nearly Lost on the Alps,' *Household Words*, 27 February 1858, 17: 241.

117 Ibid.: 242.

118 Ibid.

119 Ibid.: 244.

considerable advantage of being explosive.'[120] *Household Words*'s correspondent from Naples, Henry Wreford, described an eruption of Vesuvius earlier in 1855, and his remarkable determination, together with 'thousands of others,' to view the 'grand spectacle' from the summit itself.[121] The eruption is clearly good for business, for upon arriving in Resina he observes the 'motley crowd of guides and donkeys, facchini and torchbearers, all insisting on the necessity of their services, and forthwith attaching themselves to our persons.' Accompanied by one of these guides, he approaches the top amidst stones being shot up into the air from the new crater with flames of fire and 'a heat and light that scorched and blasted us.'[122] The grandeur of the sublime spectacle is, however, undermined by the tourist activity he encounters at the summit:

> Some were baking eggs, or lighting cigars, or hooking out lava to stick their coppers in. Some had brought baskets—ham and chicken, and such like luxuries—and had stowed themselves away under a mass of coke of some hundreds weight…The orange man and the man with cheap pastry, too, made their rounds continually; and last, though not least, the man with pieces of lava, which he was liberally offering for thirty grains each.[123]

These Vesuvian tourists disturb the sublime scene with their bathos, interrupting the atmosphere that is required for the traveller to contemplate the awesome power of the volcano. One of the key motifs identified by Buzard as contributing to the production of an overall authenticity effect for nineteenth-century Continental travellers is 'stillness,' an attribute which finds its quintessential expression in Pompeii, the city buried by an eruption of Vesuvius in 79 A.D. and only partially excavated by the 1850s. As Peter Conrad explains, Pompeii was uniquely fascinating for the Victorians 'in uncovering the domestic detail of ancient life.'[124] Bulwer Lytton's bestselling novel, *The Last Days of Pompeii* (1834), had done much to kindle interest in the buried city, eliding its historical distance from Victorian readers by drawing parallels with contemporary London and by depicting a Pompeian chamber, like Julia's dressing room, with such a detailed profusion of consumer goods—'silver basin and ewer, carpet woven from looms of the East, ornamental lamp and papyrus roll, and curtains richly broidered with gold flowers'—that it 'takes on the padded luxury of a Victorian interior.'[125] In 'The City of Sudden Death,' John Delaware Lewis mentions Lytton's 'revival' of one of the uncovered skeletons 'for our entertainment under the name of Calenus the priest,' as he describes a visit to this city of ruin.[126] Standing within the oval arena of the amphitheatre at Pompeii, with its solemn historical associations, Lewis is awed by the thought of the gladiator

---

120 Altick, *The Shows of London*, 477.
121 [Henry G. Wreford], 'Vesuvius in Eruption,' *Household Words*, 9 June 1855, 11: 436.
122 Ibid.: 437.
123 Ibid.
124 Peter Conrad, *The Victorian Treasure-House* (London: Collins, 1978), 121.
125 Ibid., 124.
126 [John Delaware Lewis], 'The City of Sudden Death,' *Household Words*, 8 May 1852, 5: 174.

who 'died for the amusement of an audience' perhaps on this very spot.[127] But like Wreford, he is continually diverted by the presence of British tourists. Passing the entrance for the gladiators and wild beasts, he notices an inscription carved on a nearby seat and speculates that it is probably 'the name of the Decemvir or Decurion who sat there,' only to find, on closer inspection, that '[b]y all that is hallowed! the British penknife has not spared even these stones of Pompeii,' and that 'J. Wilkinson, 1847' has left his mark on the monument.[128] Musing upon the various objects found strewn about in the excavation of the Soldiers' Quarter, Lewis asks 'who is there who will not construct for himself ... [from these,] some picture of what that awful moment must have been, when Vesuvius poured her boiling ashes through every pore and fibre of the city and its citizens?' 'Certainly not those two young men, beloved compatriots,' he dryly remarks, 'young Oxford students': 'One smokes a cigar, the other wields an immense sandwich; they are laughing and poking each other about with sticks, and "chaffing" their guide through the ruins.' These kinds of tourists visit sights without seeing, '[d]odging each other round the gay columns of the Alhambra—ornamenting one another with pigtails at Mount Vernon, watching intently some good-looking grisette in the galleries of the Louvre [and] dashing frantically out of St Peter's for some newly-invented pipe-light.'

In contrast, travellers like Lewis appreciate the evidence of frozen time to be seen in the objects excavated from Pompeii and now exhibited at the Museum in Naples. In 'Preservation in Destruction,' published a month later, he reflects upon the gap between the value of these goods as quotidian commodities, part of the unremarkable commerce of daily life, and as relics of historic, cultural importance: '[h]ere are more figs, cherries, plums, nuts, bits of cake. In the next cupboard are various articles of a domestic nature; soap, cotton, sponges, wax, inkstands containing dried ink, purses with coins that were never more to make a purchase; ... the value of small things; the worthlessness of great ones;—how many lessons are taught by these relics.'[129] Overwhelmed by Pompeii's archaeological evidence, Lewis is finally led to reflect upon the vicissitudes of such tourist sites, wondering whether

> in those future ages, when Mr Macaulay's New Zealander is to contemplate the ruins of London (including, as we may suppose, the remains of the still unfinished Houses of Parliament), will our descendant, in like manner, stalk uninvited through those tall and mysterious mansions, which you and I pass by with fear and trembling, or only read of in the 'Morning Post?' The splendid galleries which we enter by means of tickets our posterity may perhaps comfortably spit over ... ; they may pursue each other round the colossal fragments of the Marble Arch, armed with flasks of the liquid then in use, like the two Oxford students.[130]

Back in England, ruins were amongst the popular historic sites visited by increasing numbers of domestic tourists. Peter Mandler dates the rise of historical

---

127 Ibid.: 172.
128 Ibid.: 173.
129 [John Delaware Lewis], 'Preservation in Destruction,' *Household Words*, 5 June 1852, 5: 283.
130 Ibid.: 175.

tourism from around 1830, noting as a factor in its spread 'a kind of social compact observed by public authorities and private landowners, again increasingly from the 1840s, granting touristic access on liberal terms to historic sites whether in public or private hands, as a sign of good faith towards a deferential people.'[131] *Household Words*, however, attacked the trend according to which 'nearly all the historic relics of old England open only with silver keys, and many solemn peers of Belgravia are, in their respective counties, speculating showmen.'[132] In 'Ruins with Silver Keys,' William Blanchard Jerrold is dismayed to discover that 'six shillings and sixpence is the sum required by the noble owner of the broken Abbey walls,' before he will admit visitors to those ruins where 'the memorable battle of Pumpkinfield was fought'[133]:

> Armed with the tickets, we have a sense of a critical vocation, which refuses to depart from us. As we glance at the grey walls of the standing structure, we involuntarily look out for the check-taker's box. We expect to find placards pasted over the Gothic gateway. We speculate as to the success of the show. We reflect that it can cost the speculator nothing for gas, to begin with. We tap the walls to assure ourselves that they are not painted canvas. As we approach the doorway, it falls back, and a portly female attendant, with palms exquisitely made to receive shillings, courtesies [sic] to us. We are about to ask whether our tickets admit us to the reserved seats—but we refrain in time. We think we hear a cry of 'Apples, oranges, and ginger-beer!' but it is only our vexed brain at work, after its particular fashion. We advance into the enclosed space.[134]

For Jerrold, the commodification of the historic site inescapably colours the viewer's response, leading him to question its authenticity. Even the unavoidable tourist guide 'seems to travel over the ground mechanically, and to halt before little odd relics with the precision of an automaton. He recalls the romances of the past with the enthusiasm of a speaking doll.'[135] Arguing that 'it is hardly fair to barter the associations which belong to all Englishmen,' Jerrold condemns the transformation of the Abbey Ruins into 'Simpson's Exhibition.'

Just as Jerrold satirizes the silver keys required to open English ruins and questions the impact of such commerce on historical consciousness, Lewis's account of Pompeii shows a similar concern for the effect of tourism on the Victorian traveller's understanding of the past. He expresses an awareness of the rise and fall of empires that stands in ironic contrast to the survival of the tourist, whose failure to appreciate the significance of the site is opposed to the ideal of authenticity pursued by travellers seeking a genuine foreign encounter. Such a quest for authenticity may be linked to the perceived loss of the unity of social existence under the impact of industrial capitalism. But authenticity was also held to be a crucial property of objects: witness the souvenir. As Trilling argues, the provenance of the word itself

---

131 Peter Mandler, '"The Wand of Fancy": The Historical Imagination of the Victorian Tourist,' in *Material Memories*, ed. Marius Kwint, Christopher Breward and Jeremy Aynsley (Oxford: Berg, 1999), 127.

132 [William Blanchard Jerrold,] 'Ruins with Silver Keys,' *Household Words*, 13 September 1851, 3: 594.

133 Ibid., 592–3.

134 Ibid., 593.

135 Ibid., 594.

'is the museum, where persons expert in such matters test whether objects of art are what they appear to be or are claimed to be, and therefore worth the price that is asked for them.'[136] Whether understood in existential or empirical terms, authenticity was a cultural problem that assumed a new urgency for the mid-Victorians, and in its discussions of fake art, adulteration, the spirit trade, patent medicines, and cheap shopkeeping, *Household Words* demonstrates the extent to which uncertainty about the genuineness of goods and services is associated with the evidence of an evolving commodity culture. To be sure, the exposure of fraud, imposture and other forms of sham practice was part of the journal's more general crusade for reform. But it was also a specific response to a new world of retailing and consumption at mid-century. Such developments as the growing impersonality of the relationship between producers, retailers and consumers, innovative retail methods and the ideology of economic liberalism, are shown not only to undermine the morality of the market, but the cultural meaning invested in goods as constituents of selfhood. As Whitlock argues, the success of consumer capitalism depends upon the continuing market demand fuelled by the vicissitudes of fashion associated with goods-based status.[137] In this context, *Household Words* responded to the anxieties of those new middle-class readers who were unsure how to distinguish the real from the fake, and who sought knowledge of the constantly varying semiotic economy of goods that served to communicate social position—helping them to identify the boundary that separated the gentleman from the gent, the traveller from the tourist.

---

136 Trilling, *Sincerity and Authenticity*, 93.
137 Whitlock, *Crime, Gender and Consumer Culture in Nineteenth-Century England*, 12.

Chapter 4
'The Key of the Street'

Walking and writing were intimately entwined activities for Dickens, and city streets held a vital place in his imagination. As G.K. Chesterton put it, 'Dickens himself had, in the most sacred and serious sense of the term, *the key to the street* ... [for] [h]is earth was the stones of the street; his stars were the lamps of the street; his hero was the man in the street.'[1] So it is hardly surprising that *Household Words*, published from premises in Wellington Street just off the Strand, is so preoccupied with its metropolitan setting. However, it was not Dickens, but Sala, who wrote the article entitled 'The Key of the Street' that appeared in *Household Words* on 6 September 1851. It was this narrative of his 'enforced perambulations of the thoroughfares of the metropolis' that first brought Sala to Dickens's attention and led to his regular employment as a contributor.[2] He shared his mentor's compulsive interest in the life of the streets and many of the pieces that he wrote for *Household Words* are tales of the flâneur—that connoisseur of the urban environment who renders the city as a spectacle for consumption in his journalistic sketches.[3]

Much critical commentary has been devoted to the Parisian flâneur, and, more recently, to his London counterpart. As theorized by Benjamin, he is the observer of modernity whose urban rambling is undertaken to gather the 'fruits of idleness,'[4] the raw material for the 'panoramic literature' of the *physiologie* and the *feuilleton*.[5] In *Victorian Babylon*, Lynda Nead discusses his role in helping to create what she calls 'a new genre of metropolitan travel writing' in which London 'is written and consumed as visual spectacle.'[6] *Household Words* published such metropolitan travel writing by a range of writers—including Sala, John Hannay, William Blanchard Jerrold, John Hollingshead, and Henry Morley, besides Dickens himself—and paid its contributors at the relatively generous rate of a guinea for a two-column page of prose.[7] Michael Hollington has examined the responses to Paris in the 1850s (under

---

1   Quoted in Walter Benjamin, *The Arcades Project*, trans. Howard Eiland and Kevin McLaughlin (Cambridge, Mass.: Belknap Press of Harvard University Press, 1999), 438. My italics.
2   George Augustus Sala, *Things I Have Seen and People I Have Known*, 2 vols. (London: Cassell and Company, 1894), 1: 67.
3   As Susan Buck-Morss observes, 'in the flaneur, concretely, we recognize our own consumerist mode of being-in-the-world.' Susan Buck-Morss, 'The Flaneur, the Sandwichman and the Whore: The Politics of Loitering,' *New German Critique* 39 (1986): 104–5.
4   Benjamin, *Arcades*, 453.
5   Ibid., 5–6.
6   Lynda Nead, *Victorian Babylon: People, Streets and Images in Nineteenth-Century London* (New Haven: Yale University Press, 2000), 57.
7   John Drew notes that '*Household Words* paid amply and (no small virtue in a Victorian magazine) promptly.' John M.L. Drew, *Dickens the Journalist* (Houndmills, Basingstoke: Palgrave Macmillan, 2003), 120.

Haussmann and Louis Napoleon) published by Dickens and others in *Household Words*, noting that in 'these papers, the figure of the *flâneur* represents a kind of city dilettante of the eye, casually strolling in search of visual experience from which he will remain essentially detached.'[8] Such detachment is also observed by Richard Sennett in his description of the formation of public life in mid-nineteenth-century Paris and London:

> Public behaviour was a matter of observation, of passive participation, of a certain kind of voyeurism. The 'gastronomy of the eye,' Balzac called it; one is open to everything, one rejects nothing a priori from one's purview, provided one needn't become a participant, enmeshed in a scene.[9]

However, many of the accounts of London street-walking in *Household Words* show a level of social engagement and purpose that link such rambling with the rise of investigative journalism. Even as he relishes the contrasts, the mixture of old and new and the chance encounters of the city, the *Household Words* flâneur may be stopped short in his urban wandering by a reminder of deprivation or mortality. 'Every street in London has a character,' remarks the narrator in 'Play.' 'There are wealthy streets, starving streets, pious streets, comic streets, mortuary streets, proud streets, slavish streets, drunken streets, thievish streets, shameful streets, shameless streets,'[10] and the *Household Words* flâneur traverses most of them, offering his ethnographic observations upon their inhabitants. The journal's engagement with flânerie can also be seen in the kind of 'mobilized "*virtual*" gaze' that Anne Friedberg has identified as a precursor of cinema spectatorship.[11] As Friedberg argues, 'during the mid-nineteenth century, the coincident development of department store shopping, packaged tourism, and protocinematic entertainment began to transform this mobilized gaze into a commodity, one sold to a consumer-spectator.'[12] Many of these forms of 'commodified visual mobility' are represented in *Household Words*'s accounts of window-shopping, exhibitions, balloon-flights, and shows, such as the panorama. Even as it describes the many ways in which visual experience was being commodified, the journal offers forms of imaginary flânerie to its consumer-readers in its representation of the city as spectacle for consumption.

Urban spectatorship was, of course, a popular topic for many Victorian writers, as it had been for eighteenth-century essayists like Addison and Steele. As John Fisher Murray exclaims in his 1843 two-volume study of metropolitan life, '[h]ow pregnant with instruction, to the mind seeking wisdom, are the very streets!':

---

8   Michael Hollington, 'Dickens, *Household Words*, and the Paris Boulevards (Part One),' *Dickens Quarterly* 14 (1997): 155. See also Michael Hollington, 'Dickens, *Household Words*, and the Paris Boulevards (Part Two),' *Dickens Quarterly* 14 (1997); Michael Hollington, 'Dickens the Flâneur,' *Dickensian* 77 (1981): 71–87.

9   Richard Sennett, *The Fall of Public Man* (Cambridge: Cambridge University Press, 1977), 27.

10   [George A. Sala], 'Play,' *Household Words*, 25 November 1854, 10: 358.

11   Anne Friedberg, *Window Shopping: Cinema and the Postmodern* (Berkeley: University of California Press, 1993), 2.

12   Ibid.

> I know not how it is, but books and men are so jumbled together in the chambers of my brain, that even now, as I saunter idly down Ludgate Hill, I seem to encounter a living library. A dapper spruce *octavo*, in drab cloth, gilt, but not lettered, runs against me full tilt. I have scarcely escaped him, when I am pushed into the kennel by a dusty-faced *folio* of divinity. A pair of robust *quartos*, handsomely bound, with half-a-dozen chubby *duodecimos*, block me up at the corner; half-starved pamphlets, seedy and thin, with ragged covers, flit by me in all directions.[13]

The ubiquity of nineteenth-century interest in 'reading' the streets had multiple causes, as Mary Cowling explains, including rapid urban population growth, the mingling of different classes in public places and the striking contrasts which such conjunctions produced: 'all contributed to the intensification of feelings of curiosity, even antagonism, towards strangers thus encountered, and belief in the real, physiognomical distinctions between the three major classes to which they variously belonged.'[14] The most prolific *Household Words* contributor in the genre of metropolitan travel writing was Sala, who self-consciously articulates his penchant for loitering in a number of pieces. In 'Down Whitechapel Way,' he declares 'I am of the streets, streety. I love to take long walks, not only down Fleet Street, but up and down all other streets, alleys, and lanes'[15]; in 'Cities in Plain Clothes,' he confesses to a train of thought that 'is essentially of a Bohemian and desultory nature'[16]; in 'The Secrets of the Gas,' he claims that '[a]s I walk about the streets by night, endless and always suggestive intercommunings take place between me and the trusty, silent, every watchful gas, whose secrets I know'[17]; and in 'A Journey Due North,' he describes 'what in Bohemian euphuism is known as the Grand Scud.'

> This, though difficult of exact translation, may be accepted as implying a sort of purposelessness journeying—a viatorial meandering—a pilgrimage to the shrine of our Lady of Haphazard—an expedition in which charts, compasses, and chronometers have been left behind as needless impediments, and in which any degree of latitude the traveller may happen to find himself in, is cheerfully accepted as an accomplished fact.[18]

Such leisured looking does not, however, characterize his first contribution to *Household Words*, 'The Key of the Street,' which instead throws the aloof and idle gaze of the flâneur into question. The article describes a 'nocturnal misadventure' in which Sala was accidentally locked out of his lodgings in Upper Wellington Street with only ninepence in his pocket, and had to walk the streets till seven o'clock the next morning. Eking out a living as a 'necessitous engraver' at the time, and describing himself as 'utterly unknown and obscure,'[19] he nevertheless decided to

---

13   John Fisher Murray, *The World of London*, 2 vols. (London: Blackwood, 1843), 1: 33–4.
14   Mary Cowling, *The Artist as Anthropologist: The Representation of Type and Character in Victorian Art* (Cambridge: Cambridge University Press, 1989), 120.
15   [George A. Sala], 'Down Whitechapel Way,' *Household Words*, 1 November 1851, 4: 126.
16   [George A. Sala], 'Cities in Plain Clothes,' *Household Words*, 17 July 1852, 5: 418.
17   [George A. Sala], 'The Secrets of the Gas,' *Household Words*, 4 March 1854, 9: 46.
18   [George A. Sala], 'A Journey Due North,' *Household Words*, 6 December 1856, 14: 493.
19   Sala, *Things*, 1: 67, 66.

write an account of his forced 'evening out,' sent it to *Household Words* and was amazed to receive from the editor a letter of acceptance with a 'Bank of England note for five pounds—the largest sum [he] had ever earned by a single article.'[20]

Looking forward to the undercover investigative journalism published by later practitioners of slumming, like James Greenwood, in the 1860s, 'The Key of the Street' explores the spatial and temporal dynamics of the city by night, and their disturbing impact on the subjectivity of the peripatetic observer, to offer a compelling analysis of urban alienation. The OED's first recorded usage of the phrase 'to have the key of the street' is from the 1837 *Pickwick Papers,* and the irony of the expression calls into question the opposition between bourgeois interior and the exterior of the street that Benjamin was later to critique in his account of the Paris arcades and boulevards. Insisting upon the material reality of the street for those who have its key, Benjamin asks: 'For what do we know of streetcorners, curb-stones, the architecture of the pavement—we who have never felt heat, filth, and the edges of the stones beneath our naked soles, and have never scrutinized the uneven placement of the paving stones with an eye toward bedding down on them.'[21] Like Benjamin, Sala provides a view from the pavement, and is preoccupied with the description of urban thresholds in space and time, as he notes the 'weary waste of hours yet to traverse'[22] before, as he puts it, 'I can obtain access to my penates.'[23] He describes watching the 'whole process of closing the "Original Burton Ale House," from the sudden shooting up of the shutters, through the area grating, like gigantic Jacks-in-a-box, to the final adjustment of screws and iron nuts'[24]; he gazes at the 'departing equipages' transporting opera patrons home from Covent Garden Theatre and the closing of its 'heavy portals'; led by exhaustion to try a 'villanous ramshackle' lodging-house advertising beds for '"single men at fourpence per night,"' he is driven out in horror by 'the smell of the bugs'[25]; he remarks the doors of the flash public-houses and oyster-rooms letting out 'detachments of choice spirits all down the Haymarket.'[26] All of these descriptions mark thresholds—between opening and closing, entrance and departure, inside and outside—to convey a heightened awareness of boundary order that is symptomatic of the narrator's vagrancy.

Sala's preoccupation with these spatial and temporal points of transition may be linked to the impact of such vagrancy upon his subjectivity, affecting his pose as flâneur. He manifests an uneasy awareness of the dissolving boundaries of identity as city inhabitants merge imperceptibly with the surrounding built environment. Drury Lane is said to be distinguished by its preponderance of street-corners, all of which 'have posts, and nearly all the posts are garnished with leaning figures.'[27] In a description that anticipates Dickens's later account of the ambiguous subjectivity

---

20 Ibid., 1:68.
21 Benjamin, *Arcades,* 517.
22 [George A. Sala], 'The Key of the Street,' *Household Words,* 6 September 1851, 3: 567.
23 Ibid.: 569.
24 Ibid.: 566.
25 Ibid.: 568.
26 Ibid.: 570.
27 Ibid.: 567.

of the 'five bundles of rags' he observes outside a Whitechapel workhouse in 'A Nightly Scene in London,'[28] Sala remarks that '[s]ome of the doorways have heaps of something huddled up within them; and ever and anon a policeman will come and stir them up with his truncheon, or more probably with his boot.'[29] While 'The Key of the Street' begins with the impressionistic, physiognomic viewing of the flâneur—what the narrator describes as 'a species of lazy curiosity' with which he watches the closure of the ale house or 'contemplate[s] a cab-stand'—the essay traces a shift from this position of distant, disinterested and dispassionate observation to an acknowledgement of proximity and social relatedness. The 'amusement and instruction' he claims to derive 'from watching the performances in the ham and beef shop at the corner of Bow Street'[30] gradually give way to a sense of marginality that is disturbingly transformative: 'I feel myself slowly, but surely, becoming more of a regular night-prowler—a houseless, hopeless, vagrant, every moment. I feel my feet shuffle, my shoulders rise towards my ears; my head goes on one side; I hold my hands in a crouching position before me; I no longer walk, I prowl.'[31] Vagrancy is experienced as metamorphosis. The body seems to regress to a more primitive, brute form. This transformation in subjectivity is ironically confirmed by the compassionate gesture of 'a passing figure, in satin and black lace' who flings him a penny; a mongrel dog who 'joins company' with him, being, as he says, 'without a bed, like I am'; and finally, a fear of policemen that unaccountably grows upon him.[32] The narrator is temporarily drawn by the 'contagious' influence of a speeding fire-engine to join the excited throng in a narrow street off Soho where a pickle-shop is fiercely burning: 'I have been watching the blazing pile so long—basking, as it were, in the noise and shouting and confusion; the hoarse clank of the engines—the cheering of the crowd—the dull roar of the fire, that the bed question has been quite in abeyance, and I have forgotten all about it and the time,' he writes.[33] While the anonymous merging with the noisy crowd provides distraction and a temporary escape from solitude, however, self-awareness returns with the extinguishing of the fire, and his experience of transformation seems to be complete as he lies down to sleep upon a bench in St James's Park beside 'a tramp of some eighteen summers' who, he says, 'wakes, eyes me for a moment, and muttering "hard lines, mate" turns to sleep again.' Underlining the gesture of companionship in vagrancy, Sala remarks: 'In the mysterious free-masonry of misery, he calls me "mate."'[34]

While 'The Key of the Street' details the view from the pavement, Henry Morley provides a contrasting perspective on the city in 'Looking Out of Window.' Narrated by a 'bachelor,' 'sedate, stout, and far gone in years,' the sketch mounts an argument for viewing the world from within, through one's window, that illustrates the crucial

---

28 [Charles Dickens], 'A Nightly Scene in London,' *Household Words*, 26 January 1856, 13: 25.
29 [Sala], 'The Key of the Street,' 568.
30 Ibid.: 567.
31 Ibid.: 568.
32 Ibid.: 569.
33 Ibid.
34 Ibid.: 570.

role of the home and its contents in fashioning the middle-class self. 'From the eye a man looks out of his raw self; from the window he looks out of his dressed and garnished self, upon the world without,'[35] he writes. The narrator's insistence upon the superior merits of an interior position of spectatorship, framed for the viewer at the window by 'his household gods on his right hand and on his left,' illustrates the peculiar concern with 'dwelling' identified by Benjamin as characteristic of the nineteenth-century: 'It conceived the residence as a receptacle for the person, and it encased him with all his appurtenances so deeply in the dwelling's interior that one might be reminded of the inside of a compass case, where the instrument with all its accessories lies embedded in deep, usually violet folds of velvet.'[36] In contrast to Sala's transformative encounter with vagrancy on the streets, Morley's narrator remains safely detached from the scene outside, which is artfully framed for the delectation of the spectator: 'From a foreground of wife, children, personal surroundings, his embodied social state, he looks between his window curtains to the moving spectacle of life beyond.... the world in its own colours, breathing, throbbing, full of latent mysteries and beauties in its light and shade.'[37] Like watching a moving panorama, 'looking out of window' provides a form of imaginary flânerie for the viewer, like the journal reader, comfortably housed within doors.

While 'Looking Out of Window' advocates the view from inside, and 'The Key of the Street' describes the view from without, *Household Words* was also interested in those new panoptic positions of spectatorship which afforded a prospect of the city from above. As Judith Wechsler observes, 'the mid-nineteenth century is the period of the bird's-eye view.'[38] Balloon ascents were one of the popular shows of London at mid-century, featuring regularly at Vauxhall and Cremorne Gardens. *Punch* poked fun at the fad in 1850, proposing, amongst other 'Summer Novelties in Balloons,' that the hippopotamus just arrived at the London Zoo be taken aloft to provide a launching pad for fireworks.[39] In a more serious vein, Richard H. Horne's 1851 leader on 'Ballooning' in *Household Words* attempts to convey the unique unity of perspective obtained in viewing the metropolis from above. The effect of the balloon ascent is an intensification of visual awareness, the quintessential sensory experience of the city: as Simmel argued, '[i]nterpersonal relationships in big cities are distinguished by a marked preponderance of the activity of the eye over the activity of the ear.'[40] In the complete absence of any sensation of movement or sound, the city becomes pure spectacle for the balloonist: 'Everything below is seen in so new a form, so flat, so compressed, and simultaneously—so much too-much-at-a-time—that the first look is hardly so satisfactory as could be desired.'[41] But

---

35 [Henry Morley], 'Looking out of Window,' *Household Words*, 1 March 1856, 13: 166.

36 Benjamin, *Arcades*, 220–21.

37 [Morley], 'Looking out of Window,' 167.

38 Judith Wechsler, *A Human Comedy: Physiognomy and Caricature in 19th Century Paris* (London: Thames and Hudson, 1982), 20.

39 Richard D. Altick, *Punch: The Lively Youth of a British Institution 1841–1851* (Columbus: Ohio State University Press, 1997), 536.

40 Quoted in Walter Benjamin, *Charles Baudelaire: A Lyric Poet in the Era of High Capitalism*, trans. Harry Zohn (London: Verso, 1983), 38.

41 [Richard H. Horne], 'Ballooning,' *Household Words*, 25 October 1851, 4: 99.

the overwhelming effect of simultaneity gives way to an apparent clarity of vision: 'Away goes the earth, with all its objects—sinking lower and lower, and everything becoming less and less, but getting more and more distinct and defined as they diminish in size. But, besides the retreat towards minuteness, the phantasmagoria flattens as it lessens,' he writes, until 'the Great Metropolis itself is a board set out with toys.'[42] Then 'floating clouds fill up the space beneath' and 'all is lost in air.' The effect of miniaturization is repeated in Sala's whimsical account of London's suburban sprawl as seen from a balloon in 'The Great Invasion': 'The Monument is a Christmas Candlestick; the Tower is a Doll's House. There is not a man in London as large as Shem, Ham, or Japhet, in the toy Noah's Ark.'[43] Such views from above on the one hand appear to objectify the city as a tableau of arrested life, offering a perspective that seems to promise holistic knowledge through specular dominance over the scene laid out below; on the other hand, they render everything 'indistinct' and dreamlike. Sala describes the smoke of London, 'that transparent blue haze hanging quite over the City, like a gauze drapery to the golden houses, cut exactly to the shape of the City, thinner, and almost ragged where parks, or squares, or open places are.'[44] Mixing images both solid and insubstantial, Horne is amazed by the 'noiseless cataract of snowy cloud-rocks falling around you'—and the boundaries of observing subject and observed object appear to dissolve in the profound silence and serenity: 'We hear the ticking of our watches. Tick! Tick!—or is it the beat of our own hearts?'[45]

Such disorienting experience of spatial transcendence is explored with more awareness of social contrasts in a leader written by John Hollingshead recounting a New Year's Eve spent on the London Monument. Built to commemorate the Great Fire of 1666, the Monument was listed as a 'must see' tourist attraction in a number of mid-century guidebooks, offering panoramic views of the city and costing threepence for admission. The narrator of 'All Night on the Monument' begins by describing the bird's-eye view as a culturally informed perspective in which all below him appears to be 'merged in one mass of indistinguishable equality.'[46] Such social levelling is acknowledged as an effect of aerial distance that may render the spectator detached and indifferent to those he observes on the ground. But the Monument affords an elevated view that lies somewhere in between the panoptic gaze of the balloonist and the viewpoint of the walker at street level: 'while it is high enough to impress you with a firm belief in your immeasurable superiority to your diminutive fellow-worms beneath, it is not so lofty that it quite removes you from all sympathy with the doings and movements of those very contemptible, but very interesting creatures to whom you belong.'[47] Hollingshead's account of the clouds which have a colouration that outdoes the masterpieces of 'Martin' and 'Turner' (Turner, of course, the master

---

42 Ibid.
43 [George A. Sala], 'The Great Invasion,' *Household Words*, 10 April 1852, 5: 72.
44 Ibid.: 71–2.
45 [Horne], 'Ballooning,' 100.
46 [John Hollingshead], 'All Night on the Monument,' *Household Words*, 30 January 1858, 17: 145.
47 Ibid.: 146.

at dissolving and transfiguring the solid world of matter), his wonder at the 'ever-changing, glowing, Rembrandt-like effects' of the fog, and his delight in the 'puppet men [who] now hurry to and fro, lighting up the puppet shops; which cast a warm, rich glow upon the pavement,'[48] are shadowed by an awareness of the misery of life on the streets that abruptly dispels the sublime illusion: 'Then the bridges throw up their arched lines of lamps, like the illuminated garden-walks at Cremorne—like the yellow buttons on the page's jacket, or the round brass-headed nails in a coffin.'[49] While the city below is transformed into an ever-changing light show, the sequence of similes—from pleasure garden to graveyard—cuts short the moment of transcendence with a grim reminder of mortality. As the clocks of the churches mark the passage of the last night of the year, the narrator's meditative gaze upon the spectacle below him is disturbed by images of guilt and secrecy. Watching the stream of homeward-bound commuters, he remarks that 'many of those hurrying men fly from the city as Cain did from the murdered body of Abel'; the coming of dawn carries suggestions of the apocalypse as 'whole thoroughfares seem to sink into the earth, bit by bit'; and finally, with a startling note of dread, as the 'thin spires of churches struggle upward,' he writes, 'you can almost fancy you see men cling to them in their agony, to be saved.'[50]

The bird's-eye view was one of a number of new positions of observation explored by *Household Words* in its representation of the city as commodity spectacle. Like these aerial experiences, the crowd-pulling panoramas of the period also worked to produce rather ambiguous effects in offering an all-encompassing view by destabilizing the viewer's sense of perspective. The panorama removed all impediments to verisimilitude in order to make the spectator feel part of the scene itself. The original form of exhibition was a 360-degree cylindrical painting, viewed by an observer placed in the centre of a room that was lit from above. The optical illusion was produced by blocking sight of the top and bottom edges of the painting, so that the observer lost his or her bearings and seemed to merge with the surrounding space. The lack of framing produced a continuum between the viewer and the world viewed, challenging the subject position of the spectator. Their popularity was widely noted in the press, *Punch* remarking 'The Monster Panorama Mania' associated with the arrival from America of a moving panorama depicting a trip along the Mississippi in 1849. Subsequent accounts of 'A Cheap Excursion up and down the Nile,' 'Putting a Panorama around the Earth,' and 'Constantinople Removed to Regent Street' attest to the popularity of such shows at the commencement of the 1850s.[51] At the end of the decade, *Chambers's Journal of Popular Literature, Science and Arts* provided a rather dull history of the panorama's development, beginning with an account of its inventor, 'Mr Barker, an ingenious artist, and a man of singular energy and enterprise,' who was impelled to produce a panorama of Edinburgh, viewed from Arthur's Seat, by the scepticism of Sir Joshua

---

48   Ibid.
49   Ibid.
50   Ibid.: 147.
51   Altick, *Punch*, 614.

Reynolds for the project.[52] The staidness of the *Chambers's* essay throws into relief the humour and originality with which *Punch* and *Household Words* had treated the topic ten years earlier.

In 'Some Account of an Extraordinary Traveller,' published as the leader on 20 April 1850, Dickens satirizes the vogue for panoramas and dioramas in a description of Mr Booley's imaginary globe-trotting. The comic effect of his account depends upon the blurring of the distinction between representation and reality produced in the panorama. Thus Mr Booley is described as 'participating in an affray between the natives and the English soldiery' during his trip to New Zealand, before 'he plunged into the Bush and there camped out for some months, until he made a survey of the whole country.'[53] The illusion thus produced is then comically disrupted by details that draw attention to the framing context. For example, Mr Booley's trip to New Zealand follows immediately after his journey along the Ohio River with only a day back in London in between. Delighted one minute to encounter 'Miss Creeble, of The Misses Creebles' Boarding and Day Establishment for Young Ladies, Kennington Oval' with three of her young ladies in the midst of the New Zealand Bush, the next he returns to England 'where the ladies were safely put into a hackney cabriolet by Mr Booley, in Leicester Square, London.'[54] At least three of the panoramas viewed by Mr Booley were moving exhibits: Banvard's panorama of the Mississippi, and Bonomi, Fahey and Warren's Nile Panorama (two of those satirized earlier by *Punch*) were shown at the Egyptian Hall, and the 'Overland Route to India' appeared at the Gallery of Illustration. These consisted of long canvasses, wound around a hidden spool, which were unwound horizontally across a proscenium onto another spool. They lent themselves perfectly to river journeys.[55] Like the original 360-degree exhibitions, and other optical entertainments such as the diorama, stereoscope, and magic lantern show, the moving panorama was part of an emerging mass visual culture in which forms of consumable 'realism' were manufactured for sale.

Another example is described in 'A Globe in a Square,' Henry Morley's account of James Wyld's model of the earth, where the narrator, Jones, and his companion, Tomkins, find the effect of the globe's realism comically disrupted by some of the equipment used to generate it: observing the 'circle of gas jets with reflectors' used to illuminate the display, Jones also notes that a 'judicious hole in the model there [in the Polar Sea] admits a ventilator; except the door in the Pacific Ocean, by which we entered, and this ventilator, the model, I believe, is air-tight, and the heat reflected on all sides from the concave surface rises to make a little Sahara of the North Pole Station.'[56] *Punch* made the same complaint, observing that the 'heat of the Globe is equal to that of any baker's oven.'[57] For all its imperfections, however, Jones acknowledges the model as a marvel:

---

52 'Panoramas,' *Chambers's Journal of Popular Literature, Science and Arts*, 21 January 1860, 13: 33.

53 [Charles Dickens], 'Some Account of an Extraordinary Traveller,' *Household Words*, 20 April 1850, 1: 75.

54 Ibid.

55 Ralph Hyde, *Panoramania: The Art and Entertainment of the 'All-Embracing View'* (London: Trefoil, 1988), 131.

56 [Henry Morley], 'The Globe in a Square,' *Household Words*, 12 July 1851, 3: 370.

57 'A Journey Round the Globe,' *Punch*, July–December 1851, 22: 4.

We walk about the surface of our globe, tread the hot flagstones of its towns, or crush the soft grass of its forests, bathe on the margin of its seas, float on its rivers, look abroad from its mountain-tops, and, like good common-place folk, here we say we are in town, there by the sea-side, there we are in the country. We walk into Leicester Square, and enter a neatly made brick packing-case, look at the world boxed up in a diameter of sixty feet, and say, Ah, here is a colossal Globe! here is a work of beauty! what a clever man its maker, Mr Wyld, must be![58]

Punch likewise declared its delight in 'travelling round the Globe':

First of all, there is not a single turnpike on the road. There is no dust, nor any throwing of eggs nor flour, as on the journey from Epsom; and again, there are no beggars, as in Ireland,—no revolutions, as in France,—no monks or mosquitoes, as in Italy,—and no insults, as in America…. All the World is before you; you have only to choose where to go to.[59]

And all this for the passport of only a shilling! All of Mr Booley's pictorial forays similarly transport him—at low cost and without the usual inconveniences of travel—overseas, demonstrating the role of the panorama and its related forms, like Wyld's globe, as a middle-class substitute for the expense and danger of journeying abroad, replacing foreign tourism with commodity spectacle at home. Reporting on his 'gigantic-moving-panorama or diorama mode of conveyance' to the club-members of the 'Social Oysters' upon his return, Mr Booley remarks his delight that 'new and cheap means are continually being devised for conveying the results of actual experience to those who are unable to obtain such experiences for themselves; and to bring them within reach of the people.'[60] Dickens's account of the panorama and Morley's visit to Wyld's globe describe a replacement of experience with representation, a virtual reality, that anticipates Debord's society of the spectacle.[61] But in satirising the peculiar way in which these exhibits blend imagined and material experience for the spectator, their accounts also register the ambiguous distinction between self and other, subject and object, that I argue is a feature of the journal's engagement with commodity culture more generally.

As demonstrated in Mr Booley's travels, the visual ideology of the panorama is one in which the all-encompassing representation provides an imaginary illusion of mobility that the spectator pays to consume. Relying upon giving the impression of 'really being there,' it raises questions about subject-object relations, and the opposition between interior and exterior, that are explored elsewhere in the journal's many accounts of window-shopping. Shop display, of course, was part of the new visual culture that linked city spectacle with commodity consumption, and it was a common subject in the periodical press. As an essay on 'Shop-Windows' in *Chambers's* explains, 'to the real epicurean of the joys of meandering in metropolitan shade, there can be no happiness on the cool side of the street where shop-windows are not': they are 'galleries of art, science, and marvels, and treasures of never-

---

58 [Morley], 'The Globe in a Square,' 370.
59 'A Journey Round the Globe,' 4.
60 [Dickens], 'Some Account of an Extraordinary Traveller,' 77.
61 Guy Debord, *The Society of the Spectacle* (New York: Zone Books, 1994).

failing enjoyment; exhibitions where there is no fee for admission, where we are constrained to purchase nor catalogue nor programme of the entertainment, where there are no reserved seats and no fees to attendants.'[62] However, such pleasures as the *Chambers's* writer gleans from print-shops and bonnet-shops seem limited by their unadventurous ambit when compared with the spectacle of the shops described in *Household Words*.

In 'Down Whitechapel Way,' for example, Sala's ethnography of London's 'Far East' begins at the emporium marking the western boundary of Whitechapel for him—the 'establishment of Messrs. Aaron and Son'—with its displays that beggar description:

> Gas, splendour, wealth, boundless and immeasurable, at a glance. Countless stories of gorgeous show-rooms, laden to repletion with rich garments. Gas everywhere. Seven hundred burners, they whisper to me. The tailoring department; the haberdashery department; the hat, boots, shawl, outfitting, cutlery department. Hundreds of departments. Legions of 'our young men' in irreproachable coats, and neckcloths void of reproach. Corinthian columns, enriched cornices, sculptured panels, arabesque ceilings, massive chandeliers, soft carpets of choice patterns, luxury, elegance, the riches of a world, the merchandise of two, everything that anybody ever could want, from a tin shaving-pot to a cashmere shawl.[63]

As Linda Nead remarks of this passage, for Sala, the 'conspicuous merchandising of the Jewish trader, symbolised by the over-ornate, over-bright gas chandelier, turns modern London into an oriental bazaar.'[64] But as well as conveying the exoticism and excess of these new display techniques, Sala's description captures the peculiar quality of *multum in parvo* that characterizes the emporium. Like the panorama, or the city viewed from above, the wonder of it lies in the prospect of being able to encompass the whole 'at a glance.' Piling up superlatives with his inventory of departments and decorative features, Sala describes the emporium as a vast spectacle in which the goods themselves merge with the technologies used to display them. *Chambers's* 'peripatetic philosopher' may claim that shop-windows not only 'furnish fresh matter for our musings' and 'cheer us by the exhibition of some of the pleasant varieties of life,' but 'bring us down to the sobering level of reality if our fancy is indulging in too fantastic a flight.'[65] But Sala's account shows otherwise.

The splendours of Moses and Son contrast vividly with the shops encountered in 'Butcher Row.' Sala describes a 'city of meat' where the gas 'lights up a long vista of beef, mutton, and veal.'[66] His account of the buyers and sellers observed there once again suggests a changing relationship between people and things. While 'legs, shoulders, loins, ribs, hearts, livers, kidneys, gleam in all the gaudy panoply of scarlet and white on every side,' the variety and abundance of the goods are matched

---

62 'Shop-Windows,' *Chambers's Journal of Popular Literature, Science and Arts*, 11 April 1857, 27: 225.
63 [Sala], 'Down Whitechapel Way,' 127.
64 Nead, *Victorian Babylon*, 89.
65 'Shop-Windows,' 225.
66 [Sala], 'Down Whitechapel Way,' 127.

in his account by the range of butchers who sell them: 'There are eloquent butchers, who rival Orator Henley in their encomiums on the legs and briskets they expose; insinuating butchers who wheedle the softer sex into purchasing, with sly jokes and well-turned compliments; dignified butchers (mostly plethoric, double-chinned men, in top-boots, and doubtless wealthy), who seem to think that the mere appearance of their meat, and of themselves, is sufficient to ensure custom, and seldom condescend to mutter more than an occasional 'Buy!'"[67] Similarly, the customers are numerous and diverse in type, ranging from 'the portly matron—housekeeper, may be, to some wealthy, retired old bachelor' to 'the newly-married artisan's wife—a fresh, rosy-cheeked girl, delightfully ignorant of housekeeping, though delighted with its responsibilities—charmingly diffident as to what she shall buy, and placing implicit, and, it is to be hoped, not misplaced, confidence in the insinuating butcher.'[68] Sala's persistent inventorying of types, applied equally to the buyers and sellers, and to the wares they deal in, establishes a peculiar kind of ontological equivalence between them that has the effect of populating the city with lively goods.

The arcades—which for Benjamin provided a paradigm for the fragmentary nature of modernity in the arbitrary profusion of their commodity displays—are also a source of fascination for Sala. Surveying the history of these 'plate-glass-adorned and nick-nack-crowded covered thoroughfares' in 'Arcadia,' he follows their spread from Paris to Milan, Florence, Vienna, Berlin, and finally, London, where he describes them according to physiognomic type.[69] One of the first to be built, the Burlington Arcade manifests its aristocratic pretensions in the status-announcing commodities sold there. Eschewing 'the useful arts,' writes Sala, 'luxury was almost exclusively purveyed for': 'Boots and shoes and gloves were certainly sold; but they fitted only the most Byronically small and symmetrical hands and feet; none but the finest and most odoriferous leathers were employed in their confection, and none but the highest prices charged for them.'[70] The 'one active handicraft' practised in the arcade was hair-cutting, but even this was characterized by deception: 'fallacious mural paintings of impossible Grecian landscapes' decorated the 'sophisticated saloons' of the hair-cutters, while '[b]elow they inveigled you to buy drugs and potions wherewith to dye the grey hairs you should be proud of, blue black; and stuffs to make you emulate the smell of civet, or the musk rat, and hog's-lard condimented into bear's grease, and wigs;—woven lies made from dead men's hair to thatch live fools.'[71] The goods and services proffered bespeak the identity of their consumers, since '[s]carcely a fashionable vice, an aristocratic frivolity, or a Belgravian caprice, but had (and has) a representative in the Burlington Arcade.'[72] This is as close as Sala comes to suggesting the Burlington's connection with prostitution, located as

---

67 Ibid.
68 Ibid.
69 [George A. Sala], 'Arcadia,' *Household Words*, 18 June 1853, 7: 376.
70 Ibid.
71 Ibid.: 377.
72 Ibid.: 376–7.

it was within the zone of West End clubland.[73] 'It was paraded by padded, tight-booted, tight-girthed, wigged old beaus trying to look like boys of twenty; by boys aping the vices of old men; by carpet-warriors, and by nights fresh from Almack tournaments,'[74] he writes. The evidence of dissimulation and belatedness marks it as an early example of the antediluvian landscape, the 'ur-landscape of consumption,' found later by Benjamin in the dying Paris arcades.[75]

For Benjamin, the outdated objects of desire that collect in arcades are clues to the truth of the fetishized commodity and the transitoriness of capitalist culture. Sala's account of the 'desolation, silence and despair' found in Exeter Change anticipates this awareness in detailing with grim comedy the feeble attempts made by 'some ghastly artist' to decorate the arcade with 'mural arabesques':

> These 'arabesques' ('mauresques' would be more appropriate, for they are very mortuary) twist themselves into horrible skeleton presentments, all in a leaden, deadened, dusky tone of colour; and, high over gas-lamps, and grimly clambering about shop-fronts, are melancholy dolphins and writhing serpents, and attenuated birds of paradise; all looking intensely wretched at the positions in which they find themselves.[76]

The shops '*are* tenanted; but not much,' he writes, as he recalls the many occupiers who doubtless 'had many good and sufficient reasons for so persistently continuing not to remain.' In contrast to the aristocratic physiognomy of the Burlington, and the desolation of the Exeter, however, the Lowther Arcade, opened in the Strand in 1830, is 'resonant with the pattering of feet, the humming of voices, the laughter of children, the rustling of silk dresses, and buying, selling, bargaining, and chaffering.'[77] Sala classifies the commodities vended in this, his favourite arcade, under three heads, 'Toys, Jewellery, and Minor Utilities.' A world in miniature, the Lowther Arcade is distinguished by the 'cosmopolitanism' of its toys: 'Look at the honest, hearty, well-meaning toys of old England. The famous cock-horses of such high blood and mettle, that the blood has broken out all over their skins in an eruption of crimson spots; so full of spirit that their manes stand bolt upright, and their tails project like comets'; while the 'German toys, which like everything else coming from Deutschland, are somewhat quaint, and somewhat eccentric, and a thought misty,' are exemplified by 'queer old carved men and women, in queer attitudes, and animals whose anatomy is likewise of the queerest kind, and who yet have a queer expression of life and animation about them.'[78] Then there are the dolls' houses, those 'desirable family mansions, … with the capital modern furniture, plate, glass and linen, … [a]nd the glorious kitchens, with that bottle-jack and meat screen and dripping pan, at

---

73   Jane Rendell, '"Industrious Females" and "Professional Beauties" or Fine Articles for Sale in the Burlington Arcade,' in *Strangely Familiar: Narratives of Architecture in the City*, ed. Joe Kerr, Iain Borden, Alicia Pivaro, and Jane Rendell (London: Routledge, 1996), 35–6.

74   [Sala], 'Arcadia,' 377.

75   Susan Buck-Morss, *The Dialectics of Seeing: Walter Benjamin and the Arcades Project* (Cambridge, Mass.: MIT Press, 1989), 65.

76   [Sala], 'Arcadia,' 378.

77   Ibid.: 379.

78   Ibid.

which was roasted the wooden sirloin of beef, painted and varnished.'[79] The 'most consummate of miniatures,' the dollhouse, Susan Stewart writes, 'has two dominant motifs: wealth and nostalgia.'[80] Together with the 'red-handled carpenters' tools,' tea-sets, dolls, and accordions, the dollhouse is depicted nostalgically by Sala as a souvenir of childhood, offering a spatial and temporal transcendence to the adult urban spectator in its miniaturization of the world of everyday life.

Turning to Lowther's jewellery department, Sala notes that while it 'may want the intrinsic value of the productions of Howell and James or Hunt and Roskell,' and while its 'brilliants may not be of a water so fine as those of Regent Street or Cornhill,' 'the jewellery of my Arcade is as sparkling and as showy, as gay and as variegated, as any assemblage of gems you like to mention.'[81] Lowther boasts cameos too: 'none of your shrinking, shamefaced, genuine Roman ones—but great, bold, bouncing, pictorial pancakes: heads of Minerva as big as Bristol Channel oysters, and trios of Graces vying in size with bread-and-butter plates.' Unlike the dissimulation associated with the intensely aristocratic displays housed in the Burlington Arcade, and unlike the sham goods sold in 'Cawdor Street,'[82] Sala finds the jewellery exhibited in the Lowther '[none] the worse for being unreal—sham is hardly the word,' for this arcade boldly proclaims its cheapness and 'there is a difference between a sham deliberate, a wilful sophistry or wanton piece of casuistry, and a lie confessant; a work of fiction for instance—a novel, a fable, or a pleasant tale. As such, I consider the jewels of Lowther.'[83] As well as demonstrating the democratization of luxury and fashion effected by the accessibility of such 'eighteenpenny finery,'[84] Lowther attests to the success of consumer capitalism in creating new demands by convincing customers to make apparently unnecessary purchases amongst its 'minor utilities.' As the 'Bagdad of housekeeping odds and ends,' Lowther can supply any minor want or wish from 'the delightfully egregious farrago of fancy hucksteries here collected.'[85] And while the outmoded goods in the Burlington Arcade betray fashion's transience, the Lowther is more versatile and responsive to market trends in its vending of fancy goods: 'I may hint fugitively,' writes Sala, 'that some attenuated vases of artificial flowers under glass shades, I have known as Queen Adelaide's Own, Victoria's Wreath, The Jenny Lind Bouquet, and the Eugenia Vase.'[86]

Sala's appreciation for the way in which Lowther puts 'innocent adornments' within the reach of 'my pretty tradesman's daughter, my humble milliner or sempstress[,] even my comely cook, housemaid, or damsel of all work,'[87] finds a

---

79 Ibid.
80 Susan Stewart, *On Longing: Narratives of the Miniature, the Gigantic, the Souvenir, the Collection* (Durham: Duke University Press, 1993), 61.
81 [Sala], 'Arcadia,' 380.
82 [George A. Sala], 'Travels in Cawdor Street,' *Household Words*, 21 February 1852, 4: 517–21. See the discussion in Chapter 3.
83 [Sala], 'Arcadia,' 380.
84 Ibid.: 381.
85 Ibid.
86 Ibid.: 382.
87 Ibid.: 381.

parallel in his praise for the anti-hierarchical quality of the streets. In 'Music in Paving Stones,' he describes the charms of rambling on Regent Street—'the only boulevard of which London can boast'—and relishes the simultaneous affirmation and levelling of social distinctions to be found in the promenade of fashion:

> Between three and six o'clock every afternoon, celebrities jostle you at every step you take in Regent Street. The celebrities of wealth, nobility, and the mode, do not disdain to descend from their carriages and tread the flags like ordinary mortals. Science, Literature, and Law, walk arm-in-arm three abreast. Dethroned kings, expatriated generals, proscribed republicans, meet on a neutral ground of politics, and paving-stones. It is pre-eminently in a crowded street that you see that equality which will assert itself at times—etiquette, William the Conqueror, and Burke's Peerage and Baronetage, notwithstanding. The Queen of Spain has legs in Regent Street, and uses them. The Duke of Pampotter cannot usurp a larger share of the pavement than the plebeian in a velveteen shooting jacket who sells lap-dogs. Every gent in a Joinville tie, irreproachable boots, and a successful moustache, can be for the nonce the shepherd Paris, and adjudge the golden apple to the most beautiful bonnet, and the most beautiful face, whether their possessor be a fashionable marchioness or a fashionable milliner.[88]

While revelling in the equality imposed by the mingling and jostling of pedestrians on paving-stones, Sala's description also evokes the allure of celebrity, fashion, and cosmopolitanism. The promenade exerts its appeal through the paradoxical intensification and erasure of social contrasts, as Sala's delight in the spectacle of class and national difference at the heart of the imperial metropolis is registered in sartorial display—'the most eccentric hats, the wildest pantaloons, the craziest extravagances of braiding, the most luxuriant beards; glistening with pomatum, electroplated jewellery, and boot-varnish; swelling down Regent Street, making the air redolent with foreign perfumes and the smoke of foreign cigars'—and in the 'brilliant shops' opened by foreigners 'for the sale of perfumes, gloves, cambric pocket-handkerchiefs, Vanille chocolate, ormolu clocks, Strasburg pies, St. Julien claret, and patent leather boots.'[89] Regent Street was unique in having been planned in the early decades of the nineteenth century as a 'bespoke' shopping avenue intended 'to rival the newly created Rue de Rivoli, in Paris.'[90] It was a parade ground for 'the fireflies of fashion,' as the *Illustrated London News* observed in 1866,[91] and this brought the gents in Joinville ties and the sellers of lapdogs noted by Sala onto the pavements to mingle with the *bon ton*, and the many foreigners, 'often associated with the Opera or concert rooms,'[92] who frequented the area. Like the extraordinarily varied cross-sections of society presented in Frith's great panoramic paintings of *Derby Day* or the *Railway Station*, Sala's ethnographic account of Regent Street revels in the spectacle constituted by the striking mixture of types.

---

88 [George A. Sala], 'Music in Paving Stones,' *Household Words*, 26 August 1854, 10: 37.
89 Ibid.
90 Hermione Hobhouse, *A History of Regent Street* (London: Macdonald and Jane's, 1975), 10.
91 Quoted in Ibid., 108.
92 Ibid., 72.

Such responsiveness to social contrasts is also demonstrated in Sala's perambulation of 'Leicester Square,' whose chequered history may be read in the buildings that line its perimeter.[93] Marvelling that Saville House was 'a palace once, for George the Third's sister was married from thence,' Sala describes the successive exhibitors to have inhabited what is now a 'palace of showmanship,' the 'greatest booth in Europe':

> Serpents both of land and sea;– panoramas of all the rivers of the known world; jugglers; ventriloquists; imitators of the noises of animals; dioramas of the North pole, and the gold-diggings of California; somnambulists (very lucid); ladies who have cheerfully submitted to have their heads cut off nightly at sixpence per head admission; giants; dwarfs; sheep with six legs; calves born inside out; marionettes; living marionettes; lecturers on Bloomerism; expositors of orrery—all these have by turns found a home in Saville House. In the enlarged cosmopolitanthropy of that mansion, it has thrown open its arms to the universe of exhibitions. One touch of showmanship makes the whole world kin; and this omni-showing house would accommodate with equal pleasure, Acrobats in its drawing-rooms, Spiritual Rappers in its upper rooms, the Poughkeepsie Seer in the entrance hall, and the Learned Pig in the cellar.[94]

The expansiveness of Sala's heterogeneous list imitates the metamorphic history of the building. He relishes the striking juxtapositions that characterize the disparate occupants and marvels at their mutability as one show rapidly succeeds another. Like the catalogues of advertisements discussed in Chapter 2, such lists encapsulate the paradoxical nature of commodification—celebrating the exhilarating diversity of the things listed, while at the same time indicating their interchangeability. Dickens makes a similar point about the temporal mobility of urban sites in 'An Unsettled Neighbourhood,' where a new railway terminus produces a continuous process of transformation:

> There are not fifty houses of any sort in the whole place that know their own mind a month. Now, a shop says, 'I'll be a toy-shop.' Tomorrow it says, 'No I won't; I'll be a milliner's.' Next week it says, 'No I won't; I'll be a stationer's.' Next week it says, 'No I won't; I'll be a Berlin wool repository.' Take the shop directly opposite my house. Within a year, it has gone through all these changes, and has likewise been a plumber's, painter's and glazier's, a tailor's, a broker's, a school, a lecturing-hall, and a feeding-place, 'established to supply the Railway public with a first-rate sandwich and a sparkling glass of Crowley's Alton Ale for threepence.'[95]

These shops have a mind of their own, even if they do not know it properly, and their personification once again registers the peculiar interchangeability of people and things. Notwithstanding the narrator's ironic complaint, like Sala, he relishes the spectacle provided by these metamorphoses, the incongruous identities successively assumed by the shops. The motif is repeated in 'The Great Red Book,' as Sala describes

---

93 [George A. Sala], 'Leicester Square,' *Household Words*, 19 March 1853, 7: 63.
94 Ibid.: 64–5.
95 [Charles Dickens], 'An Unsettled Neighbourhood,' *Household Words*, 11 November 1854, 10: 291.

such transformations in the suburbs: 'The newsvendor's shop, where literature was not so long ago mixed with kites, hoopsticks, marbles, Abernathy biscuits, and bleary bullseyes in bottles, has grown into a circulating library and fancy stationers; the old chandler's shop has become a grocer's and Italian warehouse, and armies of coloured bottles start from the plate-glass windows of chemists and druggists.'[96]

London's shops, exhibitions, and shows display a fluidity of identity that challenges the flâneur's efforts to interpret and codify the physiognomy of the city. In all of these accounts of urban spectatorship, the journal illustrates a more widespread nineteenth-century development in which visual experience was turned into commodity forms with a particular interest in the sights of London. As Sala expatiates regarding the numerous 'picturesque, humorous, or descriptive sketches upon the sights, characters, and curiosities, moral and physical, of the Great Metropolis, the Great Wen, the Modern Babylon, the World of London, the Giant City, the Monster Metropolis, the Nineveh of the nineteenth century, et cetera, et cetera, et cetera' that have 'poured unceasingly from the press since the time of the Great Revolution,' the 'question is, whether we are yet arrived at the troppa scrittura, or too much writing stage'—to which he emphatically answers, no![97] London clearly makes good copy, and there is more than a hint of territorial self-interest and professional rivalry in this account of the print market. Sala is *Household Words*'s pre-eminent flâneur, and can rightly claim, as he does here, to have 'seen London asleep and awake in the early morning, and in the dead night; in rags, and in state liveries, in sickness and in health, in murder and sudden death': 'For I have had the key of the street, and have known the secrets of the gas, and have communed with the paving-stones. And, perhaps, with some fifty thousand others, I may be a curiosity of London myself.'[98] Fascinated by such new forms of commodity spectacle as the panorama, balloon ascents, or window-shopping, writers of London, like Sala, expose elements of this phantasmagoria to critique, even as they simultaneously provide an imaginary form of flânerie that the journal's readers—browsing amongst its pages in lieu of the streets—paid twopence a week to consume. With mock self-deprecation, Sala laments: 'I have not the advantage of a thick octavo volume, as a museum for *my* curiosities. A poor little essayist, I am limited to columns. I can offer no mighty sirloin to my readers, but must be content with a modest cut off the joint. Yet, to employ the homely language of the proprietor of the ham-and-beef warehouse opposite, I am privileged to "cut and come again."'[99] And indeed he does, always finding narrative interest in the life of goods on the streets—and of those who sell or buy them—rather than in the stories of their birth and manufacture. For biographies of production in *Household Words*, we must turn to the process articles.

---

96 [George A. Sala], 'The Great Red Book,' *Household Words*, 9 December 1854, 10: 408.
97 [George A. Sala], 'Curiosities of London,' *Household Words*, 23 June 1855, 11: 497. The article is a response to John Timbs's *Curiosities of London* (1855).
98 Ibid.: 499.
99 Ibid.: 502.

Chapter 5

'Men Made by Machinery'

The title of Henry Morley's leader, published on 31 January 1857, plays with the idea of the prosthesis, the joining of humans and machines, that, as Tamara Ketabgian, Erin O'Connor, Herbert Sussman, and others have shown, became an issue of increasing concern during the industrial transformations of the early to mid-nineteenth century.[1] But rather than imagining a Victorian version of the cyborg, Morley is concerned here with improvements in mechanization and their positive effect upon the livelihood of workers. He argues that far from displacing labourers and driving them to the workhouse, the introduction of machinery in British manufacture works 'for the elevation of their class'[2]: it has led to an increase in skilled labour, higher wages, and the establishment of wider and more durable markets through the cheapening of commodities—all as a result of the reduced costs of production associated with mechanization: 'While articles are by their costliness especially confined to the use of the rich, the market for them is uncertain, because it is affected by the freaks of fashion. When the demand for them passes from a higher to a lower class of consumers, the use of them is established on a wider and a firmer ground.'[3] Thus he concludes that 'the tendency of machinery is not to convert poor men into machines, but that [sic] the steam-engine is in fact their steady helper, tending to no end so much as the making of them men indeed.'[4] For Morley, in this essay at least, the human-machine relation is not just benign, but beneficial, supplementing or extending the skills of workers to increase national productivity for the good of all.

Morley's argument in favour of mechanization contrasts with the critique of industrialism provided three years earlier in *Hard Times*, where Dickens attacked the view of the Coketown workers, 'generically called "the Hands,"' as prostheses of factory machinery—an industrial coupling evident in the 'odd sensation' that 'the stoppage of the machinery always produced' upon Stephen Blackpool: 'the sensation

---

[1] See Tamara Ketabgian, 'The Human Prosthesis: Workers and Machines in the Victorian Industrial Scene,' *Critical Matrix* 11 (1997): 4–32; Erin O'Connor, *Raw Material: Producing Pathology in Victorian Culture* (Durham: Duke University Press, 2000); Herbert Sussman, 'Machine Dreams: The Culture of Technology,' *Victorian Literature and Culture* 28 (2000): 197–204; Herbert Sussman and Gerhard Joseph, 'Prefiguring the Posthuman: Dickens and Prosthesis,' *Victorian Literature and Culture* 32 (2004): 617–28. My discussion of the human-machine relation in this chapter is particularly indebted to Ketabgian's stimulating article, which considers three of Harriet Martineau's process articles for *Household Words*.

[2] [Henry Morley], 'Men Made by Machinery,' *Household Words*, 31 January 1857, 15: 97.

[3] Ibid.: 97–8.

[4] Ibid.

of its having worked and stopped in his own head.'[5] It also contrasts with Morley's own campaign against factory accidents, begun alongside the fourth instalment of Dickens's novel, as we shall see below. Nevertheless, while men may not be turned *into* machines by mechanization in Morley's 1857 essay, the steam engine, which 'makes' them 'men indeed,' is shown to possess agency and to produce a certain kind of subjectivity in those who are its 'operatives.' As Ketabgian argues, in Marx's analysis of Capital, 'user-instrument relations undergo a critical reversal' which results not just from the use of machinery itself, but the division and abstraction of labour associated with manufacturing,[6] and Morley's elaboration of the interdependence of men and machines replicates this abstraction. 'When men work with a will, machines do more than they can when the men want energy,' he writes, 'and it is true in machine-labour as in handicraft that the high-priced English workman is, so to speak, a cheaper article than the low-priced labourer of other countries.'[7] Members of the late Philanthropic Congress at Brussels (Edwin Chadwick's report upon which forms the source for his information), 'compared notes with one another on this subject,' and 'found one German labourer to be equal to two Polish labourers, but that it required three Polish labourers—and those not serfs—to do the average day's work of an Englishman.'[8] While Morley advocates the improvements for workers in skills and wages associated with the introduction of machinery, his account also exposes the abstraction of labour and the prosthetic joining of humans and machines in a way that exemplifies *Household Words*'s ambivalent response to the processes involved in the industrial production of commodities.

That paradigmatic celebration of the 'Works of Industry of All Nations'—the Great Exhibition of 1851—marked a crucial moment in the development of Victorian commodity culture, and in the formation and dissemination of industrial knowledge, as many scholars have noted. Commodification involves the decontextualization of goods in the exchange between producer and consumer, and while commentators like Andrew Miller have remarked the way in which the Great Exhibition contributed to a separation of the spheres of production and consumption—juxtaposing goods from across the globe, 'eliminating their original contexts and constructing new meanings in its austere space'[9]—Clare Pettitt has argued that the 'Machinery in Motion' section of the Exhibition was a countervailing 'attempt to represent *process*,'[10] and 'pointed towards a new economy in which the processes of production were growing increasingly difficult for non-experts to understand.'[11] Like the Great Exhibition, *Household Words* also worked to restore awareness of the processes involved in the mass-production of goods, often taking its cue for an essay topic from the raw materials or manufactures described in the Jury reports. As Miller puts it, 'the habit

---

5   Charles Dickens, 'Hard Times,' *Household Words*, 29 April 1854, 9: 240.
6   Ketabgian, 'The Human Prosthesis,' 10.
7   [Morley], 'Men Made by Machinery,' 99.
8   Ibid.
9   Andrew Miller, *Novels Behind Glass: Commodity Culture and Victorian Narrative* (Cambridge: Cambridge University Press, 1995), 51.
10   Clare Pettitt, *Patent Inventions: Intellectual Property and the Victorian Novel* (Oxford: Oxford University Press, 2004), 90.
11   Ibid., 94–5.

of mind that sees in objects the labor required for their manufacture produced the many articles in *Household Words* and *All the Year Round* (among other periodicals) that explain to readers the manufacture of common objects.'[12] But such insight is not always uniformly evident. The imaginative narrative techniques used to expose the machine-like operations of industrial labour sometimes camouflage its status *as* labour through the figurative language of the description. Ironically, while *Household Words* sought to differentiate itself from such a 'cast iron and utilitarian' competitor as *Chambers's Edinburgh Journal*[13]—sought, that is, as Dickens's epithets imply, to distinguish its journalism from any resemblance to the machine-made commodity that might otherwise be seen in its identity as a cheap periodical, designed for a mass readership and produced by a team of authors who were part of a larger division of labour in print production and (except for salaried staffers) paid by the column—the imaginative narrative techniques used to achieve this distinction also serve at times to conceal the nature of industrial labour. In marvelling at the aesthetics of factory architecture, or admiring the precisely coordinated repetitions of the production line, the journal seeks to secure its own success as a commodity within the periodicals market while at the same time disguising the alienating effects of the division of labour elsewhere. As a commentator on the craze for cheap series noted earlier in the century in the *Athenaeum*, '[t]his is the age of subdivision of labour: four men make a pin and two men describe it in a book for the working classes.'[14]

Dickens was not the first to develop the journalistic form of industrial tourist tale he referred to as the 'process article.' Brian Maidment remarks a 'lengthy tradition of rendering industrial processes as graphic narratives, narratives which are polemical and propagandist as well as documentary and informative.'[15] The 'Days at the Factories' series written by George Dodd and published in *The Penny Magazine* under the editorship of Charles Knight during the 1840s was an important precursor for the accounts of industrial visits written for *Household Words* by a range of contributors. As Dodd notes in his introduction to the 1843 revised and reprinted volume collection of his 'Days,' 'the bulk of the inhabitants of a great city, such as London, have very indistinct notions of the means whereby the necessaries, the comforts, or the luxuries of life are furnished'[16]; and his series is addressed 'to those who, although not engaged in these manufactures, would like to know by whom, and from whence,

---

12 Miller, *Novels Behind Glass*, 123.

13 Letter to Mrs S.C. Hall, 23 April 1844, in Madeline House, Graham Storey, and Kathleen Tillotson, eds., *The Letters of Charles Dickens*, 12 vols. (Oxford: Clarendon Press, 1965–2002), 4: 110.

14 *Athenaeum*, 28 September 1833, quoted in Richard D. Altick, *The English Common Reader: A Social History of the Mass Reading Public, 1800–1900*, Second ed. (Columbus: Ohio State University Press, 1998), 275. My thanks to Robert Dingley for alerting me to this quotation.

15 Brian Maidment, 'Entrepreneurship and the Artisans: John Cassell, the Great Exhibition and the Periodical Idea,' in *The Great Exhibition of 1851: New Interdisciplinary Essays*, ed. Louise Purbrick, (Manchester: Manchester University Press, 2001), 93.

16 George Dodd, *Days at the Factories; or the Manufacturing Industry of Great Britain Described, and Illustrated by Numerous Engravings of Machines and Processes* (1843; Wakefield: EP Publishing, 1975), 1.

and in what manner, the familiarly known commodities of life are produced.'[17] Other mid-century miscellanies also contributed to the genre. In *Chambers's Edinburgh Journal*, for example, the discovery of a new method of treating 'caoutchouc'—'bestowing upon it a vast increase of its valuable peculiarities, besides endowing it with some new properties'—prompts an 1847 account of 'Vulcanisation' that *Chambers's* believes 'will interest our readers.'[18] Remarking in 1855 the 'national importance' of the 'manufacture of what is commonly taken as the type of everything worthless and insignificant—straw,' *Chambers's* provides an 'Industrial History of a Straw-Bonnet,' tracing the process of manufacture and the 'various kinds of labour necessary to produce in perfection that bane of all indulgent husbands and fathers'[19]; and a writer on 'Needles' in 1856 imagines his readers 'quite unable to picture to themselves the manifold transitions through which this little wonder-worker arrives at perfection,' and proceeds to enlighten us accordingly.[20] In their attempts to make industry accessible, however, these accounts rely upon second-hand descriptions of workers, raw materials, manufacturing processes, and products, eschewing the imaginative devices that characterize the genre in *Household Words*.

Dickens recruited Dodd and Knight as contributors to his journal, and they brought with them the admiration for diligent work, the division of labour, and the 'march of intellect' associated with the publications of the Society for the Diffusion of Useful Knowledge. This ethos is also promulgated in the various process articles contributed by Harriet Martineau. Her essays, however, are distinguished by the vividness of their eye-witness reporting techniques. With the assistance of her brother's contacts, she visited a number of Birmingham manufactories making a wide range of goods—electro-plating, nail and screw making, flour milling, gold refining, glass-blowing, button-making, brass-founding, and carpet-weaving, amongst others—and she describes in minute detail their production processes, conditions of employment, wages and fluctuations of trade. More than 20 of these 'factory tourist tales'[21] were published in *Household Words* between 1851 and 1855. Their number suggests both the extraordinary interest with which Victorians regarded the new modes of commodity production[22] and the 'epistemological crisis' remarked by Pettitt that saw a 'shift in expertise from the consumer, who handled the finished product with a knowledge of its provenance for evidence of its quality, to a professional expertise about production technologies that guaranteed consistent quality.'[23] In 'An Account of Some Treatment of Gold and Gems,' for example, Martineau's visit to a Birmingham gold refinery emphasizes the importance of knowledge of industrial processes for a proper appreciation of the enterprise and its products: 'It is a strange

---

17   Ibid., 15.
18   'Vulcanised Caoutchouc,' *Chambers's Edinburgh Journal*, 3 July 1847, 8: 5.
19   'Industrial History of a Straw-Bonnet,' *Chambers's Journal of Popular Literature, Science and Arts*, 26 May 1855, 3: 327.
20   'Needles,' *Chambers's Journal of Popular Literature, Science and Arts*, 17 May 1856, 25: 316.
21   The phrase is Elaine Freedgood's. See the introduction to her edited volume, *Factory Production in Nineteenth-Century Britain* (New York: Oxford University Press, 2003), 12.
22   Ibid., 13.
23   Pettitt, *Patent Inventions*, 98.

murky place; a dismal enclosure, with ugly sheds, and yards not more agreeable to the eye. Its beauties come out by degrees, as the understanding opens to comprehend the affairs of the establishment.'[24] She laments the common assumption, born of ignorance, that Birmingham manufactures are 'sham': 'Because the citizens have at their command extraordinary means of cheap production, and produce cheap goods accordingly, the world jumps to the conclusion, that the work must be deceptive and bad.'[25] Repudiating the 'Brummagem' label, she writes in the hope that 'some of the prejudice may be removed by a brief account of what a Birmingham manufacture of gold chains is at this day.'[26] Although Martineau extols the virtues of political economy, the technological improvements of the factory system and the increased range, quality and quantity of goods produced, however, other process articles in *Household Words* register unease about the material confusions of people and things entailed in industrial production. While extending the exploration of commodity culture, the process articles reveal an ambivalence in the journal's response to mass production: on the one hand, recovering the labour invested in the manufacture of goods, and demystifying the commodity in the process; on the other, complicating the question of subject-object relations through its representation of the human-machine complex associated with industrial manufacture. The journal's imaginative treatment of industrial processes is instrumental in conveying this ambivalence.[27]

While the industrial tourist tales published in *Household Words* derive from *The Penny Magazine*, the techniques employed for the representation of commodity production in each journal differ markedly. To begin with, the *Penny Magazine* was illustrated while *Household Words* was not. Vivid description substitutes for illustration in Dickens's journal, and its process articles are distinguished by the effects of immediacy and drama associated with its first-hand reporting techniques, as well as other imaginative devices used to respond to the transformations being wrought by industrialism. The contrast may be seen by comparing the account of a plate glass factory co-authored by Dickens and W.H. Wills, 'Plate Glass,' with

---

24 [Harriet Martineau], 'An Account of Some Treatment of Gold and Gems,' *Household Words*, 31 January 1852, 4: 449.
25 Ibid.: 450.
26 Ibid.: 451.
27 In a recent article, Jonathan V. Farina pursues an argument similar to my own in remarking the ambivalence of *Household Words*'s engagement with the factory system and the way in which Martineau's factory-tourism articles infuse mass-produced 'common goods with uncommon effects.' While I share Farina's view regarding the remarkable way in which the process articles endow commodities with some of the subjectivity that fictional characters exhibit, however, the journal's mystification of industrial processes is more uneven than he acknowledges. Even a proponent like Martineau does not uniformly 'suggest that like the novel the factory system enriched the individuality of its operatives, consumers and guests.' Jonathan V. Farina, 'Characterizing the Factory System: Factory Subjectivity in *Household Words*,' *Victorian Literature and Culture* 35 (2007): 41–2. Goods are often shown to acquire life at the expense of those who operate the machinery that makes them, and rather than seeing the anthropomorphism of commodities as peculiar to the factory system, I argue that it is part of the changing relationship between people and things manifested in the journal's engagement with commodity culture more generally.

Dodd's 'A Day at a Flint-Glass Factory.' It seems likely, as Harry Stone notes, that Dickens and Wills drew upon the *Penny Magazine* article, since they reproduce the long quotation from Dr Johnson regarding the origin of glass-making with which it begins, as well as echoing some of its technical descriptions.[28] But the resemblances are less striking than the differences. While Dr Johnson's 'forcible and beautiful paragraph'[29] is quoted by Dodd with respect, not to say veneration, Dickens and Wills put it into the mouth of a pompous 'Stentor,' or 'what the modern school would call a Stunner,' who shares the railway carriage with them on the way to Gravesend, and whose delivery of 'the rounded periods of his author' is comically interrupted by the station-master's booming announcement of their arrival at Blackwall.[30] Dodd eschews such fictional framing for his brief history of glass-making and tour of the Blackfriars flint-glass factory of Mr Pellatt. After describing the raw materials of flint-glass and their sources, Dodd recounts the various stages of production in painstaking detail, beginning with the 'mixing-room,' proceeding to the work of the pot-makers, the processes connected with the melting furnaces, and the activity of the glassblowers and cutters. The technical detail of the descriptions is supplemented and clarified by illustrations and diagrams, such as a vertical cross-section and ground plan of a melting furnace, showing the positions of pots and flues. Geoffrey Tweedale argues that while 'the tours and woodcuts perhaps lack the technological sophistication and detail of the major reference works of the period,' Dodd's series was highly accurate, dealt with 'the most technically advanced and successful firms' and 'possesses a vitality that is often lacking' in the standard encyclopaedias.[31] Such vitality may be glimpsed in the woodcuts of men at work, or the occasional allusion—to 'Cassim Baba's oil-jars' peopled 'with forty (or twice forty) thieves,'[32] for example—but such flights of fancy are self-conscious indulgences held in check by a narrator whose objectivity and distance are ensured by the use of past-tense narration and the editorial plural.

While Dodd's account is a monologue, Dickens and Wills cast their visit to the works of the Thames Plate Glass Company as both a narrative and conversation involving the 'vociferous admirer of Dr Johnson,'[33] named Bossle (presumably, a joking allusion to Boswell), the director of the Company and their combined voice as narrator. They share with Dodd much of the same technical information about glass-making processes. But the techniques of first-person narrative, characterization, and dialogue give a liveliness to the account that is supplemented by other rhetorical devices. Some of these are conventional, such as the description of the hall of melting furnaces as a Hellish kitchen, with 'unearthly-looking instruments hanging on the

---

28 Harry Stone, ed., *Charles Dickens' Uncollected Writings from 'Household Words,' 1850–59*, 2 vols. (Bloomington: Indiana University Press, 1968), 1: 205.

29 Dodd, *Days at the Factories*, 257.

30 [Charles Dickens and W.H. Wills], 'Plate Glass,' *Household Words*, 1 February 1851, 2: 433.

31 Geoffrey Tweedale, '"Days at the Factories": A Tour of Victorian Industry with *The Penny Magazine*,' *Technology and Culture* 29 (1988): 897.

32 Dodd, *Days at the Factories*, 262.

33 [Dickens and Wills], 'Plate Glass,' 434.

walls, and strewn about, as if for some diabolical cookery.'[34] But the imaginative figuration also reveals features of the commodity-production process that Dodd's more objective account does not. The process of plate-glass production commences with the description of some surprising raw materials which the narrator introduces circuitously to prolong the mystery of their possible relevance: 'The first ingredient in the making of glass, to which we were introduced, was contained in a goodly row of barrels in full tap, marked with the esteemed brand of "Truman, Hanbury, Buxton, & Co."' While the puzzle is quickly explained—that seven pints of beer per day, per man, has been found 'to be absolutely necessary to moisten human clay, hourly baked at the mouths of blazing furnaces'—the device merges the workers' bodies with the raw materials of glass-making, as if to give literal expression to political economy's labour theory of value. In Marx's account of the commodification of labour, the value of labour-power is determined by the 'value of the means of subsistence necessary for the maintenance of the labourer,'[35] and such self-renewal is registered in the equivalence Dickens and Wills establish between the ingredients for making glass and for *re*making the workers. Dodd's allusion to Ali Baba reappears in the description of the storage room for the pots, but Dickens and Wills also introduce references to fairytale that serve to miniaturize the adult observer and thereby convey a sense of the enormous scale of the operations witnessed. Such allusions shade into 'a scene from an Oriental Story-Book,' when a door is pushed open to reveal the 'smoothing' operations:

> so elegant and graceful were the attitudes into which a bevy of some fifty females—many of them of fine forms and handsome features—were unceasingly throwing themselves. Now, with arms extended, they pushed the plates to one verge of the tables, stretching their bodies as far as possible; then, drawing back they stood erect, pulling the plate after them; then, in order to reach the opposite edge of the plane, they stretched themselves out again to an almost horizontal posture. The easy beauty of their movements, the glitter of the glass, the brilliancy of the gaslights, the bright colours of most of the dresses, formed a *coup d'oeil* which Mr Bossle enjoyed a great deal more than Mrs Bossle, had she been there, might have quite approved.[36]

The labour of the women is eroticized and exoticized as it shapes their bodies into postures of 'easy beauty' that form an alluring spectacle for the male observers. Like the corporeal equivalence established between the sustenance of the male workers and the raw materials from which they make glass, the bodily formation of the women by the labour of smoothing suggests a new understanding of identity as shaped by the processes of commodity production and as partaking of the nature of the objects made. But while acknowledging the industrial assimilation of the women, the description converts their labour into the gracefully choreographed movements of a dance, aestheticizing it and disguising its status *as* labour. There is no awareness shown here that their repetitive movements might actually be boring and physically exhausting. Rather, the precisely coordinated repetition of the production-line

---

34 Ibid.: 435.
35 Karl Marx, *Capital: An Abridged Edition*, ed. David McLellan, World's Classics (1867; Oxford: Oxford University Press, 1995), 111.
36 [Dickens and Wills], 'Plate Glass,' 436–7.

becomes a form of art, concealing the substitution of automatic process for individual skill through metaphor.

A similar rhetorical move to assimilate workers to the processes of industrial production is made by William Blanchard Jerrold in 'Food for the Factory,' which warns of the risks associated with Britain's dependence on America for its supply of cotton and criticizes colonial agriculturalists who have been 'too busy abusing the home Government for its mismanagement, or squabbling amongst themselves about local matters' to produce more for the mills of 'the parent country.'[37] As the title suggests, the factory is likened to a ravenous body, and worker and raw material are conflated as the cotton is automatically translated into the bodily sustenance of the 'mill spinner and power-loom weaver': 'when the cotton-fields of the Southern States yield less than their average quantity of cotton, the Manchester operative eats less than his average quantity of food. He flourishes or decays with the cotton-pod.'[38] Martineau uses the figure of corporeal machinery in 'The Wonders of Nails and Screws,' as she describes the process of cutting nails: 'A most vigorous and certain process of digestion it is. There is a sharp steel tooth at what may be called the mouth of the machine, the ledge on which the strip is laid.'[39] Likewise, the steam-press that prints *Household Words* is described in 'H.W.' as a 'devouring engine': 'As fast as they are put into its mouth, like great square lozenges, [the sheets of paper] are all sucked away at the rate of nine hundred an hour.'[40] In 'A Paper Mill,' Dickens and Mark Lemon enliven the goods, rather than the machinery that makes them, by describing the transformation of rags into paper from the perspective of the raw materials. Contemplating the 'grave of dress' represented by the rags that await processing and the 'lesson of vanity it preaches'—'The coarse blouse of the Flemish labourer, and the fine cambric of the Parisian lady, the court dress of the Austrian jailer, and the miserable garb of the Italian peasant; the woollen petticoat of the Bavarian girl, the linen head-dress of the Neapolitan woman, the priest's vestment, the player's robe, the Cardinal's hat, and the ploughman's nightcap; all dwindle down to this, and bring their littleness or greatness in fractional proportions here'—the narrator is led by the evidence these cast-offs present of an intermingling of selves with their clothes, to merge his identity with the raw materials: 'I am to go, as the rags go, regularly and systematically through the Mill. I am to suppose myself a bale of rags. I *am* rags.'[41] Imagining himself going through all of the processes of paper-making, the narrator expresses his wonder for the anthropomorphic machine that 'draw[s] me out, when I am frailest and most liable to tear, so tenderly and delicately, that a woman's hand—no, even though I were a man, very ill and helpless, and she my nurse who loved me—could never touch me with so light a touch, or with a

---

37 [William Blanchard Jerrold], 'Food for the Factory,' *Household Words*, 30 November 1850, 2: 226.

38 Ibid.: 225.

39 [Harriet Martineau], 'The Wonders of Nails and Screws,' *Household Words*, 1 November 1851, 4: 139.

40 [Charles Dickens and Henry Morley], 'H.W.,' *Household Words*, 16 April 1853, 7: 149.

41 [Charles Dickens and Mark Lemon], 'A Paper-Mill,' *Household Words*, 31 August 1850, 1: 530.

movement so unerring!'[42] Detailing the surpassing sensitivity of the machine, and endowing the raw materials with sentience, the essay depicts an industrial scene in which objects start to usurp the subjectivity of those who work them.

Such a perception of the superior skill owned by the machine and expressed in the improved quality of the final product is also evident in some of the process articles written by Charles Knight, who began his contributions to *Household Words* with a series of 'Illustrations of Cheapness.' These five articles—on the Lucifer match, globes, eggs, tea, and the steel pen—are case studies illustrating the principles of manufacture that, he argues, provide the conditions of 'cheapness.' Knight identifies these as 'science, careful employment of capital in profitable exchange, certainty and rapidity of communication, [and] extension of the market.'[43] Devoted to the 'illustration' of a theory of manufacture that has consumer benefit as its focus, his descriptions of the production process tend to ignore the inventors and workers involved in favour of personified 'Science.' In the history of the Lucifer match, for example, 'Chemistry' makes the discovery that is the 'foundation of the cheapness'[44]: 'When Chemistry saw that phosphorus, having an affinity for oxygen at the lowest temperature, would ignite upon slight friction,—and so ignited would ignite sulphur ...; or when Chemistry found that chlorate of potash by slight friction might be exploded so as to produce combustion, and might safely be used in the same combination—a blessing was bestowed upon society that can scarcely be measured by those who have had no former knowledge of the miseries and privations of the tinder-box.'[45] Dodd offers similar praise in advocating 'Penny Wisdom,' the creation of 'a something out of a commercial nothing': 'Chemistry is here the grand economiser. Chemistry is indeed Nature's housewife, making the best of everything,'[46] as horse-shoe nails are recycled to make gun-barrels, plumbago dust is turned into pencils, and the refuse of slaughter-houses is converted into 'gorgeous sheets of coloured gelatine.'[47] Knight's 'Illustrations' celebrate the reach of cheap mass-produced goods across all classes: 'for the retail expenditure of three farthings per month, every house in London, from the highest to the lowest, may secure the inestimable blessing of constant fire at all seasons, and at all hours'[48]; similarly, if 'a globe were not made upon a principle involving the scientific combination of skilled labour, it would be a mere article of luxury from its excessive costliness. It is now a most useful instrument in education.'[49] But his regard for the comfort and convenience of the workingman who can now afford to buy these goods is accompanied by a figurative erosion of the boundary between human and machine

---

42 Ibid.: 531.

43 [Charles Knight], 'Illustrations of Cheapness [iv]: Tea,' *Household Words*, 8 June 1850, 1: 256.

44 [Charles Knight], 'Illustrations of Cheapness [i]: The Lucifer Match,' *Household Words*, 13 April 1850, 1: 57.

45 Ibid.: 55.

46 [George Dodd], 'Penny Wisdom,' *Household Words*, 16 October 1852, 6: 101.

47 Ibid.: 99.

48 [Knight], 'Illustrations of Cheapness [i]: The Lucifer Match,' 56–7.

49 [Charles Knight], 'Illustrations of Cheapness [ii]: A Globe,' *Household Words*, 20 April 1850, 1: 85.

that conceals, with metaphor, the capacity of industrial processes to alienate workers. In the production of Lucifer matches, he remarks 'the amount of skill required in the labourers, and the facility of habit, which makes fingers act with the precision of machines.'[50] When he arrives at the point in the globe-making process where the sphere is to be 'endued with intelligence,' he describes 'two skilled workers, who may take rank as artists, but whose skill is limited, and at the same time perfected, by the uniformity of their operations.'[51] The skill of these workers—the precision and uniformity of their labour—is simultaneously acknowledged (they 'may take rank as artists') and undercut (their 'skill is limited, and at the same time perfected') as it is gauged through their likeness to machines. Knight implicitly endorses the assimilation of human operatives to machines, while at the same time offering the reassurance that the workers retain full potential for individual self-realization through their artistry. The realities of industrial labour are masked by the figurative language used to describe them.

Victorian commentators on industrialism typically negotiated 'the complexities of human-machine relations through prosthetic metaphors: parts and wholes, supplements and bodies, organs and bodies, organs and machines'[52]: hence the anthropomorphic paper-making machine described by Dickens and Lemon above. Proponents, like Knight and Martineau, identify the ways in which machines extend or perfect the abilities of those who operate them. In her account of the Birmingham gold refinery, Martineau admires the adaptation of bodily parts involved in the burnishing of ornamental chains: 'What curious finger-ends they have—those women who chafe the precious metals into their last degree of polish! They are broad—the joint so flexible that it is bent considerably backwards when in use; and the skin has a peculiar smoothness: more mechanical, we fancy, than vital.'[53] She notes the remedy that mechanization has brought to the 'disadvantage of great waste of time, of effort, and of gold' formerly incurred in the making by hand of gold chains. Now, 'there are cutting, and piercing, and snipping machines—all bright and diligent; and the women and girls who work at them are bright and diligent too. Here, in this long room, lighted with lattices along the whole range, the machines stand, and the women sit, in a row—quiet, warm and comfortable.'[54] Sharing the attributes of discipline and order, quietness and comfort, as Ketabgian notes, 'the striking resemblance between these machines and factory-girls hints at a concealed, internalized exchange between the two, in spite of their orderly separation on the factory floor.'[55] Likewise, needle-making is shown to improve human capacities as Martineau describes the work of 'handling' the needles according to length: 'It is altogether an affair of tact; and fine must be the touch, and long the experience, required to do such sorting with accuracy.'[56] Such bodily transformations elide the distinction between the commodity and the worker as both are 'made' by machinery.

---

50 [Knight], 'Illustrations of Cheapness [i]: The Lucifer Match,' 57.
51 [Knight], 'Illustrations of Cheapness [ii]: A Globe,' 86.
52 Ketabgian, 'The Human Prosthesis,' 5.
53 [Martineau], 'Gold and Gems,' 452.
54 Ibid.: 451.
55 Ketabgian, 'The Human Prosthesis,' 26.
56 [Harriet Martineau], 'Needles,' *Household Words*, 28 February 1852, 4: 545.

However, not all accounts of industrial processes in *Household Words* are so admiring, especially those appearing in the first half of the decade. 'A Voice from the Factory' complains about his sense of alienation from the Great Exhibition as a result of his subjection to the machine:

> My labour, leagued with poverty, estranges
> Me from this mental marvel of our time.
> I cannot share the triumph and the pageant,
> I, a poor toiler at the whirling wheel,
> The slave, not servant, of a ponderous agent,
> With bounding steam-pulse, and with arms of steel.[57]

The anthropomorphism of the machine, with pulse and arms of steel, and the familiar synecdoche of workers as 'hands' convey anxieties about identity and agency in the industrial coupling of people and things. Notwithstanding her support for the factory system throughout her process articles, in 'Shawls' Harriet Martineau acknowledges the alienation experienced by the worker who is effectively supplanted by his machine. She describes a visit to a Paisley manufactory where, on the one hand, amongst other examples of industrial progress, she admires the saving of 'vast time and labour' through the recent invention of a machine to twist the fringes of cloth shawls: 'Till a month ago this work was done by girls, in not the pleasantest way, either to themselves or the purchaser, by their wetting their hands from their own mouths, and twisting the threads between their palms.'[58] On the other hand, she also notes the way in which the Jacquard loom and lacing machine have displaced the weaver in the process of making the 'true and venerable woven shawl':

> Thus the work is really all done before-hand, except the mere putting together of the threads; done, moreover, by anybody but the weaver, who is, to say the truth, a mere shuttle-throwing machine. The poor man does not even see and know what he is doing. The wrong side of the shawl is uppermost; and not even such a wrong side as we see, which gives some notion of the pattern on the other.[59]

As well as lamenting the overmastering of worker by machine, Martineau gestures towards recognition of the embodiment of labour within the finished goods in admiring their patterns. But her description also illustrates the shifting relationship between people and things already noted as a feature of the journal's engagement with commodity culture:

> The bundles of weaving-strings and netting which regulate the pattern, are called 'flowers'. From the quantity of labour and skill wrought up in their arrangement, they are very valuable. A pile of them, on a small table, were, as we were assured, worth one thousand

---

57 [John Critchley Prince], 'A Voice from the Factory,' *Household Words*, 5 April 1851, 3: 36.
58 [Harriet Martineau], 'Shawls,' *Household Words*, 28 August 1852, 5: 553.
59 Ibid.: 554.

pounds. We may regard each as the soul or spirit of the shawl,—not creating its material, but animating it with character, personality and beauty.[60]

Martineau's account interposes several layers of processing between the labour of the worker and the final shawl, and while acknowledging the way in which the worker's skill is 'wrought up' in the 'flowers,' the commodity itself is endowed with life, with 'character, personality and beauty.' Gradually taking on a life of its own, the shawl emerges as a Marxian 'social thing' while the labour of the worker embodied in it is abstracted. While attempting to recover the otherwise unseen labour of the manufacturing process, and regretting the supplanting of worker by machine evident in the weaver's fate, Martineau's effort to breach the gap opened up by industrialization between producer and consumer cannot avoid representing the animism and autonomy of the commodity criticized by Marx.

Household Words also identified a problematic relationship between humans and machines in its vigorous campaign against preventable factory accidents. Henry Morley began the journal's attack upon the failure of mill-owners to implement the safety requirements of the 1844 Factory Act to fence their machinery in 'Ground in the Mill.' Appearing a week before the instalment of *Hard Times* that introduces Stephen Blackpool, who will become the victim of an industrial accident later in the novel (albeit from a disused mine shaft rather than machinery), Morley's essay begins with the grim account of a boy 'whom his stern master, the machine, caught as he stood on a stool wickedly looking out of window at the sunlight and the flying clouds. These were no business of his, and he was fully punished when the machine he served caught him by one arm and whirled him round and round till he was thrown down dead.'[61] Deploring the consequences of the machine's brutal mastery, Morley reserves his greatest scorn for the commercial interests that permit such an outrage. He attributes the dereliction of the manufacturers to a cost-benefit analysis that finds the requirement of fencing an 'unnecessary' expenditure. '[W]e hope,' he writes, the resulting credit to the manufacturers 'is enough to balance the account against mercy made out on behalf of the English factory workers thus':

> Mercy debtor to justice, of poor men, women, and children, one hundred and six lives, one hundred and forty-two hands or arms, one thousand two hundred and eighty-seven (or, in bulk, how many bushels of) fingers, for the breaking of one thousand three hundred and forty bones, for five hundred and fifty-nine damaged heads, and for eight thousand two hundred and eighty-two miscellaneous injuries.[62]

The workers' bodies are shown to be commodified through the subjection of their dismembered parts to weighing and calculation, like any other bulk goods. Similarly, the promise of compensation for 'death or loss of limb,' together with the application of fines to culpable mill owners, continues to put a price on the worker's body by assigning a pecuniary value (of a derisively small amount) for harm to it. Morley attacks such commensuration a year later in 'Fencing with Humanity,' where the

---

60 Ibid.
61 [Henry Morley], 'Ground in the Mill,' *Household Words*, 22 April 1854, 9: 224.
62 Ibid.: 225.

'price of life' is set at 'twenty pounds; and lower damage costs but a trifle to the person whose neglect has inflicted it.'[63] The 'cost' to the sufferer, he suggests, is incommensurable. Compensation for preventable accidents is held to be a kind of 'trading in death,' a form of contested commodification to be considered in Chapter 7.

Elsewhere in *Household Words*, however, the improvements brought by mechanization are shown to include a reduction in the pathological effects of industrial production. Harriet Martineau rarely finds evidence of industrial accidents in the manufactories she visits, and when she does, the injuries are attributed to the carelessness of the workers. As K.J. Fielding and Anne Smith wryly remark, Martineau uses 'what are now some of the familiar techniques of advertising or public relations,' erasing any unpleasant aspects of factory production 'by pleasing contrasts with other parts of the work or by thoughts of their ultimate contribution to progress. Miss Martineau herself was not only deaf but had no sense of smell (she was assisted on her visits by her sister-in-law and nieces): thus much unpleasantness may have escaped her notice.'[64] Cases of industrial disease, like the consumption long suffered by needle-pointers, whose 'noses, throats and windpipes were infested, like their dress and their skin, with myriads of sharp points of cruel steel,'[65] are explained by Martineau as due to the perversity of the workers themselves: the 'very high wages' paid for such hazardous work engendered the desire for 'a short life and a merry one' and led them to refuse to wear masks, since they 'were sure their employers were in reality wanting to lower their wages,' and to insist 'upon their right to die early, if they chose.'[66] But 'A.W.,' describing 'Needlemaking' in *Once a Week* later in the decade, makes the same point about the recalcitrance of the needle workers, whose 'lives have to be saved, even against their will; as even now, if not closely watched, they would disconnect the fans, and thus deliberately renew the old danger: indeed some of them look upon the danger as so much capital with which they think that the masters have no right to interfere, exclaiming with the Sheffield fork-grinders, that the trade is "so overfull already," that these fans will "prevent them getting a *living*."'[67]

In the gold refinery at Birmingham, Martineau notes the nerve damage previously caused in workers by the action of cutting and polishing stones and now prevented by mechanization: '[h]ere the wear and tear is deputed to that which has no nerve. As the proprietor observes, it requires no sympathy.'[68] Such machines overcome the limitations of human sentience, extending productive capacity and, as Ketabgian

---

63 [Henry Morley], 'Fencing with Humanity,' *Household Words*, 14 April 1855, 11: 241.
64 K.J. Fielding and Anne Smith, '*Hard Times* and the Factory Controversy,' in *Dickens Centennial Essays*, ed. Ada Nisbet and Blake Nevius (Berkeley: University of California Press, 1971), 36.
65 [Martineau], 'Needles,' 542.
66 Ibid.
67 A.W., 'Needlemaking,' *Once a Week*, 19 November 1859, 1: 424. The author is possibly Andrew Wynter, who contributed two articles to *Household Words* in 1852, the first of them, 'Saint George and the Dragon' in the same instalment as Martineau's 'The New School for Wives': see *Household Words*, 10 April 1852, 5: 77–80 and 84–9.
68 [Martineau], 'Gold and Gems,' 452.

notes, 'meriting' the 'anthropomorphic metaphors' applied to them.[69] In 'The Iron Seamstress,' William Blanchard Jerrold explains that the invention of the sewing machine resulted from the effort to contrive 'some kind of seamstress that would show no pale cheeks, and demand no morsel of bread': 'Flesh and blood seamstresses having become insufficient instruments, it was time to see whether a seamstress could not be formed of solid iron.'[70] An invention produced by 'Mr Ellis Howe, of Boston' unfortunately failed to work and 'fairly tired out with the iron obstinacy of his seamstress, [he] gave her up as an incorrigible sloth and dunce.'[71] However, in 1851 a 'Mr C.T. Judkins took her in hand' and 'so corrected her revolutionary tendencies that she became docile, and began to work her iron fingers admirably.' Regarded as an iron substitute for the seamstress, Jerrold's description of the sewing machine indicates both the difficulty of rendering new production processes legible to mid-century metropolitan readers, and the desire to humanize them. Benjamin has described the way in which new technologies imitate the old forms they are destined to overcome and quotes Marx's observation of 'the attempts, before the invention of the present locomotive, to construct a locomotive that actually had two feet, which, after the fashion of a horse, it raised alternately from the ground.'[72] Accordingly, Jerrold continues to personify the sewing-machine in describing its operation: 'From one side of the lady's flat iron surface, an arm rises to the height of about ten inches, and then, bending the elbow, passes over to the opposite side. From the end of the arm, a moveable finger descends; this moveable finger holds the needle….'[73] Jerrold admits that 'the iron lady is not proficient' in the 'delicate parts of work—in those mysteries known to the erudite as flounces, gussets, frills, and tucks' and is able, 'at the present time, to take in only the plainest needlework,' just as in 'Plate Glass,' Dickens and Wills describe the limits of machine expertise formerly encountered in the smoothing operation: 'the human hand alone was capable of the requisite tenacity, to rub the slippery surfaces over each other; nay, so fine a sense of touch was requisite, that even a man's hand had scarcely sensitiveness enough for the work; hence females were, and still are, employed.'[74] But 'Mr Blake, the ingenious manager of the works, has invented an artificial female hand, by means of which, in combination with peculiar machinery, glass smoothing can be done by steam.'[75] Now capable of the requisite 'tenacity' and 'sensitiveness,' the machine has been given a prosthetic hand.

Household Words shows an abiding interest in prosthetics, and not just in terms of their supplementation of the body for the purposes of industrial labour. In 'Several Heads of Hair,' George Dodd describes the hair-markets of England and France:

---

69 Ketabgian, 'The Human Prosthesis,' 20.
70 [William Blanchard Jerrold], 'The Iron Seamstress,' *Household Words*, 11 February 1854, 8: 575.
71 Ibid.
72 Walter Benjamin, *The Arcades Project*, trans. Howard Eiland and Kevin McLaughlin (Cambridge, Mass.: Belknap Press of Harvard University Press, 1999), 155.
73 [Jerrold], 'The Iron Seamstress,' 576.
74 [Dickens and Wills], 'Plate Glass,' 436.
75 Ibid.: 437.

The market of human hair would be very insufficiently supplied if it depended solely on chance clippings. There must be a regular harvest, which can be looked forward to at a particular time. And as there are different markets for black tea and green tea, for black pepper and white pepper, for brown brandy and pale brandy,—so is there a light-hair market distinct from the dark-hair market.[76]

Like any other commodity, hair is subject to market differentiation. Dodd's account of the processes that contribute to the cost of the wholesale product ('So much does it rise in value by the collecting, the sorting, the cleaning, and other preparatory processes, that its wholesale market price is generally from thirty to sixty shillings per pound'[77]) plays with the distinction between the natural and the artificial, the organic and the ornamental, involved in the trade of hair. From the evidence of its consumption by wearers of wigs and hair jewellery, he notes, 'there is a pretty extensive range of application, useful and ornamental, of the cropped crops of human beings.'[78] William Blanchard Jerrold's account of 'Eyes Made to Order' also plays with the opposition between body and prosthesis. He reports that M. Boissonneau of Paris now 'constructs eyes with such extraordinary precision, that the artificial eye, we are told, is not distinguishable from the natural eye': 'The report of his pretensions will, it is to be feared, spread consternation among those who hold in abhorrence, and consider artificial teeth incompatible with Christianity; yet the fact must be honestly declared, that it is no longer safe for poets to write sonnets about the eyes of their mistresses, since those eyes may be M. Boissoneau's.'[79] Significantly, the greater naturalism of these artificial eyes is attributed to their hand-making: formerly, a 'patient was left to pick out the eye he would prefer to wear, as he would pick out a glove' as 'manufacturers sold eyes by the gross, to retail-dealers, at a low price'; but the new artificial eyes are tailor-made, thus removing their manufacture 'from the hands of clumsy mechanics, to the superintendence of the scientific artist.'[80] Regarded as a form of 'scientific art,' the handmade eye stands apart from the mass produced commodity.

It is, however, to the exploration of mass-produced goods that *Household Words*'s process articles are primarily devoted in their attempt to wrestle with the new gaps in knowledge created by industrialization. The sheer scale of industrial production prompts the journal's efforts to find new ways of representing such magnitude. Statistics regarding the numbers of workers, quantities of raw materials, size of factory buildings, or value of exports are often invoked to convey the monumental scale. George Dodd marvels at the Leeds Flax Mill of Messrs. Marshall which boasts a 'monster room' that was based upon designs derived by M. Bonomi 'from the temple architecture of Egypt.' It has an 'entrance like an Egyptian temple, a façade of stone, surmounted with a bold cornice; a chimney having the form and proportions of the far-famed Cleopatra's needle' and an interior 'nearly four hundred feet in length,

---

76 [George Dodd], 'Several Heads of Hair,' *Household Words*, 4 March 1854, 9: 62–3.
77 Ibid.: 63.
78 Ibid.: 65.
79 [William Blanchard Jerrold], 'Eyes Made to Order,' *Household Words*, 11 October 1851, 4: 65.
80 Ibid.

by more than half of this in breadth—five times as large in area as Westminster Hall,' whose roof is 'supported by half a hundred pillars, and is lighted by ten thousand square feet of conical skylights, occupying the summits of small domes or ground arches.'[81] Martineau is equally awestruck by the 'architectural grandeur in these long lofty rooms' found at the ribbon manufactory of Messrs. Leavesley and Hands,[82] and at the scale of production such buildings house. She is astounded by the vast quantities of needles that may be made by one factory, as she contemplates a single packet in a Redditch warehouse: 'The effort to imagine their contents, when in use, was like undertaking to count the grains of a square yard of sea-beach. Yet this was only one room of one manufactory of one little town!'[83] In order to comprehend the scale of nail production in Britain, she offers a carefully graduated calculation: 'let us think of a handful of tacks, or the household box of nails, and follow these up to the pound, and the hundred-weight, and the twenty hundred-weights which make a ton, and think of five hundred of these tons, as a weekly supply; and we shall be full of wonder as to what becomes of such heaps of uncountable masses of nails.'[84] In their account of the editorial and printing processes involved in the production of *Household Words*, Dickens and Morley describe 'the acres of white paper and the ponds of writing ink, the mileage of finger movement that precede the issue of each week's allowance of print to the world.'[85] The vast labour involved in the editorial process of selecting material from 'Voluntary Correspondents' may be gauged, they argue, by the fact that in 'the last year, we read nine hundred manuscripts, of which eleven were available for this journal, after being entirely re-written. In the same period, we received and answered two thousand letters, and made appointments with an odd two or three hundred more of our fellow creatures.'[86]

Such efforts to comprehend and represent the scope of mass-production lead into speculation about the global consumption of such vast quantities of goods, as Martineau, for example, wonders where the nail she has seen made 'will next be struck on the head':

> whether in some shed on the banks of the Danube, or in the cabin of some peasant on the bleak plains of Russia, or in some Indian bungalow, or in a cattle-fold on the grassy levels of Australia, or in some chalet on the Alps, or on the brink of some mine high up in the Andes, or under the palm-roof of some missionary chapel in the South Sea islands. As the nails are snipped off and fashioned, much faster than the nimblest fingers can snip paper, it is wonderful to think how they will be spread over the globe, nowhere meeting, probably, with a single person who will think of where their heads were last struck.[87]

---

81 [George Dodd], 'Wallotty Trot,' *Household Words*, 5 February 1853, 6: 501.
82 [Harriet Martineau], 'Rainbow Making,' *Household Words*, 14 February 1852, 4: 489.
83 [Martineau], 'Needles,' 543.
84 [Martineau], 'The Wonders of Nails and Screws,' 139.
85 [Dickens and Morley], 'H.W.,' 147.
86 Ibid.: 146.
87 [Martineau], 'The Wonders of Nails and Screws,' 140.

It is to help remedy such ignorance of origins that Martineau writes in *Household Words*.[88] On a visit to the button factory of Messrs. Allen and Moore, she cautions against this sort of obliviousness on the part of consumers: '"I don't care a button," we say: but, little as a button may be worth to us, one single specimen may be worth to the manufacturer long days of toil and nights of care, and the gain or loss of thousands of pounds.'[89] An informed observer of the factory system, Martineau interprets it for readers otherwise unfamiliar with the new processes that produced the goods they used every day, finding within the commodity—even in 'an article so small as to be a very name for nothingness'[90]—the tale of its manufacture. Examining the 'broad shell' used in the manufacture of pearl buttons, she imagines the labour of the divers—'the plunge, and the wrenching of the shells from the rocks, the putting them into the pouch at the waist; and the ascent, amidst a vast pressure of water, causing the head to seethe and roar, and the ears to ache, and the imprisoned breath to convulse the frame'—and the subsequent career of the shell:

> And then must have followed the sale to the Singapore merchant; and the packing and shipping to England; and the laying up in London, to gather an enormous price—the article being bought up by a few rich merchants—and the journey to Birmingham, where the finest part of the shell is to be kept for buttons, and the coarser part sent on to Sheffield, to make the handles of knives, paper-cutters, and the like.
> Through such adventures has this broad shell gone, which we now hold in our hand.[91]

Endowed with such a biography, the raw materials are given a narrative form normally reserved for human subjects. While Martineau's factory tourist tales imagine both ends of the manufacturing process in an effort to make readers appreciate the production and consumption of goods which might otherwise be taken for granted, they also suggest a sometimes disturbing shift in the relationship between people and things. When those things are imported—such as the 'broad shells' from Singapore—the essays that describe their processing into manufactured goods not only contribute to the formation and spread of industrial knowledge, but help to bring the world back home, as the next chapter will show.

---

88 As she writes of the finished carpets woven at Kendal, for example, there 'is something almost painful in seeing by how gradual and laborious a process every hair's-breadth of the carpets we tread upon so carelessly, is made. We buy a good Brussels carpet at four shillings and sixpence a yard, or a Wilton (called Velvet) at five shillings and sixpence, and we do not think of the wool coming down the Indus to Bombay; nor of the dyes from the Pacific; nor of the linen thread, sown, grown, and prepared near Belfast; nor of the mill processes; nor of this weaver, who has to give his mind to every cast of the shuttle; nor of this boy, who is now heaving at the cord—now thrusting in his "sword," and turning, and withdrawing it—for every new loop of the whole fabric.' [Harriet Martineau], 'Kendal Weavers and Weaving,' *Household Words*, 15 November 1851, 4: 189.
89 [Harriet Martineau], 'What There Is in a Button,' *Household Words*, 17 April 1852, 5: 108.
90 Ibid.
91 Ibid.: 110–11.

Chapter 6

Worldly Goods

Just as she ponders the far-flung origin of pearl buttons or the remote destiny of nails, Harriet Martineau marvels at the extent to which 'our English needles of to-day are spreading all over the known world, wherever exchange of commodities is going on.'[1] Remarking the cosmopolitanism associated with global commodity culture, she imagines the illustrations on the 'gay boxes' containing the needles are 'probably to be seen on the walls of many a log cabin in America, and chalet in Switzerland, and bungalow in India, and home of exiles in Siberia. It seems as if all the world of needlewomen, of every clime, were supplied by England.'[2] Her comment not only draws attention to the growing importance of international trade to Britain's economy throughout the nineteenth century, but suggests the cultural imperialism that may be associated with the transnational migration of commodities. While on the one hand serving to represent the national identity of their place of origin, on the other, these goods are seen by Martineau to unite the peoples of the world in a global society of consumers. Victorian novels are full of the spoils of international trade, deriving much of their realism from the cornucopia of consumer goods displayed in their fictional settings: furniture, clothing, utensils, and comestibles such as tea, coffee, and sugar. Indeed, Elizabeth Gaskell's *Cranford,* first published serially in *Household Words*, has been widely acknowledged as an exemplary portrait of such material culture, illustrating the key role of consumer goods in the formation of domestic identities—from the oranges eaten by the Misses Jenkyns, to the 'large, soft, white India shawl' sent by Peter to his mother and the tea sold in Miss Matty's front parlour.[3] Just as Edward Said has described empire functioning 'as a codified, if only marginally visible, presence in fiction, very much like the servants in grand households and in novels, whose work is taken for granted but scarcely ever more than named, rarely studied,'[4] these sorts of goods form an almost imperceptible background to the narrative.[5] They are there in the homes of the Misses Jenkyns, or

---

1 [Harriet Martineau], 'Needles,' *Household Words*, 28 February 1852, 4: 540–41.
2 Ibid.: 545.
3 [Elizabeth Gaskell], 'A Love Affair at Cranford,' *Household Words*, 3 January 1852, 4: 350; [Elizabeth Gaskell], 'Memory at Cranford,' *Household Words*, 13 March 1852, 4: 596. On material culture in *Cranford*, see Tim Dolin, '*Cranford* and the Victorian Collection,' *Victorian Studies* 36 (1993); Lorna Huett, 'Commodity and Collectivity: *Cranford* in the Context of *Household Words*,' *Gaskell Society Journal* 17 (2003) and Andrew Miller, *Novels Behind Glass: Commodity Culture and Victorian Narrative* (Cambridge: Cambridge University Press, 1995).
4 Edward W. Said, *Culture and Imperialism* (London: Chatto and Windus, 1993), 75.
5 As Freedgood's recent study compellingly demonstrates: Elaine Freedgood, *The Ideas in Things: Fugitive Meaning in the Victorian Novel* (Chicago: University of Chicago Press, 2006).

the Honourable Mrs Jamieson, without elaboration, without explanation of the way in which empire underwrites the domestic world of the novel. For this, we must turn to the non-fictional articles that surround *Cranford* and the other novels serialized in *Household Words*, such as *North and South* or *Hard Times*. The suppression of discussion about imperial and colonial issues in the journal's fiction contrasts markedly with the detailed consideration of these matters elsewhere.

Commodities not only cross thresholds between the marketplace and the home, but state borders, and in an era of imperialism and international competition, they are freighted with national significance. Describing the foreign tobacco shops found in the 'Patmos of London' inhabited by refugees from the continental revolutions of 1848, Sala attests to the cosmopolitanism of the foreign goods sold in the city while at the same time acknowledging the cultural displacement and exile such goods represent.[6] The plight of the Germans, French, Italians, Hungarians, Russians, and Austrians seeking refuge in the area bounded by Soho, Leicester Square, Golden Square and Lincoln's Inn Fields, is expressed through the commodities they consume: clothing, coffee-houses and 'slatternly printed foreign newspapers and periodicals,'[7] all bespeak their exile. For while foreign goods may help the European refugee to retain some semblance of national identity and make a new home in London, they too partake of his displacement. Thus Sala describes the 'vain attempt' of the inhabitants of Patmos 'to delude themselves into the belief that they are consuming the *fricassées* and *ragouts*, the suet puddings and *sauerkraut*, the *maccaroni* and *stuffato* of France or Germany or Italy.... But alas! These dishes, though compounded from foreign recipes and cooked by foreign hands, are not, or, at least, do not taste by any means like foreign dishes. Cookery, like *amor patriae*, is indigenous. It cannot be transplanted.'[8]

Just as *Household Words* published process articles that sought to restore awareness of the labour involved in commodity production, it also included a remarkable number of contributions on the geographical and social lives of a wide range of foreign goods that sought to improve understanding of what it was people were consuming and the conditions under which it was produced. Many of these goods were imperial—some coming from the colonies, such as raw materials like cotton, rice, cocoa, and spices from India and Ceylon; others were manufactured in Britain for export to the far reaches of the empire, such as the needles described by Martineau above. As well as the processes of their production, the journal describes their storage and display in warehouses, shops, and international exhibitions. To be sure, other contemporary miscellanies show a similar awareness of the worldliness of modern goods. *Chambers's Edinburgh Journal*, for example, remarks of the shops of London in 1850:

> In the space of a single mile [the shopper] may travel from the North Pole to the Polynesian Isles—from Western Europe to Japan, and contemplate, and handle if he choose, the infinite productions of every latitude and every race. If he be an Englishman, he will

---

6   [George A. Sala], 'Perfidious Patmos,' *Household Words*, 12 March 1853, 7: 28.
7   Ibid.: 27.
8   Ibid.

probably feel some justifiable pride in the universal extent of that commerce, the evidence of whose success is in all directions so abundantly manifest.[9]

But in *Household Words* these worldly goods are given a narrative form in which the movement of commodities becomes a form of sociability between peoples and nations. As foreign goods are shown to get together in *Household Words*, they display a vibrant transnational dynamic that raises questions about the effects of imperialism, and about the relationship between people and things in the formation of national and cosmopolitan identities.

The Great Exhibition was not only a celebration of industrial knowledge, as noted in the previous chapter, but the first truly international display of the Works of Industry of all Nations, and a monument to the interconnection between industrial capitalism and empire.[10] Representing their places of origin, the goods in the Crystal Palace bridged vast global distances and brought the world 'home' to London. Launched at a planning meeting on 30 June 1849,[11] eight months before the first appearance of *Household Words*, the preparations for the official opening of the Great Exhibition (on 1 May 1851) coincided with the journal's first year of publication. However, as Deborah Wynne has noted, partly because the journal was unillustrated and therefore unable to compete with the enticing images of exhibits published in magazines like the *Illustrated London News*, and partly because of Dickens's objections to the self-congratulatory narrative of national progress that characterized the spectacle, *Household Words* 'discussed only the circumstances surrounding the event, rather than the event itself,' mentioning 'everything but what was actually happening inside the Crystal Palace.'[12] Nevertheless, attention to the Great Exhibition is evident not only in the accounts of the construction of Joseph Paxton's Crystal Palace, the 'invasion' of foreign visitors and debate about the future of the Exhibition building, but in the many articles by George Dodd which use the Jury reports on exhibits as the occasion for narratives investigating the transformation of raw materials into manufactured goods.

Richard H. Horne describes preparations for the event, as well as the current debate surrounding the classification and arrangement of exhibits, in 'The Wonders of 1851.' 'Should the productions of each country be kept separate?' he asks. Prince Albert favours 'a fusion of the productions of all nations,' believing this to be 'more in accordance with the broad general principle of the Exhibition—more tending to amalgamate and fraternise one country with another.' But Horne fears that 'it would cause utter confusion, and amidst the heterogeneous masses, nobody would be able

---

9 'Shops, Shopkeepers, Shopmen, and Shop Morality,' *Chambers's Edinburgh Journal*, 14 September 1850, 14: 161.

10 As Paul Greenhalgh observes, like 'everything else at the Great Exhibition, Empire was a commodity, a thing more important than but not dissimilar to shawls, ironwork, flax or indeed sculpture.' Paul Greenhalgh, *Ephemeral Vistas: The Expositions Universelles, Great Exhibitions and World's Fairs, 1851-1939* (Manchester: Manchester University Press, 1988), 54.

11 Jeffrey Auerbach, *The Great Exhibition of 1851: A Nation on Display* (New Haven: Yale University Press, 1999), 23.

12 Deborah Wynne, 'Responses to the 1851 Exhibition in *Household Words*,' *The Dickensian* 97 (2001): 228.

to make a study of the productions of any particular nation.'[13] Sabine Clemm argues that this 'debate about classification highlights the key contradictions that riddled both the Exhibition itself and *Household Words*' treatment of it': contradictions relating, first, to the Exhibition's simultaneous promotion of international brotherhood and nationalist competition, and second, to its investment in class boundaries.[14] For my purposes, however, what is of particular interest in Horne's remarks is the way in which discussion regarding the classification and arrangement of exhibits becomes mixed up with the assortment of visitors. What starts out as a concern about the categorization of goods becomes a vision of disordered crowds, as people and things become interchangeable in the exhibition space of the Crystal Palace.

A similar transformation in the relationship between people and things can be seen in Henry Morley's article on the official catalogue. Couched as an autobiography in which the Catalogue proposes to tell 'the story of my early life,' the essay begins with a description of its parentage and the multiple editions into which it has since been transformed: 'the Illustrated edition, the official edition, the French edition, the German edition, and the twopenny edition.'[15] To be sure, the Catalogue's decision 'to unbend; if I may say so, to un-catalogue myself' and engage in gossip about the problems that have beset its compilation might be interpreted as the 'quirky, humorous style of writing' that Morley knew suited Dickens's taste, as Wynne notes.[16] But it also demonstrates an anthropomorphism that typifies the journal's engagement with commodity culture more generally. The Catalogue outlines the process by which the 'returns of exhibitors from divers parts began to meet each other in the compiler's office' where they were edited and proofed,[17] and 'while all this work was going on, I was being taught to speak in French and German, by gentlemen engaged especially for that purpose.'[18] Concluding with a summary of itself that dwells upon the vast quantity of matter it comprises—'My "Official" self makes three hundred and twenty pages, or twenty sheets of double foolscap folded into eight. Two hundred and fifty thousand copies of this having been printed; one hundred and five tons of paper have been consumed therein; and, upon this paper, the duty paid is one thousand four hundred and seventy pounds'—it lists the number of pages printed in each of the publications connected with the catalogues to arrive at a grand total of 5010 pages. Like W.H. Wills's account of the vast 'printed surface' sent forth by the British press in 1848 described in Chapter 1,[19] these remarkable statistics regarding the material substance of the Catalogue emphasize its identity as a thing, even as its anthropomorphism appears to endow it with subjectivity.

Sala's essay on the anxieties associated with 'The Foreign Invasion' of visitors to the Great Exhibition also illustrates this curious interchange between people and

---

13 [Richard H. Horne], 'The Wonders of 1851,' *Household Words*, 20 July 1850, 1: 391.

14 Sabine Clemm, '"Amidst the Heterogeneous Masses": Charles Dickens's *Household Words* and the Great Exhibition of 1851,' *Nineteenth-Century Contexts* 27 (2005): 208.

15 [Henry Morley], 'The Catalogue's Account of Itself,' *Household Words*, 23 August 1851, 3: 519.

16 Wynne, 'Responses to the 1851 Exhibition in *Household Words*,' 233.

17 [Morley], 'The Catalogue's Account of Itself,' 521.

18 Ibid.: 522.

19 [W.H. Wills], 'The Appetite for News,' *Household Words*, 1 June 1850, 1: 239.

things as it remarks the international understanding promoted by the event. His discussion of the spectators crowding the exhibition spaces focuses on their clothing and accoutrements:

> The fezzes still in a woful minority. No signs of the bernouse, the snowy camise, or the shaggy capote yet. Sunburnt Lancashire faces, Manchester wide-awakes, Agricultural red cotton pocket-handkerchiefs, decidedly in the ascendant. Here and there the eccentric chapeau, or the enticing bonnet, with the inevitable beard or moustache, show me the male and female alien passing.[20]

Such use of synecdoche blurs the distinction between spectator and spectacle in the display spaces of the Great Exhibition. Like 'Grandville's fetishistically animated objects'[21] that Benjamin connects with the world exhibitions, the visitors in Sala's account appear as animated hats and cloaks. He goes on to speculate that 'from this mutual sight-seeing and metropolis-visiting, this international-fete-giving, and hand-shaking,' an increase in world harmony may be anticipated: 'Altogether, I think that a little brotherhood among nations will result from the foreign invasion.'[22] Similarly, in 'Three May-Days in London,' Charles Knight casts the Great Exhibition as an international festival of peace 'to which all the nations brought the trophies of their arts': 'Belgium exhibits her richest laces—it is her ancient and proper pride; India brings her silk and golden shawls; Tunis her embroidered tissues; Persia her gorgeous carpets.' But alongside these treasures 'are also the ribbons of Coventry, the shawls of Paisley, the calicoes of Manchester, the broadcloths of Leeds. They are for the comfort and the decent ornament of the humblest in the land.'[23] Such home-grown displays are valued by Knight for their illustration of cheapness, of the potential mass-consumption of affordable goods, thus contributing to what Thomas Richards calls the Exhibition's 'invention of a democratic ideology for consumerism.'[24]

The spectacle of the goods on display was enhanced by the architecture of the Crystal Palace, described by Knight as 'a wondrous fabric; sublime in its magnitude, beautiful in its simplicity. The venerated elms of Hyde Park are budding in their vast conservatory, and their leaves will welcome our May-Day. Singular effects of light are produced by the character of the building; and in the dim perspective of its roofs the prevailing blue shows like an aerial vault.'[25] Benjamin quotes an equally admiring description of the Crystal Palace with the elms in its midst: 'Under these glass arches, thanks to awnings, ventilators, and gushing fountains, visitors revel in a delicious coolness. In the words of one observer: "You might think you were under the billows of some fabulous river, in the crystal palace of a fairy or naiad."'[26]

---

20 [George A. Sala], 'The Foreign Invasion,' *Household Words*, 11 October 1851, 4: 62.
21 Walter Benjamin, *The Arcades Project*, trans. Howard Eiland and Kevin McLaughlin (Cambridge, Mass.: Belknap Press of Harvard University Press, 1999), 195.
22 [Sala], 'The Foreign Invasion,' 64.
23 [Charles Knight], 'Three May-Days in London. (iii) The May Palace (1851),' *Household Words*, 3 May 1851, 3: 123.
24 Thomas Richards, *The Commodity Culture of Victorian England: Advertising and Spectacle 1851–1914* (Stanford: Stanford University Press, 1990), 61.
25 [Knight], 'Three May-Days in London. (iii) The May Palace (1851),' 123.
26 Benjamin, *Arcades*, 162.

An earlier *Household Words* essay by Wills on 'The Private History of the Palace of Glass' records the ingenuity involved in 'converting a conservatory for plants into a resort for breathing beings, and a depôt for articles emphatically "to be kept dry."'[27] The artificiality of this environment produces what Anne Friedberg describes as 'a new form of *public interior*, dissolving the separations between private and public space.'[28] Such spaces produced by the introduction of iron and glass construction—like the market hall of Paris, Les Halles (1853), or the arcades—encouraged the mobilized gaze of the window-shopper, as Knight anticipates in his description of the exhibition's final preparations: 'Bazaars were springing up in the enclosed divisions; and cases were being constructed in the galleries, brilliant with plate-glass, tasteful and substantial.'[29]

Household Words published a number of articles satirizing the commodity culture encouraged by the Great Exhibition. In a comic piece about the future of the exhibition buildings, Morley purports to reproduce some of the 'answers' sent to *Household Words* in response to Mr Paxton's pamphlet asking 'What is to become of the Crystal Palace?' While one correspondent seeks 'compensation' for the loss of value to his property adjacent to the 'Monster Nuisance,' another 'dated from the shop of a distinguished quack professor' complains (ungramatically) about the medals unjustly awarded to Morison's Pills 'when my discovery is noninwentus, where I didn't send it in. It is a mixture of which, one teaspoonful took fasting will reduce a fracture, and dislocations are reduced in one minute by smelling at the bottle.'[30] Another is 'a short note from a young lady' ironically underlining the fact that despite its lofty aspirations to commemorate industrial progress and international peace, the Great Exhibition was in reality all about encouraging consumption:

> 'Do, please, dear, dear sir, put in a word for those lovely shawls, and those sweet muslin dresses. It is so tiresome having to stop in those nasty streets, where people smoke and push about; and it's so dusty always that one cannot see for dust, or else so dirty that one is knee-deep in puddle. I never enjoyed shop windows till now, and I have looked at many. O dear Exhibition, where you look at all the shops and need not buy! But if you can persuade Dear Pa to get you anything, there's always the address attached, and you know where to tell him to go.'[31]

The account makes explicit the link between window-shopping and the Crystal Palace spectacle, between the world exhibitions and the new department stores, that has been analyzed by a number of commentators.[32]

---

27 [W.H. Wills], 'The Private History of the Palace of Glass,' *Household Words*, 18 January 1851, 2: 390.

28 Anne Friedberg, *Window Shopping: Cinema and the Postmodern* (Berkeley: University of California Press, 1993), 64.

29 [Knight], 'Three May-Days in London. (iii) The May Palace (1851),' 122.

30 [Henry Morley], 'What Is Not Clear About the Crystal Palace,' *Household Words*, 19 July 1851, 3: 400.

31 Ibid.

32 In addition to the studies by Thomas Richards, Andrew Miller, and Anne Friedberg, see Rachel Bowlby, *Just Looking: Consumer Culture in Dreiser, Gissing and Zola* (New York: Methuen, 1985).

The association of the Exhibition with an emerging commodity culture was continued in the subsequent re-erection of the Crystal Palace at Sydenham, as W.H. Wills reveals in a leader describing the preparation of this 'Fairyland' that will open in 1854. Entrance is 'not effected by rubbing a lamp or clapping the hands three times' but 'a commutation is accepted in the shape of five shillings current money of the realm.'[33] The displays to be housed in this Fairyland provide a form of virtual tourism and time travel, reminiscent of the panorama, as a 'burly Djin in a white hat and a frock coat with a huge lily in the button-hole' explains:

> 'You shall be made as well acquainted with an Egyptian tomb as you are with St Clement's church-yard, and shall wander into the *cella* of a Nubian temple as familiarly as you would enter your own parish church. You shall sit awe-struck on the steps of an Assyrian palace; you shall draw hard breath in a Grecian temple; you shall slake your thirst at the fountain in a Byzantine court; you shall tread on the prayer-carpet in a Moorish mosque; you shall wag your beard in the hall of a Medieval castle; and you shall be hospitably entertained in a Pompeian house.'[34]

Like Dickens's account of Mr Booley's panoramic form of globe-trotting, discussed in Chapter 4, the description of Fairyland plays with moments of comic deflation where a discrepancy between reality and illusion is made apparent, as in Wills's observation of the 'wonders of the Forum and the Acropolis standing on wooden plinths (afterwards to be plasterified) labelled "Fragile, with care, this side up."'[35]

In addition to its discussion of such topics as the disposal of the Crystal Palace, *Household Words* engaged with the commentary surrounding the Great Exhibition in articles on free trade and protectionism. The first Christmas number contained a story by Charles Knight, 'A Christmas Pudding,' that Paul Young has linked to the Great Exhibition, showing the way in which the dialogic character of the narrative problematizes the mid-nineteenth-century ideology of free trade industrial capitalism associated with the Crystal Palace display.[36] The story concerns a Mr Oldknow, whose anxiety about a Christmas pudding stimulates a dream after he falls asleep in the kitchen 'musing over the mercantile history of the various substances of which that pudding was composed.'[37] The ingredients of the pudding are anthropomorphized in his dream, appearing as a series of genie, all of whom engage in a debate with Mr Oldknow on the merits of free trade. Thus the Raisin addresses him as the 'son of a vineless land' to complain about the depredations of fruit from the south wrought in the name of English commerce. Mr Oldknow responds by explaining the importance of English commodities in stimulating global production and consumption, avowing that 'Man only worthily labours when he labours for exchange with other labour'

---

33 [W.H. Wills], 'Fairyland in 'Fifty-Four,' *Household Words*, 3 December 1853, 8: 313.
34 Ibid.
35 Ibid.: 315.
36 Paul Young, 'Economy, Empire, Extermination: The Christmas Pudding, the Crystal Palace and the Narrative of Capitalist Progress,' *Literature and History* 14 (2005): 25.
37 [Charles Knight], 'A Christmas Pudding,' *Household Words*, 21 December 1850, 2: 301.

and that the Christmas pudding—'the emblem of our commercial eminence'—is itself proof of this:

> 'The artisan of Birmingham and Manchester—the seaman of London and Liverpool—whose festive board will be made joyous, tomorrow, with that national dish, has contributed, by his labour, to make the raisins of Malaga and the currants of Zante—the oranges of Algarve, the cinnamon of Ceylon, and the nutmegs of the Moluccas—of commercial value; and he has thus called them into existence as effectually as the labour of the native cultivator.'[38]

The idea that global free trade makes the world go round through the commodification of labour is expressed elsewhere in Edmund Saul Dixon's 'Quite Revolutionary,' where he asks:

> what is any exchange of benefits or goods but an exchange of concentrated labour? Does not the Chinaman who gathers, dries, and twists the tea-leaves, give a hand's turn to the English seamstress who drinks the infusion made from them? Do not the farmers who grow Norfolk barley, and the brewers who brew it into pale bitter ale, lend a helping hand to their friends in India, who are to drink and enjoy it at the end of its voyage? Is not the exportation of the wine and brandy of France a simple export of the labour of Frenchmen and the sunshine of France, for which we can return a friendly day's work in the shape of flannels, coals, cutlery, sugar, calicoes and muslins?[39]

In such descriptions of global trade, commodities mediate between nations: substituting for those who produce and consume them, they effect an international sociability. However, as Young notes, while Knight's story appears to promulgate the logic of an international division of labour that will encourage the world to work together in harmony, the dialogic character of the narrative works against this vision: 'scornful of the goods it receives from Britain,' the Raisin is an unwilling trade partner, 'an imperial problem,' exposing 'the fact that a metropolitan agenda to create a rational world was an endeavour driven to incorporate terrains irrespective of the opinions voiced by their inhabitants.'[40]

Dialogism is also a defining feature of the periodical context of the story, and accompanying Knight's tale is an account of 'Christmas in India' by Joachim Heywood Siddons that betrays no such recognition of imperial problems. Siddons smugly proclaims that 'the tide of European conquest, and, better still, the tide of European civilization, has carried to the benighted land knowledge, and a large spirit of toleration,'[41] so that the English Christmas and its traditions have been able to colonize their Indian setting: the house is decorated with 'wreaths and branches of laurel—the tropical substitute for holly' and the presentation of Christmas boxes is converted to a ceremonial exchange of gifts between the 'saheb' and his various

---

38 Ibid.
39 [Edmund Saul Dixon], 'Quite Revolutionary,' *Household Words*, 16 June 1855, 11: 475.
40 Young, 'Economy, Empire, Extermination,' 25; 27.
41 [Joachim Heywood Siddons], 'Christmas in India,' *Household Words*, 21 December 1850, 2: 305.

employees.[42] Such transformations of local culture are part of the imperial process. Other stories in the number are devoted to 'Christmas in Lodgings,' 'in the Navy,' 'in the Frozen Regions,' and 'in the Bush,' bringing together members of the empire in a common celebration of what was fast becoming a national institution. The leading story, Dickens's 'A Christmas Tree,' describes such a cornucopia of toys and gifts in its reminiscences about Christmases past, that it anticipates the growing commercialization of the festival (which itself became an index to the 'globalization' of consumption in the twentieth century).[43]

Like Knight's currants and raisins, anthropomorphized ingredients are also used to present Edmund Saul Dixon's advocacy of free trade in beer and wine between England and France in 'Jean Raisin.' Personifying the English barleycorn and the French grape, the narrator describes the differences in their appearance—'John [Barleycorn] has a yellow complexion, and is garnished with a fiercely bristling beard, whereas Jean has nothing of the kind to show, and can only boast of a delicate bloom on his cheek'—and argues that while they 'have long been rivals; they have now determined to become allies.'[44] While 'standing shoulder to shoulder on every French and English sideboard without a shadow of ill-will or jealousy,'[45] they nevertheless exhibit significant differences, for although John may be a 'humbler cousin,' he is 'of a hardier constitution than Jean, and is capable of making himself more generally useful.' While he 'is an ephemeral being, bodily, ... [and] [c]omparatively pigmy, too, in stature,'[46] he has never been subject to the malady which has lately affected Jean—'Insular vigour has stood firm, while continental delicacy has pined and threatened to go into a consumption'[47]—possibly an early reference to phylloxera, which caused devastation in the vineyards of France after its accidental introduction in the 1860s. Identifying the various strengths and weaknesses manifested by John and Jean, the personification establishes an equivalence between them as sentient goods that contrasts with Samuel Sidney's account of the livestock and implements sent for display at an agricultural show in Paris in 'From Paris to Chelmsford.' Sidney also uses anthropomorphism to compare the national merits of

---

42   Ibid.: 306.

43   [Charles Dickens], 'A Christmas Tree,' *Household Words*, 21 December 1850, 2: 289–95. Indeed, the development of the Christmas number as a genre was strongly driven by commercial motives, designed to boost the circulation of its parent journal. While the first Christmas number of 1850 was part of *Household Words*'s normal run, from 1851 it became an 'extra' number; and from 1852 it was expanded to 36 pages, costing three-pence, and announced as 'containing the amount of One Regular Number and a Half.' Eight were published over the life of the journal and their popularity reflects the wider transformation in seasonal publishing from the earlier, costly and elaborate Christmas gift volumes and almanacs, to the cheap periodical issue accessible to a mass audience and designed for consumption by the purchaser. See Anne Lohrli, *'Household Words' A Weekly Journal 1850–1859 Conducted by Charles Dickens, Table of Contents, List of Contributors and Their Contributions Based on The 'Household Words' Office Book* (Toronto: University of Toronto Press, 1973), 44.

44   [Edmund Saul Dixon], 'Jean Raisin,' *Household Words*, 11 November 1854, 10: 308.

45   Ibid.: 309.

46   Ibid.

47   Ibid.: 308.

the exhibitors, but with a decided emphasis upon British superiority. 'The barriers of customs houses were thrown open for the occasion,' he writes, 'and every beast and every machine presented at the French frontier was duly armed with agricultural passports, was entitled to a free passage to Paris, to free board and lodging as long as the Exhibition lasted, and to a return-ticket to the frontier when it was over.'[48] As with the Great Exhibition, the products gathered within the palace of the Champs-Élysées represent the peoples and nations from which they were sent, and the strength of British agriculture is demonstrated in the metonymy used to describe the Swiss department:

> All the associates of the Ranz des Vaches were assembled under the Parisian roof, except the mountains; these included milk, butter and cheese, but no signs of beef in the English sense... But a British invasion is conquering the land of Tell; and, according to the opinion of the Swiss commissioner, in a few years Berne and Fribourg, and all the dappled races, will have contracted British alliances and have sacrificed their national independence to prejudices in favour of roast and boiled.[49]

Through the juxtaposition of their agricultural commodities at such international exhibitions, France, Austria, Hungary, and Gallicia are all shown to provide foils for British progress.

As well as reporting such international shows, *Household Words* contains a number of articles in which the traces of global, and especially imperial, awareness are to be found in warehoused commodities, both domestic and foreign. In 'Coats and Trousers,' Samuel Sidney records a visit to a wholesale woollen merchant in Cheapside where the assembled goods manifest Britain's global reach:

> From the dark dingy staircase we had ascended, continually went forth the stuff for clothing the armies and navies of England, the parti-coloured troops of Indian princes, the Zouaves, the Gardes Impériales, Chasseurs d'Afrique, and riflemen of Vincennes. From the same source is provided the scarlet robes of Ashantee headsmen, the camlet cloaks of Chinese mandarins, the white blankets of Kaffir chiefs, the canary-coloured pantaloons of South American infantry; the serge shirts and pea-coats of Jack, A.B.; the grey great-coat of his ally, the jolly marine. The bishop's sober black of costliest quality; the miner's flannel jacket and moleskin suit; the Derby alpaca of the sporting dandy; the blue broadcloth of the school-boy's many-buttoned jacket, and the coffin-maker's dismal baize, also continually flow into the warehouse from every manufacturing district, and out again to consumers of every class and clime.[50]

Celebrating the heterogeneous profusion of goods, such avid listing also implies their interchangeability (or exchangeability) and thereby demonstrates the paradoxical nature of commodification. Diverse clothes are sent forth from this warehouse in all directions to populate the earth. The negative impact of such trade in the colonies, however, remains unacknowledged even as Sidney describes what would seem to be

---

48 [Samuel Sidney], 'From Paris to Chelmsford,' *Household Words*, 20 September 1856, 14: 217.
49 Ibid.: 218.
50 [Samuel Sidney], 'Coats and Trousers,' *Household Words*, 3 November 1855, 12: 321.

a patently impractical export to Southern Africa where, 'among the natives, English blankets have superseded the native robe of New Zealand flax. The Kaffirs formerly wore brown cloth cloaks or karosses; they now send to our friend's warehouse for white blankets.'[51] This vast extension in trade from innumerable branches of industry has been made possible by 'our manufacturing skill, cheap iron and coal, capital and credit, by a repeal of all the monopolies and all duties on raw produce with which our staple trade was once fenced round.'[52] A month earlier, in a visit to 'A Ladies' Warehouse,' Sidney similarly marvels at the volume and variety of goods assembled, and their dispersal to 'every point of the compass—five pounds' worth to the little milliner at Penzance, a thousand pounds' worth to Madame Lafleur at Havannah, and Madame Striggs, from Paris, at Melbourne.'[53] Sidney figures his tour through the premises of Ashstock, Ahrab, and Co. as a 'voyage of discovery'[54] and the firm as an expanding empire:

> What we may call outposts of attack on woman's wants have been established by Ashstock and Ahrab in branches in the great cities of Manchester, Liverpool, Edinburgh, Birmingham, Plymouth, and Dublin; besides a muslin manufactory at Glasgow and a lace factory at Nottingham. In New York and Calcutta, independent colonies—consuming nothing but the produce of the Cheapside empire—have been established; and, in the great Australian cities, like plantations have been founded.[55]

While some interest is shown in the processes of manufacture—'French embroidered handkerchiefs, even of a very cheap kind, undergo a strange round of voyages and travels before they appear at evening parties,' which are duly described [56]— Sidney's emphasis is upon the benefits of cheap machine manufacture enabling mass consumption. His support for this expansion is most evident in the description of the lace department, where '[r]oods of counters and shelves were devoted to every description of every country and every kind.'[57] While Elaine Freedgood has demonstrated the function of handmade lace in offering resistance to mass-production and consumption for critics of industrialism,[58] Sidney is more impressed by the machine-made article, 'in which, besides many new uses, the finest descriptions are so well imitated that, at a yard distance, no person not in the trade, can tell the difference between the costly fine hand-work, and cheap machine imitation.'[59] Advances in machine-production 'have enabled the million to use goods which were once the privilege of the inactive few' and the importance of this trade 'may be measured in millions of yards': 'Five kinds of it were sold in one year to the extent

---

51 Ibid.: 323.
52 Ibid.: 322.
53 [Samuel Sidney], 'A Ladies' Warehouse,' *Household Words*, 27 October 1855, 12: 305.
54 Ibid.: 303.
55 Ibid.: 305.
56 Ibid.: 302.
57 Ibid.: 304.
58 Elaine Freedgood, '"Fine Fingers": Victorian Handmade Lace and Utopian Consumption,' *Victorian Studies* 45 (2003): 625–47.
59 [Sidney], 'A Ladies' Warehouse,' 304.

of more than six thousand miles, or more than the distance from Liverpool to New York and back.'[60]

In 'A Manchester Warehouse,' published a year earlier, James Lowe also remarks the evidence of commercial progress afforded by the assembly of goods. Here, the scale of external trade is measured not in terms of the materiality of the commodities themselves, such as the distances that fabric sold might extend to, but through the 'eighteen closely printed pages' that comprise the General Stock List. It tells 'of linens, diapers, cambrics, and all varieties of sheetings, shirtings, towellings and canvassings':

> There were Hutchinson's books (not literary productions from the pen of Hutchinson, but book-muslins woven at his looms) and Swiss books, and pale hard books, and strange fabrics called by such names as nainsooks and lenos, and smooth soft lappings, all purity, and comfort, and sanctity, not inappropriately called, bishop's lawn. There, too, we read of fustians, and moleskins, velveteens and drabbets, broadcloths, beavers, pilots, Whitneys, Petershams, friezes, mohairs, and unnumbered cloakings; nor were doeskins and cassimeres, or even paddings (to give men an athletic muscular appearance) forgotten. For the first time, we heard of vestings, called baratheas, Valentias, velvettas, scarletts and gambroons.[61]

As well as emphasizing their abundance and heterogeneity, Lowe marvels at the novelty of the goods detailed in these lists, some of which perplex in their 'unaccountable nomenclature'[62] and indicate a world of foreign imports requiring translation and interpretation for British consumers. Cotton had been imported from the East since the Middle Ages, and by the eighteenth century came principally from India. Even when British cotton textile manufacture began, Indian names continued to be used for the fabrics imitated, such as calico, gingham, chintz, and muslin.[63] The presence of such textiles within the Manchester warehouses is a reminder that imperial traffic was not one-way. Thus the 'nainsooks' mentioned by Lowe—a cotton textile named from the Hindi *nain* 'eye' and *sukh* 'pleasure'—hold within them what Deirdre David calls a story of 'cultural exchange between colonizer and colonized,' and point to the way in which Victorian Englishwomen who favoured Indian fabrics played a crucial role in this process as they helped spread demand for these goods back home.[64] The gadgets listed for sale in the small-ware department run to 34 pages and are also bewildering to Lowe in their variety and newfangledness: 'Then as to hooks and eyes; what are the patent swan bills? And in needles; how shall we distinguish the super drilled-eyed sharps from the groundowns? Or what distinguishes the round head country pins from the heavy London ditto? Or what are Lillekins?'[65]

---

60   Ibid.
61   [James Lowe], 'A Manchester Warehouse,' *Household Words*, 6 May 1854, 9: 270.
62   Ibid.
63   David Washbrook, 'From Comparative Sociology to Global History: Britain and India in the Pre-History of Modernity,' *Journal of the Economic and Social History of the Orient* 40 (1997): 417.
64   Deirdre David, 'Imperial Chintz: Domesticity and Empire,' *Victorian Literature and Culture* 27 (1999): 571.
65   [Lowe], 'A Manchester Warehouse,' 270.

The warehouse of Banneret and Co. is 'the largest' in Manchester and in the baffling variety of its goods resembles 'a little Great Exhibition' all on its own.[66]

The order evident in the extensive stock-lists classifying the goods in the Manchester Warehouse contrasts with the chaos that characterizes a Colombo bazaar. In 'Number Forty-Two,' John Capper describes the 'confused and motley' collection of wares in the shop of a Moorman trader. Designated by the numbers of their shops rather than their 'terrifyingly unpronounceable names,' the Moormen traders supply 'all descriptions of useful or fancy articles of domestic use to the English' and 'may be said, indeed, to be the Jews of India.'[67] While the bazaar shares something of the heterogeneity of the goods to be found in a Manchester Warehouse, it is a form of heterotopia—one of those 'other,' phantasmagoric spaces described by Foucault that reverse social ordering[68]—characterized by apparently arbitrary intermingling and disorder:

> Our bazaar is by no means aristocratic. On the contrary, it is most decidedly republican in all its tendencies. It admits of no distinction of ranks. The higher born wares are placed on an equal footing with the most lowly merchandise, the most plebeian of goods. Earthenware jostles cut-glass; ironmongery—and some of it is rare and rusty too—elbows the richest porcelain; vulgar tin-ware hob-nobs with silks and satins. Tart-fruits and pickles revel in the arms of forty yards of the best crimson velvet. Pickled salmon in tins are enshrined amongst Coventry ribbons.[69]

The incongruous juxtapositions noted here bespeak English perceptions of market regularity and order, as well as an ironic awareness of class. The bazaar is an emblem of the colonial city in which it sits, with its 'tropical conglomeration' of congested passageways where the verandahs are 'railed off, as open receptacles of all sorts of merchandise.' The 'natives, half-castes, and Eurasians, or country-born descendents of Europeans'[70] who inhabit these streets partake of the medley that is sold there. Capper records his continual amazement at the inexhaustible resources of Number Forty-Two, often asking for things he never dreamt of requiring just to test the limits of the trader's stock: 'I thought I had caught him once when I requested to look at a few warming-pans,' he writes; but the requisite article is eventually produced, albeit covered in dust, and Capper reports that he 'had it sent home as a real curiosity, and hung it up in my library amongst other rare articles of vertu.'[71] Comically displaced from its usual function, the warming-pan becomes a bizarre souvenir of Britain's imperial reach.

Capper contrasts such self-conscious revaluation of an English commodity with the misunderstanding of the 'real value of some goods' shown by the Indian shopkeepers: 'They can tell you to a trifle the worth of a dinner-set, or of a dozen

---

66 Ibid.
67 [John Capper], 'Number Forty-Two,' *Household Words*, 10 September 1853, 8: 18.
68 Michel Foucault, 'Different Spaces,' in *Aesthetics, Method, and Epistemology*, ed. James D. Faubion (London: Penguin, 1998).
69 Ibid.
70 Ibid.: 17.
71 Ibid.

of Dutch hoes, but in millinery and other fancy articles they are often fearfully mistaken.'[72] Such gaps in cultural knowledge may enable the canny British traveller to pick up a bargain, 'buying kid-gloves at eighteen-pence, for which in London [he] should have to pay at least four shillings; and a trifle of real Brussels lace ... at the price of the very commonest Nottingham article.' Illustrating what Arjun Appadurai has described as 'the peculiarities of knowledge that accompany relatively complex, long-distance, intercultural flows of commodities,'[73] such gaps are noted elsewhere in *Household Words* in some of John Lang's accounts of his 'Wanderings in India.' Lang observes with amusement the 'quaint' arrangement of furniture in the house of a native gentleman, where in 'the dining, or drawing-room, you will find a wash-hand stand, and a chest of drawers, and a toilet-table, while in the bedroom you will, perhaps, discover an old piano, an organ, a card-table, or cheffonier.'[74] The 'quaintness' of these comically misplaced goods implies the superior understanding of their correct use that Lang shares with his British readers. But they might also be interpreted as evidence of the way in which the meaning of foreign commodities can be transformed in accordance with the values of the receiving local culture. On the one hand regarded with amusement as evidence of a gap in cross-cultural understanding, on the other, these transplanted British goods suggest the limits of cultural imperialism as their consumption is mediated by local values and tastes. Lang's account of the 'localization' of these imperial goods provides a significant contrast to more triumphal accounts in the journal, like those by Martineau or Sidney, of the global diffusion of British products.

As demonstrated in the Indian fabrics found in Lowe's Manchester warehouse, imperial traffic was two-way, albeit asymmetrical. As David argues, if 'imperial governance introduced the niceties of English domestic life to the colonized (or at least displayed those niceties for their sometimes puzzled inspection), it also returned to the home-ground words, customs, and images appropriated from colonized cultures.'[75] The evidence can also be found in the Hales's drawing-room at Milton in *North and South*, where Mr Thornton is served tea in the sixth instalment of the novel. The room is characterized by its comfort and simplicity, showing

> a warm, sober breadth of colouring, well relieved by the dear old Helstone chintz-curtains and chair covers. An open davenport stood in the window opposite the door; in the other there was a stand, with a tall white china vase, from which drooped wreaths of English ivy, pale-green birch, and copper-coloured beech-leaves.... Behind the door was another table, decked out for tea, with a white table-cloth on which flourished the cocoa-nut cakes, and a basket piled with oranges and ruddy American apples, heaped on leaves.[76]

---

72   Ibid.: 19.

73   Arjun Appadurai, 'Introduction: Commodities and the Politics of Value,' in *The Social Life of Things: Commodities in Cultural Perspective*, ed. Arjun Appadurai (New York: Cambridge University Press, 1986), 41.

74   [John Lang], 'Wanderings in India,' *Household Words*, 14 November 1857, 16: 459.

75   David, 'Imperial Chintz,' 570.

76   [Elizabeth Gaskell], 'North and South: Chapter the Tenth,' *Household Words*, 7 October 1854, 10: 181.

The chintz-curtains, like the calico curtains in *Mary Barton* discussed by Elaine Freedgood, yoke domesticity and empire together.[77] Likewise, regarded as England's 'national beverage' by the eighteenth century, tea was transformed from 'a foreign commodity into a product of the British Empire' during the Victorian period.[78] As Charles Knight explained four years earlier in describing the history of its consumption (which expanded enormously after the 'opening of the China tea-trade in 1833, and the repeal of the excise duty in 1834'[79]), tea-drinking crosses and unites all social classes in its affirmation of English identity: 'Mrs. Piozzi making tea for Dr. Johnson till four o'clock in the morning, and listening contentedly to his wondrous talk, is a pleasant anecdote of the first century of tea; the artisan's wife, lingering over the last evening cup, while her husband reads his newspaper or his book, is something higher, which belongs to our own times.'[80] Similarly, the cocoa-nut cakes, oranges, and apples arranged on the Hales's tea-table, together with the china vase and the 'light-coloured muslin gown' worn by Margaret, display the effects of global trade without drawing attention to them; although the article that follows this chapter of *North and South* in *Household Words* might prompt such awareness in its opening remarks about the sourcing of raw materials for porcelain manufacture and the 'happy ordination' evident in commodity production and exchange: 'that we cannot afford to be independent of one another; that nation is obliged to depend upon nation; country upon country, family upon family.'[81] Indeed, it is to the non-fictional articles that surround *North and South* that readers must turn for accounts of these worldly goods.

Long-time resident in Ceylon, and connected with the press there and in India for almost 40 years,[82] John Capper contributed a number of articles on goods from these two colonies—coffee, spices, pearls, cotton, silk, rice and so on—in which he seeks to improve understanding of a commodity's origin and identity. In 'The Cocoa-Nut Palm,' for example, he describes the beginnings of the key ingredient that later in *Household Words* will be used in making the Hales's cake:

> To the town-bred Englishman, the sight of *cocus nucifora* growing in its native luxuriance, would suggest little more than untidy orange shops, in which the nut is dealt out to retailers; apple-stalls upon which the kernel is displayed, to tempt amateurs, at a penny-a-slice; coir-matting woven from the fibre of the shell, and patent candles made from the oil

---

77 Freedgood, *The Ideas in Things*.

78 Julie Fromer, '"A Typically English Brew": Tea Drinking, Tourism, and Imperialism in Victorian England,' in *Nineteenth-Century Geographies: The Transformation of Space from the Victorian Age to the American Century*, ed. Helena Michie and Ronald R. Thomas (New Brunswick: Rutgers University Press, 2003), 99.

79 [Charles Knight], 'Illustrations of Cheapness [iv]: Tea,' *Household Words*, 8 June 1850, 1: 255.

80 Ibid.: 256.

81 [George Dodd], 'Cornwall's Gift to Staffordshire,' *Household Words*, 7 October 1854, 10: 187.

82 Lohrli, *'Household Words' A Weekly Journal 1850–1859 Conducted by Charles Dickens*, 221.

expressed from the nut.... To the native of Ceylon, the cocoa-nut palm calls up a far wider range of ideas; it associates itself with nearly every want and convenience of his life.[83]

'A Cinnamon Garden' opens in a similar way:

> The Englishman sips his coffee, enjoys sugar in his tea, and spices in his pastry, wondering why such things are not cheaper; and picturing Indian planters as princes, in white calico and straw hats, having little else to do than to smoke hookahs, drink brandy-pawney, and pocket their gains. A trip to some of the coffee, sugar, or cinnamon estates in Ceylon, would at once dispel the imaginary picture ...[84]

If metropolitan readers of *Household Words* ever wondered where their oranges came from, in 'Oranges and Lemons' Capper describes the 'most luscious productions of the most distant tropical regions' eagerly stocking the fresh-fruit markets of London: 'The West India Islands furnish us with pine-apples, bananas, forbidden-fruit, and citrons. The Azores, Madeiras, Malta, Crete, as well as Spain and Portugal, send us oranges; while lemons are sent to us from several islands in the Mediterranean.'[85] His glowing descriptions of the quintas or gardens in the Portuguese colony of the Azores seem to endow the fruits grown there with all the vitality of their idyllic surroundings which they then carry into the heart of the metropolis: 'the bright blue sky above, the rich green turf below, the merry sound of pipe and tabor, the song of birds of gorgeous plumage, the laugh of children around and about, the fragrant perfume of orange, and citron, and myrtle blossoms, floating in the air,— there amidst all this grow to maturity the ripe, rich fruit that within but one short week, by the potent aid of wind and steam, shall be after some tossing and tumbling, thrust into London faces in London thoroughfares.'[86] As Appadurai has argued, analysis of transnational commodity culture needs to trace the 'social life of the thing,' focussing on the trajectory it takes from production, through distribution and exchange, to consumption.[87] This 'biographical approach to things' is precisely the tactic adopted by *Household Words* contributors, like Capper, who seek to bridge the gap in knowledge between producers and consumers, while representing elements of imperial power in the process.

Together with other contributors, such as Morley and Sidney, Capper advocates the expansion of Indian agricultural production as an economic necessity for Britain. The need for a steady supply of raw cotton that does not involve dependence upon the Southern slave states in America is repeatedly urged, betraying the continuing interrelationship between British capitalism and slavery that lasted well beyond the 1833 Abolition Act. Harriet Martineau's awareness of the relations of production led to a blunt insistence upon the moral choices involved in consumption: '[e]very

---

83 [John Capper], 'The Cocoa-Nut Palm,' *Household Words*, 15 March 1851, 2: 585.
84 [John Capper], 'A Cinnamon Garden,' *Household Words*, 1 March 1851, 2: 546.
85 [John Capper], 'Oranges and Lemons,' *Household Words*, 1 April 1854, 9: 146.
86 Ibid.: 147.
87 Appadurai, 'Introduction,' 13.

increased demand for cotton on our part rivets the chains of the slave.'[88] Britain's implication in such violence provides one basis for *Household Words*'s continuing criticism of the East India Company's failure to develop the subcontinent.[89] India is depicted as an 'anachronistic space,' a country where 'we find ourselves almost transported back to the dark ages, when our skin-clad ancestors were content to feed swine on acorns, and barter with a few adventurous foreigners a little wool and a little corn.'[90] In the manufacture of silk, Morley notes that the 'Lahore weaver works very much as the English weaver worked a hundred years ago, except that his machinery is even ruder.'[91] In 'Lancashire Witchcraft,' Capper uses a similar trope of pre-industrial simplicity in tracing the imperial commodity circuit associated with the manufacture of cotton. He transposes the magic of the orient to the 'steam-and-metal witchcraft' of the Lancashire mills.[92] From the hill-sides of Central India, the raw cottons are sent to port for shipment to Liverpool and 'so on to the restless machinery of the Lancashire factories.' The cotton is 'carded, spun, woven, dressed, pressed, packed, marked, and shipped once more to Liverpool,' before it commences its return trip, and finally 'the bales of Lancashire Witchcraft behold the very village of Central India in the gardens of which their contents first saw the light of tropical day; the ryot who grew it is still there, sowing the same patch of ground with more seed; his wife is still at the threshold of their little hut busily occupied in weaving some of the selfsame cotton crop which has made so long a double journey.'[93] Frozen in time, the 'simple Hindoo weaver' cannot afford to sell goods as cheaply as 'our Lancashire Witchcraft can,' even though 'his cloth never left his native village, and was woven beneath the shade of palm trees to the song of the nightingale, instead of within a Manchester factory to the rattle of a thousand power-looms.' Even the prized Indian fabric arts cannot compete with the mills, according to Capper: 'the rajah's many-coloured scarf, the nabob's gorgeous rainbow shawl, the sultana's head-dress, the gossamer hangings for the Zenana, all are copied and reproduced by Lancashire Witchcraft, and sold at half the cost of their originals to wondering Hindoos and astounded Mussulmen.'[94]

A symbol of developmental stasis, the Hindoo weaver has his counterpart in Capper's description of the 'apathetic Indian ploughman' who cultivates his field of rice in Ceylon with a buffalo-plough. Bearing no likeness to any modern implement, the plough is regarded as an ancient relic: 'You have seen them represented in plates of Belzoni's discoveries in Egypt, and in Layard's remains of Nineveh. There they all are—as veritable, as formal and as strange—as were the Egyptian and Ninevite

---

88 [Harriet Martineau], 'A New Plea for a New Food,' *Household Words*, 3 May 1851, 3: 140.

89 The journal's liberal stance against protectionism was another.

90 [John Capper], 'India Pickle,' *Household Words*, 9 June 1855, 11: 446. 'Anachronistic space' is the phrase Anne McClintock uses to define the imperial dynamic in which spatial distance is cast in temporal terms. Ann McClintock, *Imperial Leather: Race, Gender and Sexuality in the Colonial Context* (London: Routledge, 1995).

91 [Henry Morley], 'Silk from the Punjaub,' *Household Words*, 8 January 1853, 6: 390.

92 [John Capper], 'Lancashire Witchcraft,' *Household Words*, 4 February 1854, 8: 549.

93 Ibid.: 550.

94 Ibid.: 551.

agriculturalists, I'm afraid to say how many centuries ago.'[95] However, it was China that represented the ultimate example of backwardness and insularity according to the evidence of its commodities on display in the Crystal Palace—as the now-notorious article by Dickens and Horne on 'The Great Exhibition and the Little One' indicates. Comparing the 'two countries which display (on the whole) the greatest degree of progress, and the least,'[96] Dickens and Horne define the contrast between China and England as a difference 'between Stoppage and Progress, between the exclusive principle and all other principles, between the good old times and the bad new times, between perfect Toryism and imperfect advancement.'[97] The 'silk-weaving and cotton-spinning' industries of England are set against the 'laboriously-carved ivory balls of the flowery Empire, ball within ball and circle within circle, which have made no advance and been of no earthly use for thousands of years.'[98] Such evidence of stasis is also found in the arts of sculpture and modelling—'we have the same mandarins and the same ladies, who have sat on the same teapots and screens from time immemorial'[99]—and in China's large public edifices and works, which are 'all just as they were centuries ago, suggesting the idea of the same Emperor having sat upon the same enamelled porcelain throne during the whole time, with the same thin-arched pair of elevated eyebrows, admiring and wondering, with the same inanity, at the same inanimate perfection of himself and all around him.'[100] As Lorna Huett notes, the *chinoiserie* ostentatiously displayed in Mrs Jamieson's drawing-room in 'Visiting at Cranford'[101] not only expresses the inertia of its owner, but suggests the Chinese contribution to the Great Exhibition as satirized a year earlier in the article by Dickens and Horne.[102] Associated with Regency taste, even by the late 1830s, when the novel is set, and certainly by 1851 when it began serialization, *chinoiserie* itself was old-fashioned.

---

95 [John Capper], 'Rice,' *Household Words*, 30 June 1855, 11: 524. While Capper's reference to the excavations at Nineveh sets British progress against Indian backwardness, *Household Words* had earlier used Layard's acquisition of an Assyrian winged bull for the British Museum to attack the abominations of the Smithfield Cattle Market in a satiric poem by Richard H. Horne purporting to be an address from 'The Smithfield Bull to his Cousin of Nineveh.' The Smithfield Bull claims that the 'high mission' of his 'Royal cousin,'

To Fifty One's Great Exhibition,
Is not to show your ancient learning,
But into practice knowledge turning;
And therefore you will see us righted,
Although the 'City' be benighted.

[Richard H. Horne], 'The Smithfield Bull to His Cousin of Nineveh,' *Household Words*, 15 March 1851, 2: 590.
96 [Charles Dickens and Richard H. Horne], 'The Great Exhibition and the Little One,' *Household Words*, 5 July 1851, 3: 357.
97 Ibid.: 360.
98 Ibid.: 358.
99 Ibid.: 359.
100 Ibid.: 360.
101 [Elizabeth Gaskell], 'Visiting at Cranford,' *Household Words*, 3 April 1852, 5: 61.
102 Huett, 'Commodity and Collectivity,' 47–8.

However, such a caricature of Eastern traditions in art and architecture contrasts with Morley's description of 'Shangae' in 'Our Phantom Ship: China,' published in the previous week's issue, where he fondly remarks 'the very Chinese bridge that we have learned by heart along with the pagoda, from a willow-patterned soup-plate: steps up, steps down, and a set of Chinese lanterns.'[103] The stereotyped portrait of Chinese stagnation and insularity in the article by Dickens and Horne is also challenged by another essay appearing in the very same issue of *Household Words*: 'The "Mouth" of China,' by Thomasina Ross. A translation of Ida Pfeiffer's book detailing her world travels, *Eine Frauenfahrt um die Welt*,[104] the article describes a remarkably adventurous voyage made to Canton aboard a junk, including an intrepid excursion made to the city wall disguised in male attire. Characterized by an air of genuine cross-cultural inquiry that contrasts with the racial stereotyping evident in some of the other essays on the East in *Household Words*, Ross's essay reports the civility with which Pfeiffer was 'invited to partake' of tea aboard her junk, the 'kind' offer of a head-stool 'which in China is used instead of a pillow' and upon which 'the head rests more comfortably than might be expected,'[105] her delight in the animation of the traffic on the Pearl River as she nears the city and the 'elegant' arrangement of the shops selling provisions.[106] Ross's article illustrates the dialogic effect that may be created through the juxtaposition of contrasting narratives on the same subject within a single issue of *Household Words*.

As recent commentators on the Great Exhibition have remarked, the nations of the East displayed there were largely a product of the European imagination, shaped by Western commercial interests and the logic of an international division of labour that saw colonial possessions as sources of raw materials for the factories of the metropolis.[107] The East India Company coordinated the Indian display in such a way as to emphasize the financial benefits of empire, gathering together an impressive collection of raw materials that included 'coal, oil, precious stones, saltpetre and spices.'[108] Jeffrey Auerbach argues that what 'mattered, for Britain and for other countries with colonial or imperial ambitions, was to find new sources of raw materials and, later on, new markets for their manufactured goods,'[109] a concern that is reflected in the large number of articles written by George Dodd for *Household Words* that were based upon the Jury reports from the Great Exhibition. Each of the Exhibition's 30 classes of goods had a separate jury to award prizes and to

---

103 [Henry Morley], 'Our Phantom Ship: China,' *Household Words*, 28 June 1851, 3: 330.

104 Lohrli, *'Household Words' A Weekly Journal 1850–1859 Conducted by Charles Dickens*, 80.

105 [Thomasina Ross], 'The "Mouth" of China,' *Household Words*, 5 July 1851, 3: 349.

106 Ibid.: 350.

107 Lara Kriegel, 'Narrating the Subcontinent in 1851: India at the Crystal Palace,' in *The Great Exhibition of 1851: New Interdisciplinary Essays*, ed. Louise Purbrick (Manchester: Manchester University Press, 2001); see also Auerbach, *The Great Exhibition of 1851*.

108 Nicky Levell, 'Reproducing India: International Exhibitions and Victorian Tourism,' in *Souvenirs: The Material Culture of Tourism*, ed. Michael Hitchcock and Ken Teague (Aldershot: Ashgate, 2000), 42.

109 Auerbach, *The Great Exhibition of 1851*, 101.

report on its current state and prospects for future development.[110] Dodd uses these to provide biographies of various commodities and their constituent substances—walking-sticks, cards, umbrellas, brushes, artificial flowers, stoves, wire, India-rubber, gelatine, straw, leather, silk, and opium—explaining the origins of many of the goods that find their way into the homes of novels like *Cranford* or *North and South*. Unlike the process articles discussed in the previous chapter, which seek to recover the origins of manufactured goods in the factory organization, machinery and wage labour which produced them, these essays focus instead on the varied careers of the raw materials involved in their manufacture. Instead of a factory tour, they follow global routes in an attempt to bridge the widening international gaps in knowledge between producer and consumer. *Household Words* details the hundreds of transformations raw materials will undergo before reaching their final form, employing a kind of 'inventorial sublime' to commemorate this burgeoning global commodity culture.

Dodd's lists, like the inventories of Sidney or Lowe discussed earlier, reflect the paradoxical nature of the commodity form, revelling in the exciting variety of the things listed, while simultaneously implying their interchangeability. The effusiveness of this rhetorical technique resembles the decorative exuberance of Victorian domestic style,[111] or the ever-increasing range of goods available for the connoisseur of sartorial display to choose from. In 'Walking-Sticks,' for example, Dodd cites the Report of the Exhibition Jury on Miscellaneous Articles as evidence of the enormous variety on the market of this particular commodity which obtains its raw materials from trees and grasses representing all reaches of the globe: 'the varieties most usually selected among the growths of Europe, are blackthorn, crab, maple, ash, oak, beech, orange-tree, cherry-tree, furze-bush, and Spanish reed; from the West Indies there come vine-stems, cabbage-stalks, briar-stalks; while from other countries in the warm regions are brought rattans, calamus-stems, bamboos, Malaccas, and Manilla canes.'[112] The range of materials used for the handle multiplies this diversifying effect: 'As to the ferules, crooks, handles, and decorative appendages, who shall number them? Gold, silver, sham-gold, sham-silver, ivory, ebony, tortoiseshell, mother o' pearl, agate, cornelian, jasper, jade, leather, hair, silk, skin—all are employed.'[113] While the changeableness of fashion is attributed to the capricious behaviour of the goods themselves—'What offence crooks have given, that they should be out of favour, does not appear; but certain it is that the rectangular handle is now in the ascendant: it juts out in stern precision from the vertical stem, and ignores Hogarth's theory of the beauty of curved lines'—human agency and ingenuity are acknowledged in the 'nationality' of walking-sticks, as Dodd observes that 'Germany makes better whalebone sticks than England, ... Austria excels in

---

110 Asa Briggs, *Victorian Things* (London: Batsford, 1988), 55.

111 Thad Logan has described this as an 'appearance of "excessive" ornamental detail that declares the home to be liberated from an economy driven by necessity—to participate, instead, in a new economy of desire.' Thad Logan, *The Victorian Parlour: A Cultural Study* (Cambridge: Cambridge University Press, 2001), 205.

112 [George Dodd], 'Walking-Sticks,' *Household Words*, 11 September 1852, 5: 611.

113 Ibid.: 612.

the sticks with carved ivory handles ... [and] England bears the palm for those ornamented with silver wire, or gold and silver chasing.'[114]

'India-Rubber' details the manufacture and various uses to which this useful substance has been put.[115] The South American Indians' rude methods of collecting and processing the gum are contrasted with the inventive techniques of Western manufacture: 'It is cut into minute fragments by a savage slashing machine; it is washed in warm water, to get rid of so much dirt as chooses to take its departure on such gentle urging; and then in a dry state, it is crushed and kneaded with appalling severity: it is rolled over and over, distorted, crippled, penetrated to the heart, sliced, thinned, thumped, heaped up again into a mass, cut into lumps, squeezed again....'[116] Dodd's efforts to enliven his description according to the required 'Household' style are at times clumsy; but they nonetheless contribute to the journal's exploration of the shifting relation between people and things by implying the sentience of the material undergoing the 'tortures' of manufacture, endowing it with a mind of its own: 'Great ingenuity is called for in all these processes; for India-rubber has a strong propensity to be wayward; it becomes hot and angry when meddled with.'[117] Such liveliness is also found in the social differences attributed to the products described in 'A Good Brushing,' where Dodd marvels at the 'more than two million pounds of bristles' imported every year, 'irrespective of those which grow on the backs of true-born British hogs,' and studies their career: sourced principally from Russia, they are cropped, assorted into colours and qualities, dressed, transported to market and sold for export.[118] Dodd distinguishes between the 'common, humble, cheap, inferior, working-day brooms and brushes' made by 'pan-work,' and 'the stiff and sharp-haired family such as scrubbing-brushes, shoe-brushes, clothes-brushes, tooth-brushes, nail-brushes, hair-brushes, flesh-brushes, and so forth,' most of which are made by 'draw-work,' and are above comparison with their humbler cousins.[119] The social differences attributed to the various classes of brushes are also shared by some of the other everyday objects Dodd examines, like dolls. 'Aristocracy and democracy find their way into the doll world,' he argues, comparing the components and manufacture of 'Jane Tibbs's wooden doll' with the more delicate 'composition' doll of 'Miss Emily Augusta de Swellermode.'[120] Like walking-sticks, India-rubber, and brushes, dolls are a lesson in international commerce, as Dodd remarks the enormous 'interchange between different countries' they entail even in the materials of their manufacture: 'At Hamburgh dolls' heads are made by thousands of dozens, in wax and in papier mâché, and are exported to the doll-makers of other lands. Large numbers of English dolls have home-made bodies but foreign-made heads; and the better kinds of wooden dolls are also largely imported, from countries where

---

114 Ibid.
115 [George Dodd], 'India-Rubber,' *Household Words*, 12 March 1853, 7: 29.
116 Ibid.: 30.
117 Ibid.
118 [George Dodd], 'A Good Brushing,' *Household Words*, 8 July 1854, 9: 493.
119 Ibid.: 495.
120 [George Dodd], 'Dolls,' *Household Words*, 11 June 1853, 7: 352–3.

wood for carving can be more readily obtained than in England.'[121] Dolls are thus shown to embody forms of transnational sociability in their making, even as they shore up national differences in their responsiveness to fashion: 'The dolls'-eye makers say that, since we have had a blue-eyed Queen, blue-eyed dolls have had a more gracious reception than black—indeed the latter are scarcely admitted at all; whereas in countries in which the brilliant flashing dark eye is a prevailing beauty, dolls with blue eyes are regarded as flat, tame, and unprofitable.'[122]

Such border-crossings as those effected by dolls, or goods like tea, oranges, or cotton, attest to a fascination with the growing traffic between nations at mid-century mediated by a burgeoning range of commodities. As they are described in *Household Words*, these goods are repeatedly endowed with an agency that suggests their international sociability, whether they are everyday objects or less well-known commodities, like malachite, the 'Russian Stranger' to whom we are introduced in the article of that title. This 'illustrious stranger made his appearance in London in the year eighteen hundred and fifty-one' and when he was first seen 'in a polished green jacket, the inquiry ran around—who is he; what is his name; whence does he come; and how does he make his jacket?'[123] Dodd's biography provides the answers. But as well as embodying sociability, these global commodities may be characterized as competitors, as Dodd reveals in an article appearing earlier the same month where 'Leather' is urged to 'look to his laurels' in the face of threats from challengers like 'Papier Mâché' or 'Carton Pierre.' He remarks that 'the veteran has had more formidable attacks from two other interlopers—Meer India Rubber and Shah Gutta Percha,' who 'boast so much of their elasticity, their toughness, their indestructibility, and every other corporeal and corpuscular excellence, that Leather has had as much as he can do to maintain his ground against them.'[124]

'Papier Mâché' is the raw material for one of the more unusual exports to the colonies described by Dodd: portable houses. 'The House that Jack Built' reports the manufacture of a 'papier-maché village,'[125] designed for transport to Australia, by Messrs. Bielefield—the manufacturers of Wellington Street, Strand, who made a hit at the Great Exhibition with their 'colossal column and Corinthian capital,'[126] and whose marvellous variety of 'picture-frames, mouldings, cornices, brackets, alto-relievi, bas-reliefs, busts (apparently in plaster, in white marble, and in dark-coloured marble), figures, chimney-ornaments, monumental tablets, looking-glass frames, ceiling ornaments, and articles of furniture' had already been discussed by Richard H. Horne in 'The Pasha's New Boat,'[127] and by Harriet Martineau in 'Flower Shows

---

121 Ibid.: 354.
122 Ibid.
123 [George Dodd], 'A Russian Stranger,' *Household Words*, 24 September 1853, 8: 91.
124 [George Dodd], 'Nothing Like Leather,' *Household Words*, 17 September 1853, 8: 57.
125 [George Dodd], 'The House That Jack Built,' *Household Words*, 19 November 1853, 8: 288.
126 [Richard H. Horne], 'The Pasha's New Boat,' *Household Words*, 22 November 1851, 4: 210.
127 Ibid.: 212.

in a Birmingham Hot-House,'[128] two years earlier. Martineau had focused upon a more humble export made from papier mâché, 'the national tea-tray.' Visiting the works of Messrs. Jennens and Bettridge whose improvements have been carried 'into every sort of dwelling—from the cottage kitchen to the state rooms of Buckingham Palace,' she describes the wide range of goods made of papier mâché, but avows that 'there was nothing which charmed the eye and mind so much as a tray, of a simple form—circular, with a scalloped rim—with a handful of glowing verbenas in the middle; so natural, as to deserve to take a place in any school of flower-painting.'[129] Just such a tea-tray—arranged with 'china ... of delicate egg-shell,' 'old-fashioned silver [that] glittered with polishing' and 'eatables ... of the slightest description'—is set out at the card-party in Miss Jenkyns's parlour in the opening instalment of *Cranford*, published two months later on 13 December 1851.[130]

While the description of such exports provides a narrative of national identity and progress, *Household Words* also reveals the negative side of imperialism evident in commodity exchange. Capper exposes some of the realities of oppression and exploitation in the colonies in 'The Peasants of British India,' demystifying the function of British commodities as symbols of imperial progress:

> Travellers have found Sheffield knives selling in Bokhara; grey tweeds from Scotland in the Cabool bazaars and Birmingham wares in Cashmere villages. I have stumbled upon an empty blacking-bottle of Day and Martin, in a miserable Indian mud hut. I have found, adorning the walls of a Buddhist temple, printed cotton handkerchiefs covered with political caricatures, from Manchester: I have seen the reception hall of a Kandian chief graced by one of Rowland's picturesque Macassar labels, with a dark lady combing uncommonly long black hair. But it by no means follows, that because all these knives, and cottons and wares, are exchanged for rich spices, costly silks, and precious gums, that the country is prosperous, or that its trade is progressively remunerative.[131]

While creating the illusion that they perform the civilizing work of empire, these goods actually represent the wealth of the few, disguising the reality of oppression and poverty amongst the Indian peasantry. On his way to attend 'An Indian Wedding,' in a leader published a month later, Capper passes the shop of a carpenter and carriage-builder, where the assemblage of obsolete goods glimpsed inside implies the history of ravage in pre-colonial and colonial Ceylon:

> Every kind of conveyance that had been invented since the flood, appeared to have a damaged representative in that strange place. Children's shattered donkey-carriages, spavined old breaks, a rickety triacle of the Portuguese period, hackeries of the early Malabar dynasty, palanquins of Cingalese descent, Dutch governors' curricles, English

---

128 [Harriet Martineau], 'Flower Shows in a Birmingham Hot-House,' *Household Words*, 18 October 1851, 4: 82–5.

129 Ibid.: 82–3.

130 [Elizabeth Gaskell], 'Our Society at Cranford,' *Household Words*, 13 December 1851, 4: 267.

131 [John Capper], 'The Peasants of British India,' *Household Words*, 17 January 1852, 4: 389.

gigs, were all pent up, with irrecoverable cart-wheels, distorted carriage-poles, and consumptive springs.[132]

A junk-shop of empire, the premises belie the much-vaunted benefits of imperial trade. The ephemeral value of the derelict carriages forms a kind of allegory for the mutability and impermanence of empire. 'A long, low, rambling shed,' the shop was 'such as we might consider good enough to hold cinders or firewood: the turf-thatched roof had been patched in many places with tattered matting; the crazy posts were undermined by the pigs in the next yard, where they shared the mud and the sun with a heap of wretched children, and a score of starving dogs.'[133] This heterotopic space exposes the underside of imperial commodity culture, providing a stark contrast to the triumphalism that characterizes Harriet Martineau's account of British needle exports in the following week's issue of the journal. Uncovering the traces of imperial awareness to be found in foreign goods, *Household Words* helped to make some of the gains and losses of empire imaginable for its mid-Victorian readers.

---

132 [John Capper], 'An Indian Wedding,' *Household Words*, 21 February 1852, 4: 506.
133 Ibid.

Chapter 7

'Trading in Death'

In its July-December volume for 1852, *Punch* published the following letter regarding 'Speculative Sympathy':

'Mr. PUNCH,
Some little time since we had the misfortune to lose a relative. A day or two afterwards arrived a letter, addressed in a lady's hand, the stylish look and deep black-bordered envelope of which made us think it was one of condolence. But it proved to be from some linendrapers in Oxford Street, offering us their sincere sympathy, and enclosing specimens of crape, &c, and a card of terms somewhat as follows:–

TO THE BEREAVED.

MESSRS. GROGRAM AND TWILL

BEG to offer you their condolences upon your recent loss, and to forward you, with assurances of their sympathy, specimens selected from their large stock of Crapes, Widows' Silks, Twills, &c.

> O! Ye, whose hearts, half crushed beneath the blow
>   Of some sad loss, still struggle to be calm,
> Receive, to soothe your unavailing woe,
>   Our crape and comfort, bombazine and balm....[1]

Signed by 'Dolor,' *Punch*'s comic account of these enterprising purveyors of mourning drapery continues the satiric campaign it had waged against commercial greed in the funeral industry since the late 1840s. The self-interested opposition of undertakers to proposals for government regulation and the closure of unsanitary city churchyards elicited verse parodies, such as 'The Jolly Undertakers,' 'A Funeral After Sir John Moore's (Furnished by an Undertaker),' and 'The Song of the Undertaker,'[2] and cartoons such as '"Performers" after a Respectable Funeral,'

---

    1   'Speculative Sympathy,' *Punch* 23 (July–December 1852): 167.
    2   'A Funeral after Sir John Moore's (Furnished by an Undertaker),' *Punch* 18 (January–June 1850): 4; 'The Jolly Undertakers,' *Punch* 17 (July–December 1849): 254; 'The Song of the Undertaker,' *Punch* 18 (January–June 1850): 215.

and 'The Starved-Out Undertakers.'[3] Dickens shared *Punch*'s scorn for the elaborate customs associated with the 'respectable' Victorian funeral, so it is hardly surprising that, as a campaigning periodical, *Household Words* also devoted attention to the topical issue of funerary reform. Dickens filled his journal with articles about bodies, graveyards, monuments, epitaphs, and the like, many of which show an ambivalent response to the whole idea of trading in death and raise wider questions as to how far society should go in permitting people to buy and sell goods and services, how far the *laissez-faire* market should extend. In its consideration of the Victorian management of death, the journal takes a different direction from those accounts of commodity culture I have examined so far by revealing instances of conflict or tension concerning the commodity status of the goods and services involved. It gives attention to three areas of conflicted trade—the commercial development of the Victorian funeral, including both the state and the 'respectable' funeral; the growth of commercial cemeteries; and bodysnatching and the commodification of corpses—all of which represent, to use the term employed by property law theorist Margaret Jane Radin, 'contested commodities.'[4] All show evidence of the widening scope of the market in the nineteenth century, as an increasing range of objects and relationships came to be identified and treated as marketable goods and services.

In the essay from which I take my title, 'Trading in Death,' Dickens vehemently attacks the theatrical ostentation and commercialization of the state funeral provided for the Duke of Wellington. Written on the eve of Wellington's funeral and published as the leader in *Household Words* on 27 November 1852, the article begins by detailing a range of abuses associated with the Victorian management of death: Dickens inveighs against the 'system of barbarous show and expense' associated with the 'respectable' funeral, describing it as an association of 'the most solemn of human occasions with unmeaning mummeries, dishonest debt, profuse waste, and bad example in an utter oblivion of responsibility'; he rails against the predatory practices encouraged by Burial Clubs for the poor; the long file of middlemen associated with funeral furnishing; and the sanitary problems caused by intramural burial before finally identifying the 'culminating point of this gigantic mockery' in the state funeral.[5] Deploring the way in which this event 'encourages these shameless traders in their dealings on the very coffin-lid of departed greatness,' his article conveys a fear of degeneration, of a return to barbarism, that echoes the anxieties expressed in his powerful novelistic response to the Great Exhibition, *Bleak House*, then in progress, with its famous opening scene of London mired in primal mud and fog.[6] The decomposition of the Duke's body and contemporary fears about the proximity of decaying flesh provide a subtext to these anxieties concerning degeneration; for although he died on 14 September 1852, the Duke was not buried

---

3 '"Performers" after a Respectable Funeral,' *Punch* 18 (January–June 1850): 5; 'The Starved-out Undertakers,' *Punch* 18 (January–June 1850): 185.

4 Margaret Jane Radin, *Contested Commodities* (Cambridge, Mass.: Harvard University Press, 1996), xii–xiii.

5 [Charles Dickens], 'Trading in Death,' *Household Words*, 27 November 1852, 6: 241.

6 Dickens would later describe undertakers as the 'Medicine Men of Civilisation' in *The Uncommercial Traveller* (1860–69).

for another two months because the state funeral desired by the Queen required the formal approval of the November meeting of Parliament.[7] Dickens deplores the long-deferred state funeral for the political ends he insinuates have been served by its postponement, and, more particularly, for awakening the 'general trading spirit' all too evident in the advertising columns of the *Times*.

Wellington's funeral has received renewed critical attention in recent years as part of a scholarly interest in 'the exhibitionary complex.'[8] It was, as Harry Garlick notes, 'the greatest spectacle of the Victorian Age, and a significant expression of the national psyche.'[9] Peter Sinnema observes that Wellington's funeral was 'an arguably grander spectacle' than the Great Exhibition,[10] noting that 'exhibition and public commemoration for the heroic dead can ... be read as parts of the same cultural spectrum.'[11] Like the Great Exhibition, Wellington's funeral was to showcase British arts, craftsmanship and technology.[12] Both deployed spectacle—that mode of amplification and extravagance found elsewhere in popular theatrical performances featuring elaborate special effects, and in the crowd-pulling panoramas, dioramas, and cycloramas of the period discussed in Chapter 4. Indeed, Richard Altick reports that less than a month after the funeral, the diorama of Wellington's life that had been showing at the Gallery of Illustration had three scenes added showing the Duke's lying in state, the funeral procession and the interior of St Paul's during the ceremony.[13] Both Exhibition and state funeral thus fostered the pleasure of consuming displays. Just as the visitors to the Crystal Palace paid money for the privilege of wandering its aisles, mourners eager to see the state funeral procession had their pleasure as spectators regulated according to how much they could or would pay for seats.[14]

These elements of commodity spectacle emerge in Dickens's attack upon the funeral in *Household Words*. He derides the strategies employed by the advertisers in the *Times*, who use a form of merchandizing, a way of talking about commodities, that was a legacy of the Great Exhibition.[15] Many of the *Times* advertisements exploit the occasion of Wellington's funeral to endow their goods with symbolic value, appealing to nationalist sentiment, to the patriotic consumer who wants to be seen to be part of this great commemorative event. Dickens's scorn for the announcements

---

7   See Pearsall for a discussion of anxieties about the postponement of the Duke's burial. Cornelia D.J. Pearsall, 'Burying the Duke: Victorian Mourning and the Funeral of the Duke of Wellington,' *Victorian Literature and Culture* 27 (1999): 365–93.

8   Tony Bennett, *The Birth of the Museum: History, Theory, Politics* (London: Routledge, 1995), Chapter 2.

9   Harry Garlick, 'The Staging of Death: Iconography and the State Funeral of the Duke of Wellington,' *Australian Journal of Art* 9 (1992): 59.

10 Peter Sinnema, *Dynamics of the Pictured Page: Representing the Nation in the 'Illustrated London News'* (Aldershot: Ashgate, 1998), 180.

11 Ibid., 202n1.

12 Garlick, 'The Staging of Death,' 73.

13 Richard D. Altick, *The Shows of London* (Cambridge, Mass.: Harvard University Press, 1979), 479.

14 Sinnema, *Dynamics of the Pictured Page*, 182.

15 Thomas Richards, *The Commodity Culture of Victorian England: Advertising and Spectacle 1851–1914* (Stanford: Stanford University Press, 1990), 21.

regarding comestibles condemns the cannibalistic nature of such merchandizing techniques, as traders exploit the cultural capital of the Duke's name to sell their wares: he deplores the 'The Duke of Wellington Funeral Wine' and 'Funeral Cake,' together with the '"celebrated lemon biscuits" at one and fourpence per pound, which were considered by the manufacturer as the only infallible assuagers of the national grief.' In the typography of his article, Dickens reproduces the display technology of the *Times*'s print advertisements: use of various font sizes, capitalization, italics, and so on, to highlight desirable features in the commodities put up for sale. Such display strategies within the increasingly sophisticated discourse of advertising were, as I have argued in Chapter 2, a crucial component in the nineteenth-century development of commodity culture. Judith Roof has identified the way in which, after the late seventeenth century, 'display became increasingly separable from the object displayed, becoming visible in itself as display.'[16] Nineteenth-century print advertisements, with their mixture of iconography and letterpress, also demonstrate this emerging mode of exhibition, which can be seen—albeit at a rudimentary stage— in the print advertisements relating to Wellington's funeral in the *Times*. Dickens's article quotes more than three-dozen of these advertisements, with commentary occasionally interspersed to highlight the most piquant absurdities.

For example, among the list of advertisements proffering rooms and windows to let along the procession route Dickens remarks the following 'NOTICE TO CLERGYMEN':

> T.C. Fleet Street, has reserved for clergymen exclusively, *upon condition only that they appear in their surplices*, FOUR FRONT SEATS, at £1 each; four second tier, at 15s. each; four third tier, at 12s. 6d.; four fourth tier, at 10s.; four fifth tier, at 7s.6d.; and four sixth tier, at 5s. All the other seats are respectively 40s., 30s., 20s., 15s., 10s.[17]

As he sardonically comments, the 'anxiety of this enterprising tradesman to get up a reverend tableau in his shop-window of four-and-twenty clergymen, all on six rows, is particularly commendable, and appears to us to shed a remarkable grace on the solemnity.'[18] The ambiguity evident here in the use of shop windows—as a space reserved for a tableau of clergymen or as a vantage point for viewing the funeral parade—and the duplication of sightlines involved, increase the emphasis upon spectacle, upon the transformation of the Duke's funeral into what Dickens describes as a 'Public Fair and Great Undertakers' Jubilee,' by confusing or multiplying the objects of display.[19] Several of the advertisements for seats quoted here proffer shop-windows as vantage points in this way, their emphasis upon the presence of plate-glass suggesting the ambiguous function of the window. The introduction of

---

16 Judith Roof, 'Display Cases,' in *Victorian Afterlife: Postmodern Culture Rewrites the Nineteenth Century*, ed. John Kucich and Dianne F. Sadoff (Minneapolis: University of Minnesota Press, 2000), 118n5.

17 [Dickens], 'Trading in Death,' 242.

18 Ibid.

19 Tony Bennett notes that the 'peculiarity of the exhibitionary complex' is to be found in its incorporation of aspects of panopticism with the principles of the panorama, thus regulating the crowd by making *it* the ultimate spectacle. Bennett, *The Birth of the Museum*, 68.

mass-production techniques for the manufacture of plate-glass in the mid-1830s transformed the nature of the display window, enhancing the exhibition value of the goods arranged behind it: 'While previously it had been little more than an ordinary window that permitted people to see into and out of the shop, it now became a glassed-in stage on which an advertising show was presented.'[20] The advertisements for seats exploit the presence of plate-glass as a display technology to produce a peculiarly reversible dynamic between viewer and viewed, subject and object. They register not only the spectator's prospective pleasure in viewing the Duke's funeral from the best position, but also the desire to be viewed. Freud describes this as the 'reversal of affect'—the idea that the aim of any instinct may be reversed into its opposite—and notes that the instincts of exhibitionism and voyeurism are therefore intimately related: the voyeur really wants to be looked at.[21] As Roof notes, such a dynamic of voyeurism, operating within nineteenth-century display technologies, met the 'needs of a nascent and discerning commodity culture.'[22] For what Dickens is registering here is not just a general desire to be viewed, but a form of desire specific to commodity culture: the 'Notice to Clergymen' appeals to the consumer who wants to be seen as one who has paid for a prime location at Wellington's funeral procession. The advertisement figures a certain kind of consuming subject whose desire to be identified as such will lure him to pay for the privilege of forming part of an advertising tableaux in T.C.'s shop window.[23] Additional lures are offered to those who might wish to get up a picnic for the event, as the advertisers invite 'a few agreeable gentlemen, who are wanted to complete a little assembly of kindred souls, who have laid in abundance of "refreshments, wines, spirits, provisions, fruit, plate, glass, china," and other light matters too numerous to mention, and who keep "good fires."'[24]

A large group of advertisements quoted by Dickens concern the sale of letters or autographs of the Duke, and like the advertisements for seats, these too show evidence of emergent strategies for attracting customers in the discourses of commodity culture. The letters are various, their value held to be distinguished by a range of

---

20 Wolfgang Schivelbusch, *Disenchanted Night: The Industrialisation of Light in the Nineteenth Century* (Oxford: Berg, 1988), 146.

21 Sigmund Freud, 'Instincts and Their Vicissitudes,' in *A General Selection from the Works of Sigmund Freud*, ed. John Rickman (New York: Doubleday Anchor, 1957), 77–9.

22 Roof, 'Display Cases,' 105. My discussion of shop windows owes much to Roof's stimulating essay.

23 One of the spectators watching from the first-floor window of a stationer's on the south side of Fleet Street was another *Household Words* contributor, Sala, who used his vantage point to make sketches for a grand panorama of the state funeral, a series of steel plates, etched, and aquatinted. Commissioned by the firm of Ackermann, Sala was to work on the carriages and figures, while the sporting artist, Henry Alken, would focus on the equestrian element. The 'finished panorama extended to more than sixty-six feet and was sold at the very considerable price of two guineas,' Ralph Straus, *Sala: The Portrait of an Eminent Victorian* (London: Constable, 1942), 104. A pocket-sized edition was also produced (a continuous strip measuring 13 by 2042 cm), rendering the grand event in a miniature and more accessible, but nevertheless spectacular form.

24 [Dickens], 'Trading in Death,' 242.

factors including date, length, subject matter, and the presence or absence of an envelope with seal and post mark intact. But while individual advertisers try to draw the eye of potential customers in competition with one another in this way, all stress the value of the autograph they have for sale as 'original' and as 'characteristic' of the Duke's 'peculiar style.'[25] The autographs are proffered as souvenirs of the Duke, captivating the desire of consumers with the allure of objects that 'serve as traces of authentic experience'[26]—in this case, of British heroism. In some advertisements, letters are offered as positional goods—their alleged rarity enhancing the value they carry as potential markers of social distinction—while in others the appeal is made to the charitable impulses of the consumer. For example, an autograph letter 'written in 1830, enclosed and directed in an envelope, and sealed with his ducal coronet' is offered by 'A widow, in deep distress,' who would 'be happy to PART WITH' this treasure 'for a trifle.' Other advertisements puff relics of the Duke: while one 'lady, having in her possession a quantity of the late illustrious DUKE'S HAIR, cut in 1841, is willing to PART WITH a portion of the same for £25,' the enterprising 'son of the late well-known haircutter to his Grace the Duke of Wellington, at Strathfieldsaye, has a small quantity of HAIR that his father cut from the Duke's head, which he is willing to DISPOSE OF.'[27] Marcia Pointon observes that the 'intense social and tactile investment in hair as relic and as artefact' derives from its peculiar status as 'a bodily substance that outlives the body' and enables it to materialize memory.[28] 'Nineteenth-century writing was explicit about these associations,'[29] she argues, and George Dodd describes the importance of the sanctified lock to 'every woman' in 'Several Heads of Hair': 'By a natural affection she wishes to preserve, in the form of a locket or brooch, a little of the hair which once decked the brow of a departed sister or mother; she has a trusting faith that the jeweller has really applied that very identical hair in that identical locket.'[30] Such relics of loved ones are part of the rituals of Victorian mourning. But instead of 'materialis[ing] grief as secular reliquary' in this way, the traded hair of the Duke of Wellington, like his autograph, has become a souvenir, an object that represents 'the "secondhand" experience of its possessor/owner'[31]; and as Dodd's comment about 'trusting faith' suggests, the value of the hair—as memento of a loved one or as souvenir—depends upon its authenticity, which can be called into question by sharp commercial practices involving the substitution of other people's hair. Whether the proffered locks of his hair are genuine or not, the penultimate advertisement for personal relics of the Duke

---

25 Ibid.: 243.

26 Susan Stewart, *On Longing: Narratives of the Miniature, the Gigantic, the Souvenir, the Collection* (Durham: Duke University Press, 1993), 135.

27 [Dickens], 'Trading in Death,' 244.

28 Marcia Pointon, 'Materializing Mourning: Hair, Jewellery and the Body,' in *Material Memories*, ed. Marius Kwint, Christopher Breward, and Jeremy Aynsley (Oxford: Berg, 1999), 45.

29 Ibid., 46.

30 [George Dodd], 'Several Heads of Hair,' *Household Words*, 4 March 1854, 9: 61.

31 Stewart, *On Longing*, 135. As Stewart argues, 'We cannot be proud of someone else's souvenir unless the narrative is extended to include our relationship with the object's owner or unless ... we transform the souvenir into the collection.' Ibid.: 137.

quoted by Dickens is indeed unique. It concerns a 'very choice article,' the 'value of which may be presumed to be considerably enhanced by the conclusive impossibility of its being doubted in the least degree by the most suspicious mind':

> A MEMENTO of the DUKE of WELLINGTON.– La Morte de Napoleon, Ode d'Alexandre Manzoni, avec la Traduction en Français, par Edmond Angelini, de Venise.– A book, of which the above is the title, was torn up by the Duke and thrown by him from the carriage, in which he was riding, as he was passing through Kent; the pieces of the book were collected and put together by a person who saw the Duke tear it and throw the same away. Any person desirous of obtaining the above memento will be communicated with.[32]

Not all of the advertised mementoes of the hero of Waterloo were so risible. But neither was such commodification of his image new. Wellington's name had been used for commercial purposes since at least the 1830s. Bemoaning the rise of puffery in an 1835 short story, Mary Russell Mitford described the ubiquity of the Duke's name and image: 'We live in Wellington squares, we travel in Wellington coaches, we dine in Wellington hotels, we are educated in Wellington establishments, and are clothed from top to toe (that is to say the male half of the nation) in Wellington boots, Wellington cloaks, Wellington hats, each of which shall have been severally purchased at a warehouse bearing the same distinguished title.'[33] Wellington's death clearly provided a new occasion for canny entrepreneurs to cash in on patriotic sympathies.

Such trade in relics of the dead is described in another *Household Words* article dealing with memorial customs: 'Burns. Viewed as a Hat-Peg,' written by Wilkie Collins. Published as the leader on 12 February 1859, it criticizes the commercial exploitation of the memory of Robert Burns in various commemorative celebrations marking the centenary of the poet's birth. According to Collins, 'the honour of discovering that the memory of Burns might be profitably used in the capacity of a Hat-Peg rests with the Directors of the Crystal Palace Company,' who have sought to make money by offering cheap musical entertainment and a taste of 'cock-a-leekie and haggis, at three shillings a head' in 'honour' of the poet who was himself inadequately recognized and rewarded during his lifetime.[34] But the 'new use [thus] found out' for Burns is not confined to the entrepreneurial activities of joint-stock companies, and Collins describes a number of commemorations, throughout England and Scotland, at which relics of Burns were exhibited: 'his hair, his toddy-ladle, his wife's hair, his snuff-box, his pistols, his punch-bowl, and even a print over which he is reported to have once shed tears, were all displayed at different places,' writes Collins.

---

32 [Dickens], 'Trading in Death,' 244.
33 Mary Russell Mitford, *Country Stories*, Short Story Index Reprint Series (1896; Freeport, NY: Books for Libraries Press, 1970), 122.
34 [Wilkie Collins], 'Burns. Viewed as a Hat-Peg,' *Household Words*, 12 February 1859, 19: 241.

But the Edinburgh Gathering went a step farther, and exhibited a living relic, in the shape of a poor old man, who had lived one hundred years in this weary world, and who at that great age was hung up in public on the Hat-Peg, because he had been brought, as a carrier, into personal contact with Burns, as an exciseman. It seems scarcely consistent with the respect and the consideration which are due to great age to make a show of this old man; and, when one assembly had done staring at him, to pass him on to another.[35]

Both Collins and Dickens object to the lack of respect for personhood shown by the exhibition and trade of relics of the dead. They deplore the assimilation of personal attributes or effects to the realm of commodities. Collins remarks the objectification of the old man who is 'passed' on from one exhibition to another, while Dickens writes that 'the sanctity of a seal, or the confidence of a letter, is a meaningless phrase that has no place in the vocabulary of the Traders in Death.'[36] This kind of trade is regarded as an invasion of privacy, because it involves treating parts of the deceased hero's identity as alienable goods: a 'new use' found out in 'great men' as Collins puts it. The value of these sorts of commodities depends upon the way in which certain categories of property are bound up in historically and culturally specific ways with the constitution of the self, thus raising questions about the ethics of commodification. As Radin explains,

> In human life as we know it, self-constitution includes connectedness with other human beings and also with things in the world, with a home, for example.... When an item of property is involved with self-constitution in this way, it is no longer wholly 'outside' the self, in the world separate from the person; but neither is it wholly 'inside' the self, indistinguishable from the attributes of the person. Thus certain categories of property can bridge the gap or blur the boundary between the self and the world, between what is inside and what is outside, between what is subject and what is object.[37]

Personal relics represent one such category of property.

While Dickens's attack upon Wellington's state funeral raises questions about the relationship between commodification and identity in a particularly acute way, his protest against trading in death continues elsewhere in *Household Words*'s critique of the commercial imperatives associated with the 'respectable' funeral. Appearing in the same issue as Dickens's article, the 'Chip' by Henry Morley and W.H. Wills on 'Funerals in Paris' contrasts the regulation of the business of undertaking which prevents abuses there, with the deplorable absurdities rife in London: 'Measures have been planned more than once for the purpose of providing a reformed system of carrying the dead to burial, by which surviving relatives may be enabled to pay the last outward tribute of respect to the departed without paying a tribute too ridiculous to the good company by whom the funeral has been performed.'[38] But thus far, complain Morley and Wills, to no avail. *Household Words* earlier carried two articles in support of the General Interment Bill that was before Parliament in June 1850,

---

35 Ibid.: 242.
36 [Dickens], 'Trading in Death,' 243.
37 Radin, *Contested Commodities*, 57.
38 [Henry Morley and W.H. Wills], 'Funerals in Paris,' *Household Words*, 27 November 1852, 6: 257.

both of which reveal the ways in which issues of class inflect the commodification of death and the social meaning attached to funerals as occasions for representing identity. The first of these, written by Dickens and published on 8 June 1850, 'From the Raven in the Happy Family,' employs the voice of a Raven, whose carrion-eating nature is used to offer ironic support for the undertakers who 'furnish' the 'respectable' funeral. The Raven bluntly identifies the cultural meaning of the funeral as a consumer good that defines the social place of the deceased and his or her family as members of what he calls the 'gen-teel party.' He satirizes the use of middlemen in funeral 'performance,' observing the role of the 'Black Jobmaster' who had 'let the coaches and horses to a furnishing undertaker, who had let 'em to a haberdasher, who had let 'em to a carpenter, who had let 'em to the parish-clerk, who had let 'em to the sexton,' and so on, in a long list recalling the House that Jack built.[39] The range of funereal consumer goods required to furnish a respectable funeral is comically indicated in an exchange between the undertaker and a neighbour of 'Mrs Grundy':

> 'Hearse and four, Sir?' says [the Black Jobmaster to the bereaved gentleman]. 'No, a pair will be sufficient.' 'I beg your pardon, sir, but when we buried Mr. Grundy at number twenty, there was four on 'em, Sir; I think it right to mention it.' 'Well, perhaps there had better be four.' 'Thank you, Sir. Two coaches and four, Sir, shall we say?' 'No. Coaches and pair.' 'You'll excuse my mentioning it, Sir, but pairs to the coaches and four to the hearse, would have a singular appearance to the neighbours. When we put four to anything, we always carry four right through.' 'Well! Say four!' 'Thank you, Sir. Feathers of course?' 'No. No feathers. They're absurd.' 'Very good, sir. *No* feathers?' 'No.' '*Very* good, sir. We *can* do fours without feathers, Sir, but it's what we never do. When we buried Mr. Grundy, there was feathers, and—I only throw it out, Sir—Mrs Grundy might think it strange.' 'Very well! Feathers!' 'Thank you, Sir,' –and so on.[40]

The power of fashion to compel excessive funeral expenditure, even amongst those who cannot afford it, is attacked again in a second article on the Interment Bill published later the same month. In a mock 'Address from an Undertaker to the Trade (Strictly Private and Confidential),' Percival Leigh impersonates an undertaker protesting against the General Interment Bill as likely to destroy his trade. The Bill proposed to empower the Board of Health to provide for the management and conduct of funerals, by persons appointed by them, at fixed charges: it proposed a limit to the commodification of death, legislating for something less than a *laissez-faire* market regime. As Leigh's undertaker-narrator is made to acknowledge, 'we have always considered that a funeral ought to cost so much to be respectable at all. Therefore relations have gone to more expence [sic] with us, than they would otherwise have been willing to incur, in order to secure proper respect.'[41] In an era when social mobility could be achieved through acquired wealth, the funeral became a locus of anxiety as funeral expenditure provided a final judgement upon one's standing

---

39 [Charles Dickens], 'From the Raven in the Happy Family [ii],' *Household Words*, 8 June 1850, 1: 242.
40 Ibid.: 241–2.
41 [Percival Leigh], 'Address from an Undertaker to the Trade (Strictly Private and Confidential),' *Household Words*, 22 June 1850, 1: 303.

in the community, and *Household Words* satirizes this cultural practice.[42] Leigh's undertaker considers 'Science' a 'most dangerous enemy' to the trade, because it 'shows that the dead do not remain permanently in their coffins, even when the sextons of metropolitan graveyards will let them. It not only informs Londoners that they breathe and drink the deceased; but it reveals how the whole of the defunct party is got rid of,' and may thus lead the bereaved to 'think twice before they will spend from thirty to several hundred pounds in merely putting a corpse into the ground to decompose.'[43] He fears the regulatory provisions of the Interment Bill that will ensure the undertakers 'shall be employed simply as tradesmen, and shall obtain, like other tradesmen, a mere market price for our articles, and common hire for our labour.'[44] 'Burials may be expensive,' he protests; but '[s]o is spiritual provision; I mean the maintenance of all our reverends and right reverends.'[45] Arguing that 'Pluralities are as bad as crowded gravepits, and I don't see that there is a pin to choose between the church and the churchyard,'[46] he urges his fellow members of the trade to excite opposition to the Bill by dinning the 'objection to a burial rate' into the ears of 'church-wardens, overseers and vestrymen.'[47]

Leigh's suggestion that vested parish interests have impeded attempts to reform the unsanitary practice of intramural burial is echoed in a leader by Henry Morley, published five years later. 'An Enemy's Charge' begins by lampooning a 'well-known ecclesiastical association, having for its members the Rev. W.H. Hale, Archdeacon of London; the Rev. W. H. Hale, Canon Residentiary of St. Paul's; the Rev. W.H. Hale, Master of the Charterhouse; the Rev. W.H. Hale, Almoner of St. Paul's; the Rev. W.H. Hale, Chaplain to the Bishop of London; and the Rev. W.H. Hale, Vicar of St. Giles's, Cripplegate,' who 'has lately been made the subject of virulent satire in a something purporting to be a charge addressed to the clergy of the archdeaconry of London, by W.H. Hale, M.A.'[48] 'Only in a land where there is L.S.D. instead of I.H.S upon the pulpit-cushion, could a charge like this have been delivered,' writes Morley. The charge concerns the compensation for loss of burial fees to clergy and parochial authorities that was recommended by the government committee appointed to examine the issue of intramural burial earlier in the decade. As Morley explains, the satirist employs a 'cloak of religion and morals' beneath which is visible 'the whole figure of Mammon.'[49] 'Alas for the lost days of churchyard monopoly!' writes Morley: 'To recover this, or to get compensation for the loss of it, or if neither can be done, to hurl defiance at the persons and opinions by which so excellent a business has been ruined, is apparently the object of the charge.'[50] While the satirist deplores the 1851 'act of Parliament which favoured the commercial speculation of the

---

42 Thomas Laqueur, 'Bodies, Death, and Pauper Funerals,' *Representations* 1 (1983): 115.
43 [Leigh], 'Address from an Undertaker to the Trade,' 302.
44 Ibid.: 303.
45 Ibid.: 301.
46 Ibid.
47 Ibid.: 304.
48 [Henry Morley], 'An Enemy's Charge,' *Household Words*, 20 October 1855, 12: 265.
49 Ibid.: 267.
50 Ibid.: 268.

cemetery companies,'[51] Morley clearly supports such developments as an attempt to solve the sanitary problems associated with overcrowded city churchyards. However, *Household Words* elsewhere expresses some concern about the transformation of the burial place into a piece of real estate, a consumption good, and about the forms of commodity spectacle associated with the commercial expansion of municipal cemeteries. In 'Deadly Lively,' for example, William Blanchard Jerrold describes the way in which the great metropolitan cemeteries in Paris had become pleasant holiday venues, places of entertainment, and leisure for 'excursionists,' as much as sites for commemorating the dead.[52] Sketching the tableaux formed by various mourners, and speculating about their stories, the narrator in 'Deadly Lively' seems to enjoy the cemetery at Montmartre as a mode of exhibition or theatre, a spectacle distinguished by its 'odd incidents of mingled grief and festivity.' He describes the variety of shops serving visitors to the cemetery—'stalls devoted to the sale of sweetmeats,' 'restaurants offering a formidable list of *plâts* at wonderfully low prices,' beer and spirit shops, and traders selling immortelles:

> From the first floor to the ground, arranged in patterns the most fantastic, and in colours most grateful, are hung thousands of [these] immortelles, or circular rolls of baked and dried flowers. And, judging by the brisk trade that is going on, the stranger will not think that the supply exceeds the demand by a single immortelle.[53]

While insisting upon the 'wholesome feeling' and 'affecting tenderness' apparent in the commemorative customs he describes,[54] the language of commodification betrays the narrator's unease: he observes, for example, a 'hearty, lively bonne' approach the immortelle magazine, who 'looks in a very business-like manner at the varieties of eternal emblems about her, as she would look at a cap-ribbon.'[55]

Jerrold's discordant simile implies disapproval of the preoccupation with ornamentation and display he sees in the cemetery—a preoccupation that is also identified as a matter for concern by James Hannay in his discussion of monuments and gravestones in 'Graves and Epitaphs.' Hannay's article expresses some anxiety about the secularization of death and commemoration brought about by the cemetery movement. He discusses the importance of correct 'taste' in the monumental design of London's new commercial cemeteries, arguing 'how absurd is a monument that

---

51 Ibid.: 267.
52 [William Blanchard Jerrold], 'Deadly Lively,' *Household Words*, 25 March 1854, 9: 138. Dickens is similarly struck by the spectacle of the Paris morgue and those who seem to visit it for their amusement: 'It is wonderful to see the people at this place. Cheery married women, basket in hand, strolling in, on their way to or from the buying of the day's dinner; children in arms with little pointing fingers; young girls; prowling boys; comrades in working, soldiering, or what not.' [Charles Dickens], 'Railway Dreaming,' *Household Words*, 10 May 1856, 13: 387. As Vanessa Schwartz argues, the morgue was 'a site of pleasure and entertainment—a "spectacle"—in the French double sense of theatre and grand display.' Vanessa Schwartz, *Spectacular Realities: Early Mass Culture in Fin-De-Siecle Paris* (Berkeley: University of California Press, 1998), 59.
53 [Jerrold], 'Deadly Lively,' 139.
54 Ibid.: 138.
55 Ibid.: 139.

symbolises nothing but the statuary's bill.'[56] He distinguishes between 'a natural and an unnatural style of ornament' in the composition of epitaphs, and objects to the use of wit in epigraphy as a form of fetishism in which the person to be commemorated is 'completely sunk into the position of an object of the writer's ingenuity': instead of evoking a properly reflective disposition in the viewer, '[i]n looking at [such a] monument [he writes], you think only of the statuary.'[57] Similarly, he complains that the use of such decorative features as stone canopies, pillars, and sham urns in tomb design turns commemoration into spectacle: 'you attract passers-by, not to pause reverently and merely to look, but to stare in a *dilettante* fashion, as if they were in a wax show.'[58] For Hannay, the obtrusive materiality of the monument converts what should be respectful private tribute into public display. 'Affectations,' such as 'elaborate broken columns, with the artfully shattered fragments affectedly scattered about in a laboriously desolate way,'[59] show commodity culture distorting the commemorative function of the cemetery. In 'Deadly Lively,' the unsettling effect of Jerrold's peculiar oxymoronic title is reinforced as he remarks the incongruous mixture of grief and festivity evident in the behaviour of the cemetery excursionists, and in the trading of 'grave decorations, or pious emblems suited to the purses of all.' Indeed, the burial place is figured as a piece of real estate, Jerrold reporting that 'those graves at Montmartre which are not bought 'in perpetuity' are let for 15 years, at the expiration of which tenancy the unconscious tenant is ousted from his resting-place, and conveyed to a spot whither all fifteen-year tenants are removed in similar circumstances.'[60] As Hannay notes wryly of this new commercial enterprise for disposal of the dead, '[c]emeteries express the feelings, and meet the wants of an altered time,'[61] and *Household Words*'s discussion of their development shows a mixed response to the commodity culture associated with them.

Another area of conflicted trade in death was the commodification of the corpse itself. As Ruth Richardson has demonstrated, a 'small but important sector of the population—anatomists, artists, physicians, surgeons, articulators, dentists, and their suppliers—depended in varying degrees for their economic survival upon the ease with which the human corpse could be treated as a commodity.'[62] As any reader of *A Tale of Two Cities* or *Our Mutual Friend* knows, commerce in bodies both fascinated and revolted Dickens. *Household Words* also dealt with bodysnatching and dissection in a leader by Henry Morley entitled 'Use and Abuse of the Dead.'[63]

---

56 [James Hannay], 'Graves and Epitaphs,' *Household Words*, 16 October 1852, 6: 108.

57 Ibid.: 107. Nevertheless, *Household Words* later published an article illustrating the very epitaphic wit denounced by Hannay: [James Payn], 'Among the Tombs,' *Household Words*, 3 April 1858, 17.

58 [Hannay], 'Graves and Epitaphs,' 108.

59 Ibid.

60 [Jerrold], 'Deadly Lively,' 140.

61 [Hannay], 'Graves and Epitaphs,' 105.

62 Ruth Richardson, *Death, Dissection and the Destitute* (London: Penguin, 1988), 71–2.

63 [Henry Morley], 'Use and Abuse of the Dead,' *Household Words*, 3 April 1858, 17: 361–5. The title echoes in part Thomas Southwood Smith's influential article, 'Use of the Dead to the Living,' which was originally published in the *Westminster Review* in 1824 in the years leading up to the first Anatomy Bill and reprinted in 1832 at the time of the second

Taking as his premise the 'imperative necessity that human anatomy should be studied diligently by our surgeons and physicians,' Morley argues that it is not so difficult as it might at first appear to reconcile the 'national feelings of humanity' and the 'interests of science' in dealing with this contentious issue.[64] His retrospect of the situation prior to the 1832 Anatomy Act outlines a range of abuses involved in meeting the necessity for dissection in medical training and research: 'Churchyards were robbed, sick chambers were robbed; the high price that anatomists were compelled to pay for means of study tempted wretched men to commit murder.'[65] He describes the activity of the professional resurrectionist, who 'chose for himself a well-filled city graveyard, and then worked it, with a miner's industry, in the most systematic manner,' detailing the techniques used to extract the body from the coffin, and the range of prices that a body so stolen might fetch ('ten, twelve, and sometimes even fifteen pounds').[66] Throughout his account, Morley uses market terminology to describe the traffic in corpses: bodies are 'priced,' bought and sold, discussed in terms of supply and demand, packed in 'sacks,' 'imported' and exported. Moreover, the success with which the Anatomy Act has removed many of the abuses associated with resurrectionism is measured, at least in part, in economic terms: 'These regulations [he says] have entirely put an end to the older forms of bodysnatching, have made murder for dissection quite impossible, and have so far tended to supply the anatomist with better means of study, that the price of a subject to the student in this country is now four pounds, instead of ten.'[67]

Ruth Richardson argues that the 1832 Anatomy Act was 'in reality an advance clause to the New Poor Law' in its establishment of a nationally organized and centrally funded inspectorate, and in the way in which the threat of dissection was used to augment the popular dread of the workhouse.[68] The Act provided for the donation of corpses for dissection by any person in lawful possession of a body, unless the deceased had expressed—by writing or verbally in the presence of at least two witnesses during the illness which led to his or her death—a desire not to be dissected, or unless a surviving relative objected to the dissection.[69] In effect, it provided for dissection of those poor who died in the workhouse, thus signalling the effectual criminalization of poverty that was subsequently enshrined in the

---

bill. Smith was Bentham's physician and anatomist, an active campaigner for reform in public health and sanitation, and his 1854 pamphlet on recent *Results of Sanitary Improvements* was enthusiastically reviewed by Morley, who had himself studied medicine at Kings College: [Henry Morley], 'Your Very Good Health,' *Household Words*, 28 January 1854, 8: 524–6.

64 [Morley], 'Use and Abuse of the Dead,' 361.
65 Ibid.
66 Ibid.
67 Ibid.: 363–4. Smith also urged the importance of economic considerations, arguing that 'it is of the utmost importance that [supply of subjects] should be abundant, regular, and cheap.' [Thomas Southwood Smith], 'Use of the Dead to the Living,' *Westminster Review* 1824, 1: 91.
68 Richardson, *Death, Dissection and the Destitute*, 191–2.
69 Richardson notes that there was nothing in the Act 'to ensure that the transfer of bodies from "executor" to anatomist should be gratuitous, and no embargo upon the sale of corpses, entire or dismembered.' Ibid., 208.

New Poor Law. According to Richardson, the Anatomy Act was an early success of Benthamite/Malthusian policy, a 'class reprisal against the poor': 'only incidentally,' she argues, 'did it endorse the respectability of scientific medicine.'[70]

But Morley finds a justification for the Act in the union of science and political economy. His argument begins with the acknowledgement that while the Act has done much to remedy old abuses and reduce the price of 'subjects' for dissection, it has not 'put an end to the villainous jobbing in corpses which is still within the power of an undertaker who can get the master of a workhouse to assist his views.'[71] He attributes the problem to the clause of the Act which 'makes it simply permissive in those who have custody of an unclaimed body, to give it for dissection.' The remedy, he suggests, is not to adopt the French system under which every person dying in a hospital automatically surrenders his body to science, for this would be an infringement of personal liberty. 'In this country,' he declares, 'let no man alive or dead be denied bodily freedom.' As Richardson has shown, however, 'bodily freedom' depended upon having the economic means to obtain secure burial.

Morley's affirmation of personal freedom here highlights some of the issues at stake in an anecdote he recounts. This concerns a certain '"Caroline W."' who wrote to an anatomist 'telling him that she was an unfortunate woman weary of life, and eager to lay her burden down if she could quit the world able to pay the few pounds that she owed to creditors.'[72] The woman wished to sell her body—literally—and her story makes explicit the economic basis of prostitution that, as Lynda Nead has noted, was typically concealed within a language of social order, health, and morality in the 'respectable, public discourses of Victorian Britain.'[73] Morley's account of the woman's plight raises questions about agency and selfhood as it reveals the process of her commodification. Significantly, no direct quotation from the woman's letter is offered beyond her signature, Morley choosing instead to mediate her voice through his third person narrative. The woman informed the anatomist that 'she was of such an age—so tall, so stout—of fair complexion; and she might be seen on the Strand side of Temple Bar at a certain hour on a certain day.' In an area notorious for prostitution, the woman uses the street to display the body she proposes to sell. The wretchedness of the woman's plight and the threat to her selfhood are captured in the peculiar disjunction of identity that emerges in her reported assurance to the anatomist: 'If he would buy her for dissection she did not want any money for herself: only his word of honour that he would pay those who might bring her body to his rooms.' Arguably, this tenuous subjectivity is undermined even further by the denial of economic agency to the woman: her offer of sale is, of course, refused. Morley apparently includes the anecdote in his article as an example of potential abuse of the dead occasioned by severe social distress. But no attempt is made to deal with the distress by giving the would-be seller the financial help she requires. The response of the anatomist is to consult the police, who 'appeared at the

---

70 Ibid., 266.

71 [Morley], 'Use and Abuse of the Dead,' 364.

72 Ibid.: 363.

73 Lynda Nead, *Myths of Sexuality: Representations of Women in Victorian Britain* (Oxford: Blackwell, 1988), 99.

appointed place of meeting, and scared the wretched soul away. No more was heard of her,' writes Morley. The tragic irony of the woman's situation—unremarked by Morley—is that her body can be of value only when she no longer owns it.[74] Living, the woman apparently could neither sell her labour (nor, presumably, her sexual services) for sufficient money to pay her debts nor contract for the sale of her own corpse to cover them; dead, and unclaimed, she could become the property of the anatomist under the provisions of the Anatomy Act.

Having exposed the continuity between the commodification of women's sexuality and body-selling in this way, Morley calls for an amendment to the Anatomy Act to include an 'ordinance' rather than a 'permission' that 'the unclaimed dead shall supply the needs of science and humanity, whenever the body is not that of one who, in life, prohibited its use for such a purpose.'[75] His description of this ordinance finds a justification for the commodification of the corpse in the mutually authorizing discourses of science and economics:

> Let there ... be a plain and fixed rule, that if any man die without having expressed a wish to be dissected after death rather by worms than by his student brethren; rather to rot than be spiritualised into knowledge that shall dry hereafter many a tear, ease many a pain; if any man die without having testified a desire that his body should be useless rather than useful to society when he is gone, then let society have the benefit of the doubt.[76]

The idea of being 'spiritualised into knowledge' is certainly a long way removed from the gruesome images of dissection conjured by Dickens, describing the young medical students, Bob Sawyer and Benjamin Allen, in the *Pickwick Papers*, gorging themselves at the Christmas breakfast table at Dingley Dell while they discuss the dissection of arms and legs ('"Nothing like dissecting, to give one an appetite,"' says Bob).[77] Morley's concern that bodies should be 'useful' rather than 'useless' invokes a key Utilitarian principle and links it to the rhetoric of scientific progress to form his argument supporting the regulation of trade in corpses under the Anatomy Act. The problem for Morley is not so much whether there should be a market in bodies, but how it should be regulated to serve the ends of medical science.

In its discussion of various forms of trading in death then, *Household Words* represents a process of contested commodification that registers a number of mid-Victorian anxieties about the appropriate scope of the market. As a trained doctor, Morley, not surprisingly, endorses a narrative of economic and scientific progress in identifying the ways in which improvements in medical practice have resulted from legislation facilitating and regulating commercial activity. In contrast, Dickens's critique of the rampant commercialism of the funeral trade sets a narrative of capitalist entrepreneurship against a narrative of non-commodifiable objects, of inalienable and incommensurable values. While demonstrating the technologies

---

74 Thomas Laqueur makes this point about the bodies of the poor more generally. Laqueur, 'Bodies, Death, and Pauper Funerals,' 122.

75 [Morley], 'Use and Abuse of the Dead,' 364.

76 Ibid.

77 Charles Dickens, *The Pickwick Papers*, ed. James Kinsley, World's Classics (1836–37; Oxford: Oxford University Press, 1988), 365–6.

of display and exchange that enable new things to be apprehended and treated as commodities, he also suggests that some things cannot or should not be alienated in this way, that certain forms of commodification threaten personhood. Of course, Dickens himself was not averse to trading in death through the incorporation of emotionally charged deathbed scenes in his fiction, or in some of his popular public readings—such as Sikes's murder of Nancy. His willingness to play on the reader's heartstrings is evident in a number of the stories he wrote for *Household Words*,[78] and his sentimentality drew criticism from some reviewers. 'No man can offer to the public so large a stock of death-beds adapted for either sex and for any age from five-and-twenty downwards,' sniped the *Saturday Review* in 1858.[79] Notwithstanding the personal bias evident in James Fitzjames Stephen's reviews of Dickens in the late 1850s, such criticism reminds us that the journal's discussion of trading in death was part of its own exchange value, its success as a commodity within the periodical market. But this preoccupation was also a product of Dickens's peculiar imaginative vision. As John Carey puts it, Dickens was 'just as intrigued by dead bodies as Mrs Gamp,'[80] and his fascination with corpses, coffins, and waxworks—with objects that inhabit the borderland between people and things, the living and the non-living—suggests a deep preoccupation with those ambiguously abstracted forms that characterize industrial capitalism: a preoccupation that also drives *Household Words*'s examination of the part played by mid-Victorian commodity culture in forming the subjects who inhabited it.

---

78 See for example [Charles Dickens], 'A Child's Dream of a Star,' *Household Words*, 6 April 1850, 1: 25–6.

79 Unsigned review of the Library Edition of the *Works*, *Saturday Review*, 8 May 1858. Reprinted in Philip Collins, ed., *Dickens: The Critical Heritage* (London: Routledge, 1971), 383–4. Collins notes that the review is almost certainly by James Fitzjames Stephen, whose bitter attack on Dickens as a purveyor of 'Light Literature' continued in the *Saturday Review* from 1857 to 1859.

80 John Carey, *The Violent Effigy: A Study of Dickens's Imagination* (London: Faber, 1979), 80.

Chapter 8

'Fashion in Undress'

In 'Stopped Payment, at Cranford,' Mary Smith describes Mr Hoggins looking 'broad and radiant' following the extraordinary announcement of his engagement to Lady Glenmire:

> [He] creaked up the middle aisle at church in a bran-new pair of top-boots, an audible, as well as visible, sign of his purposed change of state; for the tradition went that the boots he had worn till now were the identical pair in which he first set out on his rounds in Cranford twenty-five years ago; only they had been new-pieced, high and low, top and bottom, heel and sole, black leather and brown leather, more times than any one could tell.[1]

As Dudley Costello declares in an article published two years later, there 'may be other integuments, equally indicative of manhood, but there are none of which a male wearer is so proud as of his boots': 'Hats and gloves are temporary adornments; other articles of clothing depend, more or less, on the skill of the tailor, but boots depend upon themselves: self-reliant, they stand alone.'[2] The idea that a man like Mr Hoggins may be made anew by the splendour of his boots points to the more general function of clothing as a symbolic expression of identity in Victorian culture, as well as to its particular use in the nineteenth-century novel to define fictional character. Dress is a sign replete with social meaning and value. As the most famous Victorian clothes-philosopher argues in *Sartor Resartus*, '"Society is founded upon Cloth,"' and Carlyle uses clothing and its fetishism to expose the fabrications of authority in modern social and political institutions.[3]

The function of clothing as an expression of selfhood is a relatively recent and distinctively urban development, as theorists such as Richard Sennett have shown. The nineteenth-century expansion and fragmentation of city life produced new anxieties about the definition and interpretation of metropolitan identities. As public behaviour became 'a matter of observation, of passive participation, of a certain kind of voyeurism,'[4] the need to decode the more nuanced languages of an increasingly homogeneous urban dress found literary expression in the figure of the flâneur discussed in Chapter 4. In the crowded metropolitan milieu of strangers, clothing became invested with character, containing subtle markers of social differentiation.

---

1   [Elizabeth Gaskell], 'Stopped Payment, at Cranford,' *Household Words*, 2 April 1853, 7: 110.
2   [Dudley Costello], 'Boots and Corns,' *Household Words*, 12 May 1855, 11: 348.
3   Thomas Carlyle, *Sartor Resartus*, ed. Kerry McSweeney and Peter Sabor, World's Classics (1833–34; Oxford: Oxford University Press, 1987), 41.
4   Richard Sennett, *The Fall of Public Man* (Cambridge: Cambridge University Press, 1977), 27.

Fashion, as Elizabeth Wilson notes, originates 'in the early capitalist city,'[5] and as Peter Stallybrass reminds us, the example with which Marx begins his analysis of commodity fetishism in *Capital* is a coat.[6] Marx tracks the coat and the linen of which it is made back through the transformations of the capitalist marketplace to identify the human labour that was appropriated in its making. Distinguishing between the use-value and the exchange-value of the coat, Marx demonstrates that the latter is created by the 'congelation' of human labour that was expended in its making and is therefore embodied in it. 'In this aspect,' he argues, 'the coat is a depository of value, but though worn to a thread, it does not let this fact show through.'[7]

Clothing has long been recognized as a key element used by nineteenth-century novelists to achieve that 'solidity of specification' associated by Henry James with narrative realism.[8] More recently, cultural critics have linked the depiction of dress and other consumer goods in Dickens's novels to the emergence of commodity culture in the nineteenth century. As noted in Chapter 1, the link is made by Murray Roston in *Victorian Contexts* (1996), where he argues that Dickens employs the possessions, homes, and habiliments of his characters 'as animated external emblems of their inner being,' 'seeing within the proprietary selection of goods a method of differentiating character.'[9] What happens, though, when the goods are recycled, when the cultural effect of their 'proprietary selection' is complicated by second-hand purchase? In particular, what cultural significance is evident in the representation of a commodity like second-hand clothing, given the central role of fashion in the definition of identity? Such questions are prompted by the recurring descriptions of once-worn clothes in *Household Words*, by Sala and other contributors, which illustrate the journal's more general preoccupation with the changing relationship between people and things as part of an attempt to come to terms with the development of urban commodity culture at mid-century.

To be sure, Dickens's interest in second-hand clothing pre-dates *Household Words*. One of his earliest and best-known pieces on it occurs in his *Sketches* where Boz wanders through the markets in Monmouth Street, among the 'extensive groves of the illustrious dead':

> We have gone on speculating ... , until whole rows of coats have started from their pegs, and buttoned up, of their own accord, round the waists of imaginary wearers; lines of trousers have jumped down to meet them; waistcoats have almost burst with anxiety to put themselves on; and half an acre of shoes have suddenly found feet to fit them.[10]

---

5   Elizabeth Wilson, *Adorned in Dreams: Fashion and Modernity*, Revised ed. (London: Tauris, 2003), 9.

6   Peter Stallybrass, 'Marx's Coat,' in *Border Fetishisms: Material Objects in Unstable Spaces*, ed. Patricia Spyer (London: Routledge, 1998), 183–207.

7   Karl Marx, *Capital: An Abridged Edition*, ed. David McLellan (1867; Oxford: Oxford University Press, 1995), 26.

8   Henry James, 'The Art of Fiction,' in *The House of Fiction*, ed. Leon Edel (London: Rupert Hart-Davis, 1957), 33.

9   Murray Roston, *Victorian Contexts: Literature and the Visual Arts* (New York: New York University Press, 1996), 83, 77.

10 Charles Dickens, 'Meditations in Monmouth Street,' in *Sketches by Boz and Other Early Papers 1833–39*, ed. Michael Slater, Dent Uniform Edition of Dickens's Journalism (London: Dent, 1994), 78.

While Boz clearly revels in the invention of stories behind the cast-off garments hanging in the Monmouth Street shops, their identification as the 'burial-place of the fashions' also suggests a peculiar relationship between discarded dress and death, an image of the city as necropolis, that recurs in a more disturbing form in Dickens's later writing. In 'Lying Awake,' for example, his fascination with the Paris Morgue leads to a recollection of its 'ghastly beds, and the swollen saturated clothes hanging up, and the water dripping, dripping all day long, upon that other swollen saturated something in the corner, like a heap of crushed over-ripe figs that I have seen in Italy!'[11] In 'Railway Dreaming,' he remembers the keeper of the morgue surrounded by pegs and hooks from which hang 'the clothes of the dead who have been buried without recognition. They mostly have been taken off people who were found in the water, and are swollen (as the people often are) out of shape and likeness.'[12] These recently inhabited clothes of the dead are inscribed with pollution taboos regarding disease and criminality, thus provoking Pip's unease, on a visit to Newgate in *Great Expectations*, when he notices the Lord Chief Justice's proprietor wearing 'mildewed clothes, which had evidently not belonged to him originally, and which, I took it into my head, he had bought cheap of the executioner.'[13] These descriptions capture the uncanniness of second-hand clothing, its disturbingly liminal quality. Cast-off clothes are inanimate things that somehow retain the vestiges of the lives of former wearers. In her study of fashion and modernity, *Adorned in Dreams*, citing the passage from Boz above, Elizabeth Wilson asks why 'clothes without a wearer, whether on a second-hand stall, in a glass case, or merely a lover's garments strewn on the floor, can affect us unpleasantly, as if a snake had shed its skin.'[14] She argues that part of the answer to this 'strangeness of dress' is that the body is a cultural organism with limits that are equivocally defined and it cannot be separated from the dress which inscribes it, producing it as a social body: thus 'Clothing marks an [already] unclear boundary ambiguously, and unclear boundaries disturb us.'[15]

Unclear boundaries disturbed the Victorians too, and the preoccupation with dress in general and second-hand clothing in particular, evident in *Household Words*, is an indication of contemporary anxieties about the blurring of divisions between categories conventionally held to be distinct. Other commentators on city life in *Household Words* besides Dickens share his interest in the residue of character that lingers in empty clothing. Sala's journalism shows a similar preoccupation with cast-off garments, and the autonomy they seem to possess, that is bound up with his exploration of the uncertainties of modern urban experience and of what Marx referred to as the 'phantasmagoria' of commodity culture.[16] The ambiguities of clothing as a liminal form, at the interface between the body and the environment,

---

11 [Charles Dickens], 'Lying Awake,' *Household Words*, 30 October 1852, 6: 147.

12 [Charles Dickens], 'Railway Dreaming,' *Household Words*, 10 May 1856, 13: 388.

13 Charles Dickens, *Great Expectations*, ed. Margaret Cardwell, World's Classics (1860; Oxford: Oxford University Press, 1994), 164.

14 Wilson, *Adorned in Dreams*, 3.

15 Ibid., 2.

16 Sala's abiding interest in clothing and fashion is also evident in his devotion of the penultimate chapter of his memoir, *Things I have Seen and People I have Known* (1894), to 'Costumes of my Infancy.'

make it a complex constituent of modern subjectivity. As Susan Buck-Morss notes of Benjamin's account of the form of fashion specific to capitalist modernity, 'In fashion, the phantasmagoria of commodities presses closest to the skin.'[17] In *The Arcades Project*, Benjamin cites the passages from *Capital* outlining the way in which the social character of the labour that produces commodities is obscured in their exchange value as part of his own critique of modernity.[18] Clothing is an exemplary commodity in this regard, hiding the evidence of the producer's labour in its purchase to express the identity of the wearer. But in its cast-off form, clothing complicates such processes of abstraction and objectification of labour by bearing the traces of the lives of former wearers. Second-hand clothing draws attention to 'the importance of the recursivity of objectification,'[19] disrupting the linearity assumed in accounts of the production-to-consumption commodity chain. It forms a kind of palimpsest, an emblem for the multi-layered nature of modernity remarked by Benjamin, where the archaic and the new, past and present, exist side by side. Ambiguously marking boundaries that were already unclear, as Wilson suggests, clothing has the potential to destabilize oppositions between the spheres of production and consumption, between ideas of individuality and conformity, between people and things.

Richard Sennett has written of the new principle of 'immanence' that arose in the nineteenth century through which clothing came to be interpreted as a statement about the personality of the wearer.[20] For Sennett, dress is an instance of a more general secularist tendency to invest attributes of intimate personality in material things. The consequence of such an investment was the introduction of 'an element of profound self-doubt into [a society's] cognitive apparatus': 'When belief was governed by the principle of immanence, there broke down distinctions between perceiver and perceived, inside and outside, subject and object.'[21] Such a loss of distinctions is explored in the accounts of cast-off clothes that appear in *Household Words*. While dress is now conventionally understood to be a sign of identity, even when serving as a disguise, the discussion of clothing in the journal suggests the new power of the commodity not simply to express or reflect, but rather to constitute modern subjectivity in ways that complicate the fetishism theorized by Marx.

Such a perception of the changing relationship between people and things is apparent in Sala's account of 'Fashion.' Published as the leader in *Household Words* on 29 October 1853, Sala's article begins by condemning the idolatry of Fashion only to pause and consider the many who

> earn their daily bread by making and vending Fashion's elegant trumpery;—gloves, fans, spangles, scents, and bon-bons: how ships, colonies and commerce, are all mixed up in a curious yet congruous elaboration with these fal-lals: how one end of the chain may be my lady's boudoir and its knick-knacks in Belgravia, and the other end a sloppy ship-dock

---

17 Susan Buck-Morss, *The Dialectics of Seeing: Walter Benjamin and the Arcades Project* (Cambridge, Mass.: MIT Press, 1989), 97.
18 Walter Benjamin, *The Arcades Project*, trans. Howard Eiland and Kevin McLaughlin (Cambridge, Mass.: Belknap Press of Harvard University Press, 1999), 181–2.
19 Nicky Gregson and Louise Crewe, *Second-Hand Cultures* (Oxford: Berg, 2003), 10.
20 Sennett, *The Fall of Public Man*, 164.
21 Ibid., 169.

on the hot strand of the Hooghly; how the beginnings of a ball supper, with its artificial flowers, its trifles, its barley-sugar temples, its enamelled baskets and ratafia cakes, were the cheerless garret and the heated cellar.[22]

In reconnecting the production and consumption ends of the chain, Sala attempts to demystify the commodity and expose its origins. But he also celebrates the restless movement of worldly goods, marvelling at the linkage of incongruous sites and the vast distances commodities can travel. While recognizing in fashionable objects the sweated labour that may be required for their manufacture, as well as the colonial exploitation that may be associated with imperial trade, Sala's empire of circulating commodities in this piece takes on a vivid, particularized life of its own. He delights in the profusion of objects, reeling off lists of disparate items, and building up alliterative phrases and co-ordinate clauses describing a process of worldwide manufacture and trade that might be extended endlessly. He emphasizes the superficiality of these fashionable goods and acknowledges their sign value— 'Fashion is not tangible or palpable,'[23] he says—which is to be contrasted with the material realities of the 'cheerless garret' and 'heated cellar.' However, although he implies the existence of the producers who inhabit these spaces, his narrative interest lies in the life of the goods themselves, which take precedence over their makers and wearers as part of the objectness of modern material culture. As a flâneur, he relishes the visual experience of such heterogeneity. His account of fashion captures a key cultural shift in the representation of commodities at mid-century, away from a focus on the relations of production to the processes of circulation and consumption.

As commentators like Thomas Richards, Andrew Miller, and Regenia Gagnier have noted, and as the preceding chapters have shown, the development of commodity culture in the nineteenth-century is distinguished by the way in which objects, once detached from those who made them, come to represent qualities of the consumer, and to acquire a sign-value over and above their use-value.[24] The labour theory of value espoused by the earlier political economists was gradually abandoned in favour of a model of consumer choice. The sign-value of clothing is, however, complicated by its recycling as second-hand goods, simultaneously affirming and disrupting its function as an interpretable expression of identity. Exploring the relationship between identity and attire in 'Fashion,' Sala uses the language of theatre to blur the distinction between world and stage, audience and actors, in contemplating the cast-offs to be found in 'Mrs Brummus's' shop. The remnants of 'Fashion's great chalked stage' include

the crimson velvet dresses of duchesses, the lace that queens have worn, our grandmothers' brocaded sacks and hoops and high-heeled shoes, fans, feathers, silk stockings, lace pocket-

---

22 [George A. Sala], 'Fashion,' *Household Words*, 29 October 1853, 8: 194.
23 Ibid.: 193.
24 See Thomas Richards, *The Commodity Culture of Victorian England: Advertising and Spectacle 1851–1914* (Stanford: Stanford University Press, 1990); Andrew Miller, *Novels Behind Glass: Commodity Culture and Victorian Narrative* (Cambridge: Cambridge University Press, 1995); Regenia Gagnier, *The Insatiability of Human Wants: Economics and Aesthetics in Market Society* (Chicago: University of Chicago Press, 2000).

handkerchiefs, scent-bottles, the Brussels lace veil of the bride, the sable bombazine of the widow, embroidered parasols, black velvet mantles, pink satin slips; ... robes without bodies and bodies without robes, and sleeves without either; the matron's apron and the opera dancer's skirt. Here is Fashion in undress, without its whalebone, crinoline, false hair, paint, and pearl powder; here she is tawdry, tarnished, helpless, inert, dislocated, like Mr Punch's company in the deal box he carries strapped behind his back.[25]

The *theatrum mundi* motif exposes the role of fashion in the performance of social identity. Sala acknowledges the function of clothing and adornment in marking distinctions of class and gender, his social classification of garments imitating the 'botanizing on the asphalt' undertaken by the flâneur.[26] Like Boz meditating upon the second-hand clothing in Monmouth Street, he constructs typologies from the garments on display, inferring the duchesses, widows, matrons, or opera dancers who once wore them. These cast-offs also signify the compartmentalized lives of their former middle- and upper-class owners: sub-divided into life stages, marking rites of passage, or defining the activities which belong to a certain time of day. But while remarking the social types and occasions that may be read from their cast-off clothing, Sala's account reveals the role of these goods in fashioning identity in such a way as to call the nature of subjectivity itself into question. Personifying Fashion, he paradoxically represents second-hand clothing as divested of its former owners: 'Here is Fashion in undress.' As Virginia Woolf later wrote of Orlando's remarkable transformation, '[clothes] change our view of the world and the world's view of us. ... There is much to support the view that it is clothes that wear us and not we them.'[27] Such an inversion of agency is also suggested in another leader by Sala, published two years earlier, where he remarks of the 'sweepings of civilisation' to be found in the old Cloth Fair,

> [a]ll the lies and the subterfuges of dress, the padded coats and whale-boned waistcoats, the trousers that were patched in places where the skirts hid them, have come naked to this bankruptcy. The surtout that concealed the raggedness of the body-coat beneath; the body-coat that buttoned over the shirtless chest; the boots which were not Wellingtons, as in their strapped-down hypocrisy they pretended to be, but old Bluchers; all are discovered, exposed, turned inside out, here.[28]

Rather than serving as an expression of selfhood, as an external sign of their owner's identity and yet another occasion for moral reflection upon the vanity of adornment, the second-hand clothes in the old Cloth Fair, or Mrs Brummus's shop, offer the more radical suggestion that modern subjectivity itself partakes of the nature of clothing, that people and things are mutually constituted.

Sartor Resartus satirizes the emptiness of modern institutional authority through Teufelsdröckh's ironic regard for second-hand clothing:

---

25 [Sala], 'Fashion,' 194.
26 Walter Benjamin, *Charles Baudelaire: A Lyric Poet in the Era of High Capitalism*, trans. Harry Zohn (London: Verso, 1983), 36.
27 Virginia Woolf, *Orlando*, ed. Rachel Bowlby, World's Classics (1928; Oxford: Oxford University Press, 1992), 180.
28 [George A. Sala], 'Old Clothes!,' *Household Words*, 17 April 1852, 5: 97.

> The gladder am I ... to do reverence to those Shells and outer Husks of the Body, wherein no devilish passion any longer lodges, but only the pure emblem and effigies of Man: I mean, to Empty, or even to Cast Clothes. Nay, is it not to Clothes that most men do reverence: to the fine frogged broadcloth, nowise to the 'straddling animal with bandy legs' which it holds, and makes a Dignitary of?... That reverence which cannot act without obstruction and perversion when the Clothes are full, may have free course when they are empty.[29]

Sala shares this clothes-philosophy in his account of a visit to the Musée des Souverains at the Louvre. Noting that 'Mr Carlyle might come hither, and find—not a new philosophy, but fresh materials for its application,' he remarks the way in which 'the coronation mantle dangles from a peg, in the long run, even as the masquerade domino, the cast-off uniform, or the threadbare great-coat.'[30] The importance of clothing as a memorializing practice is ironically exposed in these cast-offs that once fulfilled important functions in war or work, but now only signify their desuetude and the mortality of their former wearers. Sala's description of the relics of Napoleon on display emphasizes an inconsistency between the man and the 'secondhand sovereignties' represented by his clothes, a disjunction between identity and attire, that works to demystify the heroic history memorialized in the Musée des Souverains. The power of the relic is simultaneously evoked and undercut in Sala's description of Napoleon's coat:

> the famous redingote gris—the gray great coat.... I don't think, intrinsically, it would fetch more than half a dozen shillings. I am afraid Mr Moses Hart of Holywell Street would not be disposed to give even that amount for it yet here it is beyond price and purchase. It has held the body of the man whose name is blazoned on the ceiling; whose initial, pregnant with will and power, N, is on wall and escutcheon.... This common coat of coarse gray duffel hangs in the midst of velvet and silk, gold and silver embroidery, stern, calm and impassable, and throws all their theatrical glories into shadow.[31]

Set in the midst of such gorgeous display, the old coat is an uncanny object. Sala's account betrays a tension between emphasis upon its power as a relic of historical import, and a deflating recognition of its secondariness, sordidness, and triviality. Preserved in what he describes as 'a palatial Monmouth Street or Holywell Street for the display of second-hand sovereigns,'[32] the second-hand clothes of Napoleon are like Benjamin's outmoded commodities, obsolete objects that serve to expose the phantasmagoria of mythic history and to demystify the fetishism of the commodity.

Anxieties about the ambiguous relationship between second-hand clothing and identity are also evident in 'Old Clothes!,' where Sala describes the frenetic activity of the Cloth Fair and details the profusion of 'ostracised garments' jumbled together indiscriminately:

---

29 Carlyle, *Sartor Resartus*, 182.
30 [George A. Sala], 'Second-Hand Sovereigns,' *Household Words*, 13 January 1855, 10: 516.
31 Ibid.: 512.
32 Ibid.

> There, pell-mell, cheek by jowl, in as strange juxtaposition, and as strange equality, as corpses in a plague-pit, are the groom's gaiters and my Lord Bishop's splatterdashes; with, save the mark! poor Pat's ill-darned, many-holed brogues, his bell crowned felt hat, his unmistakeable blue coat with the brass buttons, high in the collar, short in the waist, long in the tails, and ragged all over. There is no distinction of ranks; no precedence of rank, and rank alone, here.[33]

The second-hand clothing shop is a form of heterotopia. Here, clothing still serves to mark types or classifications of gender and class; but as effigies of their former owners, jumbled side by side, these garments effect a promiscuous intermingling in defiance of rank and hierarchy. A similar heterotopic space is found in the lost property office of the railways, where W.H. Wills describes the hat shelf with its 'heterogeneous jumble of rank, station, character, and indicative morality which that conglomeration of castors presents. Here a dissipated-looking four-and-nine leans its battered side against the prim shovel of a church dignitary; there a highly-polished Parisian upper-crust is smashed under the weight of a carter's slouch.'[34] Such accounts of the contingency of incongruous juxtapositions effected in these spaces of storage or exchange displace the flâneur's delight in the suggestive contrast of urban types onto the clothing they once wore. Within the old Clothes Exchange, the dissolution of distinctions is compounded by the multi-ownership of the garments:

> There is my lord's coat, bespattered by the golden mud on Fortune's highway; threadbare in the back with much bowing; the embroidery tarnished, the spangles all blackened; a Monmouth Street laced coat. Revivified, coaxed, and tickled into transitory splendour again, it may lend vicarious dignity to some High Chamberlain, or Stick-in-Waiting, at the court of the Emperor Soulouque. There is a scarlet uniform coat, heavily embroidered, which, no doubt, has dazzled many a nursemaid in its day. It will shine at masquerades now; or, perchance, be worn by Mr Belton, of the Theatres Royal; then emigrate, may be, and be the coat of office of the Commander-in-Chief of King Quashiboo's body-guard; or, with the addition of a cocked hat and straps, form the coronation costume of King Quashiboo himself.[35]

Rather than serving to define and place the wearer, recycled clothing produces a mixing of social identities. Where Boz regarded the clothes displayed in Monmouth Street as an occasion for storying 'backwards' to recover the lives of their former owners, Sala looks in the other direction, tracing the biography of garments that cross social and geographical borders with a life of their own. But just as second-hand clothing blurs social distinctions at home, it reinforces other boundaries between colony and metropolis. Sala distinguishes 'three orders of "Old Clothes" as regards the uses to which they may be applied.' Garments not 'good enough to be revivered, tricked, polished, teased, re-napped, and sold, either as superior second-hand garments, in second-hand-shop streets, or pawned for as much as they will fetch, and more than they are worth' are consigned to the second class, and

---

33 [Sala], 'Old Clothes!,' 97.
34 [W.H. Wills and Christopher Hill], 'Railway Waifs and Strays,' *Household Words*, 28 February 1850, 2: 320.
35 [Sala], 'Old Clothes!,' 97.

exported to the margins of the empire.[36] As Margaret Maynard has shown, the effects of British imperialism were felt within the Australian colonial marketing structure as the competition from cheap imports posed difficulties for the expansion of the local clothing industry.[37] Sala's third class of old clothes are 'so miserably dilapidated, so utterly tattered and torn' that they are pulled apart and ground into 'devil's dust' to be re-manufactured as 'broadcloth.' Such recycled clothes may secretly effect the most remarkable social conjunctions: 'Who shall say that the Marquis of Camberwell's footmen—those cocked-hatted, bouquetted, silk-stockinged Titans—may not have, in their gorgeous costume, a considerable spice of Patrick the bog-trotter's ragged breeches, and Luke the Labourer's fustian jacket?'[38] Similarly, in 'Saint Crispin,' George Dodd describes the work of the so-called 'Translator' or 'clobberer,' who works with a 'store of pieces, derived from the uppers and unders of boots and shoes which have passed through a process of dissection, after perhaps a long career of service in a higher walk in life,' and recycles them 'to run a yet further career' in an altogether different guise.[39]

As Sennett notes, black broadcloth became the regulation street wear of middle- and upper-class men by the 1840s, and the increasing homogeneity of appearance was 'the beginning of a *style* of dressing in which neutrality—that is, not standing out from others—was the immediate statement.'[40] The mass-production of machine-made clothes afforded the means for men to blend into the crowd, but also engendered a new concern to decode appearances by looking for clues in the small details of costume. In 'Rag-Fair in Paris,' Dudley Costello remarks the uniformity evident in the discreet ready-to-wear street-dress of the professional man—'Clifford Street or the Rue de Choiseul turn out very nearly the same sort of made-up man'[41]—and Sala satirizes the homogeneity of modern dress in 'Where Are They?'—the article discussed in Chapter 2 concerning the Personal columns of the newspapers:

A chief cause for our distressing uncertainty as to where the people we are in search of are to be found, lies in the disagreeable uniformity of costume prevalent in the present day…. [M]ay I ask how we are to tell any one man from another … by his dress alone. Really, what with the moustache movement, the detective police, the cheap clothing establishments, the shirt-collar mania … nobody knows who or what anybody else is.[42]

As Sennett remarks, such anxieties about reading appearances, about making sense of the inhabitants of the street, also entail a desire to avoid detection, to control the revelation of personality through self-fashioning: 'beyond all mystification produced by the machine, the very belief that appearance is an index of character would

---

36 Ibid.: 98.

37 Margaret Maynard, *Fashioned from Penury: Dress as Cultural Practice in Colonial Australia* (Cambridge: Cambridge University Press, 1994), 122.

38 [Sala], 'Old Clothes!,' 98.

39 [George Dodd], 'Saint Crispin,' *Household Words*, 26 March 1853, 7: 79.

40 Sennett, *The Fall of Public Man*, 161.

41 [Dudley Costello], 'Rag-Fair in Paris,' *Household Words*, 25 November 1854, 10: 344.

42 [George A. Sala], 'Where Are They?,' *Household Words*, 1 April 1854, 9: 152–3.

prompt people to make themselves nondescript in order to be as mysterious, as little vulnerable, as possible.'[43] He attributes these contradictory impulses—scrutiny of the appearances of others while avoiding attention oneself—to the way in which 'the new ideas of immanent personality mesh with the mass production of appearances in public.' Thus 'does a black broadcloth suit come to seem a "social hieroglyphic," to use Marx's phrase.'[44] Sala's account gestures towards this connection between the mystification of the mass-produced commodity and of urban identity. But while he pokes fun at such fetishism here, comically lamenting the conformity of fashion and implying the possibilities for disguise and social mobility it enables, Sala also goes beyond acknowledging the function of clothing in expressing or concealing an underlying identity to explore the role of dress in both marking and throwing into question the boundaries of the self.

For Sala, garments do not merely cover, but inscribe the body, producing a complex subjectivity that is multi-layered like clothing. In 'Our Doubles,' he elaborates a theory of 'corporeal duality' as he dwells upon 'the properties we all have, more or less, of casting our skin—of being one man abroad and another at home, one character for the foot-lights and another for the greenroom.'[45] But this duality is to be found not only in the distinction between public and private life. We are 'all gifted' with a capacity for playing one part 'simultaneously with the other': 'Everybody, so it seems to me, can be, and is somebody else.'[46] Nor is this duality 'always hypocritical': 'A great many wear double skins unconsciously,' he argues; 'Such is the schoolmaster who has a cricket-loving, child-petting, laughter-exciting, joke-cracking skin for inmost covering, but is swathed without in parchment bands of authority and stern words.' Such too, is the beadle: 'The fat man knows himself inwardly, and is notoriously at home a ninny, yet, awake to the responsibility of a cocked hat and staff and gold laced coat, frowns himself into the semblance of the most austere of beadles.'[47] Like Carlyle, Sala plays upon the double meaning of 'habit' as both clothing and behaviour, remarking the tailorization of identity. For example, '[h]abit gives a double cuticle to Mr John Trett (of the firm of Tare and Trett) of the city of London, ship-broker,' for while 'one Mr Trett is a morose despot, with a fierce whisker, a malevolent white neckcloth, and an evil eye,' the other, who lives at Dalston, is surprisingly discovered to be 'something more than an amateur on the violincello, although Giuseppe Pizzicato, from Genoa, was last week brought to Guildhall, at the complaint of Mr Trett's double, charged with outraging the tranquillity of Copperbottom Court, Threadneedle Street, where the ship-brokers have their offices, by the performance of airs from Don Giovanni on the hurdy-gurdy.'[48]

Although clothes in general and uniforms in particular make the man, however, they are an inherently ambiguous signifier. The acute temporality of fashion means

---

43 Sennett, *The Fall of Public Man*, 169.
44 Ibid., 164.
45 [George A. Sala], 'Our Doubles,' *Household Words*, 10 July 1852, 5: 388.
46 Ibid.
47 Ibid.: 389.
48 Ibid.: 390.

that identity is always haunted by belatedness. In 'Mars a la Mode,' prompted by contemporary calls for reform of the costume of the British army, Sala provides a satiric survey of the history of military fashion, selecting the Duke of Wellington as a particularly noteworthy illustration of the unstable relation between identity and attire:

> [I]n his first ensigncy he must have worn hair-powder and a pigtail, a cocked hat as large as a beadle's, silver bell-pull epaulettes, tights like a rope-dancer, and ankle-jacks not unlike those of a dustman. The Duke of Wellington in a pigtail and ankle-jacks! Can you reconcile that regulation costume of the subaltern in the Thirty-third Foot with the hessian boots and roll-collar of Talavera: the gray frock, glazed hat, white neckcloth and boots named after himself, of Waterloo: the rich field-marshal's uniform, covered with orders, of the snowy-headed old patriarch who smiles upon the baby Prince, in Winterhalter's picture.[49]

The 'boots named after himself' assert the intimate connection between clothing and identity. As Dudley Costello remarks, '[l]ike the man whose name it bears,' the Wellington boot early on 'fixed itself firmly as one of the institutions of the country.'[50] But the vicissitudes of military fashion render the Duke a comic mixture of disparate parts—part beadle, rope-dancer and dustman—as time is frozen in the museum-like collection of his uniforms. Sala's account collapses historical differences across time within the space of the present in a way that demystifies the aura surrounding the hero's image and suggests the illusion of 'panoptical time' that Anne McClintock has associated with British imperialism.[51] Indeed, the account of Wellington's outmoded regalia recalls Morley's description, in his account of the slave trade, 'Our Phantom Ship: Negro Land,' of King Boy as a harlequinade decked out in the 'gifts' of cast-off clothing left behind by earlier imperial explorers: 'His Majesty with a cunning, coarse face, and red eyes, is attired in a Scotchman's dress, a present from England, the deficiency in which he has supplied with a huge pair of Turkish trowsers, fastened outside, the skirt of his kilt being tucked into them.'[52] The absurd amalgamation highlights the arbitrariness and transience of fashions' dictates as they are manifested in military costume or other regalia, exposing the myth-making operations of imperial progress through such accounts of 'the "trash" of history.'[53]

The social benefits of uniformity in dress were outlined by Dickens elsewhere in *Household Words* in his account of Urania Cottage, the 'Home for Homeless Women' he established with Angela Burdett Coutts in 1847. As Phillipe Perrot argues, clothing is a powerful element of social regulation, inducing the individual 'to merge with the

---

49 [George A. Sala], 'Mars a La Mode,' *Household Words*, 14 October 1854, 10: 194–5.

50 [Costello], 'Boots and Corns,' 350.

51 Ann McClintock, *Imperial Leather: Race, Gender and Sexuality in the Colonial Context* (London: Routledge, 1995).

52 [Henry Morley], 'Our Phantom Ship: Negro Land,' *Household Words*, 18 January 1851, 2: 404.

53 The phrase is used by Susan Buck-Morss to describe Benjamin's quarry. Buck-Morss, *The Dialectics of Seeing*, 93.

group, participate in its rituals and ceremonies, share its norms and values, properly occupy his or her position, and correctly act his or her role.'[54] Dickens's awareness of the function of uniform as a disciplinary technology is evident in the clothing that was assigned to the inmates of Urania Cottage. While the dresses he chose for them were to be 'as cheerful in appearance as they reasonably could be—at the same time very neat and modest,'[55] Dickens emphasizes the role of this particular clothing in furthering the project of reform:

> They make and mend their own clothes, but do not keep them.... Formerly, when a girl accepted for admission had clothes of her own to wear, she was allowed to be admitted in them, and they were put by for her; though within the Institution she always wore the clothing it provides. It was found, however, that a girl with a hankering after old companions rather relied on these reserved clothes, and that she put them on with an air, if she went away or were dismissed. They now invariably come, therefore, in clothes belonging to the Home, and bring no other clothing with them.[56]

In making and mending 'their' clothes, the Urania Cottage inmates were to learn the skills of domestic economy that would prepare them to become suitable wives of emigrants in the colonies. But of course they were not 'their' clothes, the slippage in the pronoun revealing the difference between making and wearing, as opposed to owning, garments: the borrowed clothes were designed to help (re)form the subjects who wore them. As Amanda Anderson has noted, there is 'a disturbing similarity' between the practices adopted in Urania Cottage and the structure of Victorian prostitution: the dress policy resembled the way in which brothel keepers were able to retain control over their employees by providing and owning their clothing.[57] This practice was described by urban investigators, like Henry Mayhew and James Greenwood, as 'dress-lodging,' and Greenwood emphasizes the miserable plight of its practitioners:

> They are bound hand and foot to the harpies who are their keepers. They are worse off than the female slaves on a nigger-plantation, for they at least may claim as their own the rags they wear.... But these slaves of the London pavement may boast of neither soul nor body, nor the gaudy skirts and laces and ribbons with which they are festooned. They belong utterly and entirely to the devil in human shape who owns the den that the wretched harlot learns to call her 'home.'[58]

---

54 Philippe Perrot, *Fashioning the Bourgeoisie: A History of Clothing in the Nineteenth Century*, trans. Richard Bienvenu (Princeton: Princeton University Press, 1994), 13.

55 Charles Dickens, 'To Miss Coutts,' in *Letters from Charles Dickens to Angela Burdett-Coutts, 1841–1865*, ed. Edgar Johnson (London: J. Cape, 1953), 106.

56 [Charles Dickens], 'Home for Homeless Women,' *Household Words*, 23 April 1853, 7: 171.

57 Amanda Anderson, *Tainted Souls and Painted Faces: The Rhetoric of Fallenness in Victorian Culture* (Ithaca: Cornell University Press, 1993), 78.

58 James Greenwood, *The Seven Curses of London* (1869; Oxford: Blackwell, 1981), 182–3.

As Greenwood's account suggests, the dress-lodger is alienated from the clothing she wears not only by a lack of ownership, but by enslavement to the keeper who rents her garments. Such finery is a badge of occupation that subsumes the selfhood of the wearer in her degraded work as a streetwalker. Dress-lodging thus represents a peculiar form of second-hand clothing, simultaneously affirming and denying the intimate relationship between the wearer and her attire. The identity of the dress-lodger would seem to be established paradoxically through her alienation from the very clothes by which she procures her livelihood and which advertise her fallen state. While the Urania Cottage inmates were not required to rent their clothes, as Dickens's article indicates, their lack of ownership and surrender of personal choice in the garments they wore were part of a disciplinary strategy designed to regulate their behaviour. Like the dress-lodgers, the identity of these women was to be (re)formed through clothes they wore but could not own, as if the possession or 'proprietary selection' of apparel (to go back to Roston's terms) enables a relationship between identity and dress that might shore up a recalcitrant self.

Dickens's use of clothing in the Urania Cottage project thus suggests a role for dress in the constitution of modern subjectivity that goes beyond the expressive value it was conventionally understood to possess. Withholding the opportunity for 'proprietary selection' or ownership that might enable the Victorian consumer in the marketplace to fashion a self, his account suggests the power of clothing to form or reform subjectivity. Likewise, Sala's acute consciousness of the role of clothing in the performance of social identity leads to an understanding of the ways in which dress is not so much an expression, as an embodiment, of the selfhood of the wearer, a selfhood that partakes of the paradoxes of fashion with its conflicting impulses towards individuality and conformity, change and continuity, past and future.

***

Cast-off clothing, of course, was not the only form of second-hand trading explored in *Household Words*. A number of the 'process articles' examine the possibilities of recycling industrial waste. 'Penny Wisdom' provides a diverse range of examples where technical ingenuity has enabled the manufacturer to 'save a penny' and create 'something out of a commercial nothing': the use of old horse-shoe nails to make gun-barrels, of old bones and bits of skin salvaged from abattoirs to make gelatine, of plumbago dust to substitute for lead in pencils, of small coal—left-over at pit mouths—to make coke, of ammoniacal liquor left over from the manufacture of gas-light to make the volatile salts kept in my lady's smelling-bottle, and so on.[59] The sheer number and heterogeneity of the examples provided emphasize the boundless possibilities of recycling to ensure industrial thrift. Similarly, in 'Waste,' John Capper describes the way in which 'Science has shown how the mere parings of daily industry may be transformed into important elements of utility; how the refuse of the smithy, the foundry, the stall, the farm-yard, the slaughter-house, the gas-factory, has in itself, a value before undreamt of.'[60] George Dodd describes the 'new branch of industry' involved in the treatment of refuse from the smelting of iron, copper,

---

59 [George Dodd], 'Penny Wisdom,' *Household Words*, 16 October 1852, 6: 96.
60 [John Capper], 'Waste,' *Household Words*, 10 June 1854, 9: 390.

lead, and zinc ores in 'Important Rubbish,' imagining 'a new Belgravia, a second Tyburnia, rising up at the bidding of some adventurous Cubitt or Peto, built with slag bricks, and faced with a polished front of surpassing brilliancy.'[61] Attacking the problem of sewage pollution in 'A Way to Clean Rivers,' Henry Morley advocates the recycling of town refuse as manure. 'Dirt itself is not gold,' he argues, 'though industry may make it so.'[62] Edmund Saul Dixon continues the campaign in a leader on 'Dirty Cleanliness' published a fortnight later, where he asks why the Seine flows 'so clean and green' compared with the filthy Thames, and argues against the short-sightedness and ignorance of supposing 'that all which congregated human beings need do, is simply to get rid of their rejectaments. The object must be to get rid of them usefully, to turn them to account, to utilize them, or the whole machinery of agricultural and horticultural production and reproduction must stop.'[63]

As oxymoronic titles such as 'Dirty Cleanliness' and 'Important Rubbish' suggest, these articles play upon the ambiguity inherent in the meaning of 'waste'—as refuse matter, or as the process of squandering goods. Driven by concerns about thrift, sanitation, and environmental degradation, they argue for the commodification of waste, a redefinition of the meaning of rubbish through its assumption of exchange-value within the market. But such large-scale re-valuation and reuse of waste contrasts with the precarious livelihoods of those marginal traders in rubbish, illustrated elsewhere in *Household Words*, who represent the underside of industrial capitalism. While the progress of industry may be trumpeted about by Dodd in his accounts of manufacturers' innovative efforts to reuse waste, recycling is pursued with more urgency in the residual economies of the 'cinder-sifters' depicted in 'Dust; or Ugliness Redeemed,'[64] or the rabbit-skin buyer of Paris, described by William Blanchard Jerrold, whose 'thin, pale face, proclaims his habit of stinting himself, and no less proclaims the trade—not too healthy—in which he is engaged.'[65] Dependent upon the casting-out that results from the ceaseless desire for the 'new' driving modern commodity culture, these traders eke out a living on the margins of capitalist enterprise. They impel the question that Geoffrey Hemstedt asks regarding the presence of such recyclers in *Sketches by Boz*: 'In the grand plot of Victorian history what part is played by those citizens who largely consume what others throw aside, or who live on waste?'[66]

As well as raising questions about forms of trade not easily assimilated into the grand narrative of the mainstream capitalist economy, the representation of recycling in *Household Words* challenges those accounts—like the factory tourist tales—that see the process of production as the key defining moment in a commodity's biography. The journal's discussion of second-hand goods suggests instead that

---

61 [George Dodd], 'Important Rubbish,' *Household Words*, 19 May 1855, 11: 378.
62 [Henry Morley], 'A Way to Clean Rivers,' *Household Words*, 10 July 1858, 18: 80.
63 [Edmund Saul Dixon], 'Dirty Cleanliness,' *Household Words*, 24 July 1858, 18: 121–2.
64 [Richard H. Horne], 'Dust; or Ugliness Redeemed,' *Household Words*, 13 July 1850, 1: 379–84.
65 [William Blanchard Jerrold], 'Rabbit-Skins,' *Household Words*, 15 July 1854, 9: 519.
66 Geoffrey Hemstedt, 'Inventing Social Identity: *Sketches by Boz*,' in *Victorian Identities: Social and Cultural Formations in Nineteenth-Century Literature*, ed. Ruth Robbins and Julian Wolfreys (London: Macmillan, 1996), 226.

commodities undertake a much wider range of biographical transformations than may be encompassed in the first cycle of production and consumption. As Nicky Gregson and Louise Crewe argue, 'unlike Marxian accounts of value, where fetishism masks the social relations of production and makes the production process (wherein value is created) remote and misperceived,' attention to second-hand cultures 'offers a useful corrective and suggests that power and value can be imbued in commodities long after the original production has ceased, through cycles of use, transformation and reuse.'[67] Conventional understandings of commodity value, as determined through the production, distribution and marketing costs of particular goods, are thus disrupted by the journal's account of relics, like Napoleon's 'redingote gris' or the Duke of Wellington's waistcoat.[68] Here, it is the imagined history vested within the commodity that creates its meaning. Representing the celebrity of the Duke, the value of the waistcoat depends not upon its raw material or manufacture, but upon ideas of authenticity and cultural capital. In other cases, as in Sala's account of the clothes indiscriminately juxtaposed in the old Clothes Exchange, the unknown others who once inhabited them—'Where are the people, I wonder, to whom these clothes belonged? Who will wear them next?' he asks—may lend garments a particular interest or allure beyond their use value.[69]

The journal's accounts of second-hand goods also provide the potential for critique of the urban commodity spectacle it celebrates elsewhere. While Sala's depiction of the old Clothes Exchange employs the figure of the flâneur in displacing the physiognomic categorization of urban types onto the clothing they once wore, this space of exchange differs significantly from the first-cycle retail precincts through which he wanders in 'Arcadia' or 'Music in Paving Stones.' Instead of the distanced consumption practices of window-shopping, which depend upon the dislocated admiration of the strolling spectator, the spaces of second-hand exchange are distinguished by jumble and disorder, by practices of rummaging and excavation. In contrast to the relations of looking that characterize the spectacular form of modern commodity culture, the old Clothes Exchange invites touch, the most liminal of senses,[70] and trades in goods that bear the imprint of previous owners. As 'the air is darkened with legs and arms of garments held up to be inspected,' Sala reports, the 'buyer pokes, and peers into, and detects naplessness, and spies out patches, and is aware of rents, and smells out black and blue reviver, and noses darns and discovers torn linings.'[71] A form of heterotopia, the old Clothes Exchange is a place where borders between interior and exterior, self and other, are put under pressure and social boundaries threaten to break down.

---

67 Gregson and Crewe, *Second-Hand Cultures*, 172.
68 [Charles Dickens], 'Trading in Death,' *Household Words*, 27 November 1852, 6: 244.
69 [Sala], 'Old Clothes!,' 97.
70 For a suggestive discussion of touch, see Susan Stewart, 'Prologue: From the Museum of Touch,' in *Material Memories*, ed. Marius Kwint, Christopher Breward, and Jeremy Aynsley (Oxford: Berg, 1999).
71 [Sala], 'Old Clothes!,' 97.

Qualifying that 'marked preponderance of the activity of the eye' in the city noted by Simmel,[72] second-hand trade complicates the shifting relationship between people and things that I have been arguing is a distinguishing feature of *Household Words*'s engagement with a developing commodity culture. Unlike Marx's coat, which comes to seem a 'social hieroglyphic,'[73] second-hand clothing is shown to be a paradoxical commodity that is 'transformed by maker and wearer alike,' that '*is* a kind of memory.'[74] Marked by the corporeal presence of their former inhabitants, second-hand clothes are like the obsolete objects sought out by Benjamin, discarded things whose afterlife can reveal the truth of the fetishized commodity.[75] Put into circulation again, these goods undergo multiple stages in their biographical journey, highlighting the narrowness of commodity accounts that focus solely upon the trajectory from production to consumption. Destabilizing the linearity of such narratives, the cast-offs found, for example, in Mrs Brummus's shop, await the moment of purchase that will be both the ending of one biographical journey and the beginning of another. They resist the 'essentialist, linear descent to "rubbish"' that will become such a damaging feature of modern consumer society.[76] As the narrative potential of their social lives is realized in *Household Words*, such goods—like the many commodities anthropomorphically described, exuberantly catalogued, or otherwise enlivened by the imaginative techniques that typify the journal's non-fiction prose—partake of the provisionality and uncertainty of the Victorian identities they help to represent. Clothes fashion identity as part of an interchange between people and things that leaves its disturbing traces in second-hand garments, and that challenges the effort to locate and fix the value and meaning of goods in the social relations of production. Studying 'Fashion in undress,' *Household Words* inverts conventional relationships between clothing and identity to reveal a deep ambivalence about the social life of goods, about the growing importance of commodities in imagining the modern self.

---

72 Quoted in Benjamin, *Charles Baudelaire*, 38.

73 Marx, *Capital*, 45.

74 Peter Stallybrass, 'Worn Worlds: Clothes, Mourning, and the Life of Things,' *Yale Review* 81 (1993): 38.

75 Graeme Gilloch, *Myth and Metropolis: Walter Benjamin and the City* (London: Polity Press, 1996), 122.

76 Gregson and Crewe, *Second-Hand Cultures* (Oxford: Berg, 2003), 202.

Bibliography

Contributions to *Household Words*

[Blanchard, Sidney Laman]. 'A Biography of a Bad Shilling.' *Household Words*, 25 January 1851, 2: 420–26.
[Capper, John]. 'A Cinnamon Garden.' *Household Words*, 1 March 1851, 2: 546–8.
———. 'The Cocoa-Nut Palm.' *Household Words*, 15 March 1851, 2: 585–9.
———. 'India Pickle.' *Household Words*, 9 June 1855, 11: 446–53.
———. 'An Indian Wedding.' *Household Words*, 21 February 1852, 4: 505–10.
———. 'Lancashire Witchcraft.' *Household Words*, 4 February 1854, 8: 549–51.
———. 'Number Forty-Two.' *Household Words*, 10 September 1853, 8: 17–20.
———. 'Oranges and Lemons.' *Household Words*, 1 April 1854, 9: 145–50.
———. 'The Peasants of British India.' *Household Words*, 17 January 1852, 4: 389–93.
———. 'A Reference to Character.' *Household Words*, 25 June 1853, 7: 390–94.
———. 'Rice.' *Household Words*, 30 June 1855, 11: 522–6.
———. 'Silken Chemistry.' *Household Words*, 9 April 1853, 7: 129–31.
———. 'Waste.' *Household Words*, 10 June 1854, 9: 390–393.
[Collins, Wilkie, and Charles Dickens]. 'Doctor Dulcamara, M.P.' *Household Words*, 18 December 1858, 19: 49–52.
[Collins, Wilkie]. 'Burns. Viewed as a Hat-Peg.' *Household Words*, 12 February 1859, 19: 241–3.
[Costello, Dudley]. 'Boots and Corns.' *Household Words*, 12 May 1855, 11: 348–54.
———. 'Picture Advertising in South America.' *Household Words*, 14 February 1852, 4: 494–8.
———. 'Rag-Fair in Paris.' *Household Words*, 25 November 1854, 10: 344–8.
Dickens, Charles. 'Hard Times.' *Household Words*, 29 April 1854, 9: 237–42.
———. 'Hard Times.' *Household Words*, 3 June 1854, 9: 357–62.
[Dickens, Charles, and Richard H. Horne]. 'The Great Exhibition and the Little One.' *Household Words*, 5 July 1851, 3: 356–60.
———. 'One Man in a Dockyard.' *Household Words*, 6 September 1851, 3: 553–7.
[Dickens, Charles, and Mark Lemon]. 'A Paper-Mill.' *Household Words*, 31 August 1850, 1: 529–31.
[Dickens, Charles, and Henry Morley]. 'H.W.' *Household Words*, 16 April 1853, 7: 145–9.
[Dickens, Charles, and W.H. Wills]. 'The Old Lady in Threadneedle Street.' *Household Words*, 6 July 1850, 1: 337–42.
———. 'Plate Glass.' *Household Words*, 1 February 1851, 2: 433–56.
———. 'A Plated Article.' *Household Words*, 24 April 1852, 5: 117–21.
———. 'Spitalfields.' *Household Words*, 5 April 1851, 3: 25–30.
[Dickens, Charles]. 'The Amusements of the People.' *Household Words*, 30 March 1850, 1: 13–15.

———. 'The Begging-Letter Writer.' *Household Words*, 18 May 1850, 1: 169–72.
———. 'Bill-Sticking.' *Household Words*, 22 March 1851, 2: 601–6.
———. 'A Child's Dream of a Star.' *Household Words*, 6 April 1850, 1: 25–6.
———. 'A Christmas Tree.' *Household Words*, 21 December 1850, 2: 289–95.
———. 'Epsom.' *Household Words*, 7 June 1851, 3: 241–6.
———. 'From the Raven in the Happy Family [ii].' *Household Words*, 8 June 1850, 1: 241–2.
———. 'The Ghost of Art.' *Household Words*, 20 July 1850, 1: 385–7.
———. 'Home for Homeless Women.' *Household Words*, 23 April 1853, 7: 169–75.
———. 'Lively Turtle.' *Household Words*, 26 October 1850, 2: 97–9.
———. 'Lying Awake.' *Household Words*, 30 October 1852, 6: 145–8.
———. 'New Year's Day.' *Household Words*, 1 January 1859, 19: 97–102.
———. 'A Nightly Scene in London.' *Household Words*, 26 January 1856, 13: 25–7.
———. 'On Duty with Inspector Field.' *Household Words*, 14 June 1851, 3: 265–70.
———. 'Our Commission.' *Household Words*, 11 August 1855, 12: 25–7.
———. 'Our French Watering-Place.' *Household Words*, 4 November 1854, 10: 265–70.
———. 'A Preliminary Word.' *Household Words*, 30 March 1850, 1: 1–2.
———. 'Railway Dreaming.' *Household Words*, 10 May 1856, 13: 385–58.
———. 'Some Account of an Extraordinary Traveller.' *Household Words*, 20 April 1850, 1: 73–7.
———. 'The Spirit Business.' *Household Words*, 7 May 1853, 7: 217–20.
———. 'Trading in Death.' *Household Words*, 27 November 1852, 6: 241–5.
———. 'An Unsettled Neighbourhood.' *Household Words*, 11 November 1854, 10: 289–92.
———. 'Well-Authenticated Rappings.' *Household Words*, 20 February 1858, 17: 217–20.
[Dixon, Edmund Saul]. 'Dirty Cleanliness.' *Household Words*, 24 July 1858, 18: 121–5.
———. 'Jean Raisin.' *Household Words*, 11 November 1854, 10: 307–12.
———. 'Quite Revolutionary.' *Household Words*, 16 June 1855, 11: 474–7.
[Dodd, George]. 'All About Pigs.' *Household Words*, 31 July 1852, 5: 471–4.
———. 'Cornwall's Gift to Staffordshire.' *Household Words*, 7 October 1854, 10: 187–90.
———. 'Dolls.' *Household Words*, 11 June 1853, 7: 352–6.
———. 'Done to a Jelly.' *Household Words*, 24 June 1854, 9: 438–40.
———. 'A Good Brushing.' *Household Words*, 8 July 1854, 9: 492–5.
———. 'The House That Jack Built.' *Household Words*, 19 November 1853, 8: 286–8.
———. 'Important Rubbish.' *Household Words*, 19 May 1855, 11: 376–9.
———. 'India-Rubber.' *Household Words*, 12 March 1853, 7: 29–33.
———. 'Nothing Like Leather.' *Household Words*, 17 September 1853, 8: 57–60.
———. 'Penny Wisdom.' *Household Words*, 16 October 1852, 6: 97–101.
———. 'A Pill-Box.' *Household Words*, 12 February 1853, 6: 517–21.
———. 'A Russian Stranger.' *Household Words*, 24 September 1853, 8: 91–4.
———. 'Saint Crispin.' *Household Words*, 26 March 1853, 7: 76–80.

———. 'Several Heads of Hair.' *Household Words*, 4 March 1854, 9: 61–5.
———. 'Splitting Straws.' *Household Words*, 11 March 1854, 9: 85–9.
———. 'Umbrellas.' *Household Words*, 13 November 1852, 6: 201–4.
———. 'Walking-Sticks.' *Household Words*, 11 September 1852, 5: 610–613.
———. 'Wallotty Trot.' *Household Words*, 5 February 1853, 6: 499–503.
[Fitzgerald, Percy]. 'Down among the Dutchmen.' *Household Words*, 24 October 1857, 16: 398–402.
[Gaskell, Elizabeth]. 'A Love Affair at Cranford.' *Household Words*, 3 January 1852, 4: 349–57.
———. 'Memory at Cranford.' *Household Words*, 13 March 1852, 4: 588–97.
———. 'North and South: Chapter the Tenth.' *Household Words*, 7 October 1854, 10: 181–7.
———. 'Our Society at Cranford.' *Household Words*, 13 December 1851, 4: 265–74.
———. 'Stopped Payment, at Cranford.' *Household Words*, 2 April 1853, 7: 108–15.
———. 'Visiting at Cranford.' *Household Words*, 3 April 1852, 5: 55–64.
[Hannay, James]. 'Graves and Epitaphs.' *Household Words*, 16 October 1852, 6: 105–9.
———. 'The Great Coffee Question.' *Household Words*, 12 April 1851, 3: 49–53.
[Hollingshead, John]. 'All Night on the Monument.' *Household Words*, 30 January 1858, 17: 145–8.
———. 'Buying in the Cheapest Market.' *Household Words*, 28 August 1858, 18: 256–8.
———. 'A Counterfeit Presentment.' *Household Words*, 3 July 1858, 18: 71–2.
———. 'Twenty Shillings in the Pound.' *Household Words*, 7 November 1857, 16: 444–6.
[Horne, Richard H.]. 'Ballooning.' *Household Words*, 25 October 1851, 4: 97–105.
———. 'The Cattle-Road to Ruin.' *Household Words*, 29 June 1850, 1: 325–30.
———. 'The Cow with the Iron Tail.' *Household Words*, 9 November 1850, 2: 145–51.
———. 'Dust; or Ugliness Redeemed.' *Household Words*, 13 July 1850, 1: 379–84.
———. 'The Pasha's New Boat.' *Household Words*, 22 November 1851, 4: 209–13.
———. 'The Smithfield Bull to His Cousin of Nineveh.' *Household Words*, 15 March 1851, 2: 589–90.
———. 'The Wonders of 1851.' *Household Words*, 20 July 1850, 1: 388–92.
[Hunt, Frederick Knight]. 'How to Spend a Summer Holiday.' *Household Words*, 6 July 1850, 1: 356–8.
———. 'The Modern Robbers of the Rhine.' *Household Words*, 19 October 1850, 2: 90–93.
[Jerrold, William Blanchard, and W.H. Wills]. 'The Subscription List.' *Household Words*, 28 September 1850, 2: 10–12.
[Jerrold, William Blanchard]. 'Deadly Lively.' *Household Words*, 25 March 1854, 9: 138–40.
———. 'Eyes Made to Order.' *Household Words*, 11 October 1851, 4: 64–6.
———. 'Food for the Factory.' *Household Words*, 30 November 1850, 2: 225–9.
———. 'The Iron Seamstress.' *Household Words*, 11 February 1854, 8: 575–6.
———. 'The Methusaleh Pill.' *Household Words*, 5 October 1850, 2: 36–8.
———. 'The Milky and Watery Way.' *Household Words*, 20 June 1857, 15: 593–6.

———. 'Rabbit-Skins.' *Household Words*, 15 July 1854, 9: 519–21.

———. 'Ruins with Silver Keys.' *Household Words*, 13 September 1851, 3: 592–4.

———. 'Why People Let Lodgings.' *Household Words*, 9 November 1850, 2: 167–8.

[Keene, John, and W.H.Wills]. 'A Golden Newspaper.' *Household Words*, 22 November 1851, 4: 207–8.

[Knight, Charles]. 'A Christmas Pudding.' *Household Words*, 21 December 1850, 2: 300–304.

———. 'Illustrations of Cheapness [i]: The Lucifer Match.' *Household Words*, 13 April 1850, 1: 54–7.

———. 'Illustrations of Cheapness [ii]: A Globe.' *Household Words*, 20 April 1850, 1: 84–7.

———. 'Illustrations of Cheapness [iv]: Tea.' *Household Words*, 8 June 1850, 1: 253–6.

———. 'Illustrations of Cheapness [v]: The Steel Pen.' *Household Words*, 7 September 1850, 1: 553–5.

———. 'Three May-Days in London. [iii] The May Palace (1851).' *Household Words*, 3 May 1851, 3: 121–4.

[Lang, John]. 'Wanderings in India.' *Household Words*, 30 January 1858, 17: 148–56.

———. 'Wanderings in India.' *Household Words*, 14 November 1857, 16: 457–63.

[Leigh, Percival]. 'Address from an Undertaker to the Trade (Strictly Private and Confidential).' *Household Words*, 22 June 1850, 1: 301–4.

[Lewis, John Delaware]. 'The City of Sudden Death.' *Household Words*, 8 May 1852, 5: 171–6.

———. 'Preservation in Destruction.' *Household Words*, 5 June 1852, 5: 280–284.

[Lowe, James]. 'A Manchester Warehouse.' *Household Words*, 6 May 1854, 9: 268–72.

[Lynn, Eliza]. 'Passing Faces.' *Household Words*, 14 April 1855, 11: 261–4.

[Martineau, Harriet]. 'An Account of Some Treatment of Gold and Gems.' *Household Words*, 31 January 1852, 4: 449–55.

———. 'Flower Shows in a Birmingham Hot-House.' *Household Words*, 18 October 1851, 4: 82–5.

———. 'Kendal Weavers and Weaving.' *Household Words*, 15 November 1851, 4: 183–9.

———. 'The Magic Troughs at Birmingham.' *Household Words*, 25 October 1851, 4: 113–17.

———. 'Needles.' *Household Words*, 28 February 1852, 4: 540–546.

———. 'A New Plea for a New Food.' *Household Words*, 3 May 1851, 3: 138–40.

———. 'The New School for Wives.' *Household Words*, 10 April 1852, 5: 84–9.

———. 'Rainbow Making.' *Household Words*, 14 February 1852, 4: 485–90.

———. 'Shawls.' *Household Words*, 28 August 1852, 5: 552–6.

———. 'What There Is in a Button.' *Household Words*, 17 April 1852, 5: 106–12.

———. 'The Wonders of Nails and Screws.' *Household Words*, 1 November 1851, 4: 138–42.

[Morley, Henry, and W.H. Wills]. 'Funerals in Paris.' *Household Words*, 27 November 1852, 6: 257–60.

[Morley, Henry]. 'Beef.' *Household Words*, 24 December 1853, 8: 385–8.

———. 'The Catalogue's Account of Itself.' *Household Words*, 23 August 1851, 3: 519–23.

Bibliography

———. 'Constitutional Trials.' *Household Words*, 17 July 1852, 5: 423–6.
———. 'Country News.' *Household Words*, 2 July 1853, 7: 426–30.
———. 'An Enemy's Charge.' *Household Words*, 20 October 1855, 12: 265–70.
———. 'Fencing with Humanity.' *Household Words*, 14 April 1855, 11: 241–4.
———. 'The Ghost of the Cock Lane Ghost.' *Household Words*, 20 November 1852, 6: 217–23.
———. 'The Globe in a Square.' *Household Words*, 12 July 1851, 3: 370–372.
———. 'Ground in the Mill.' *Household Words*, 22 April 1854, 9: 224–7.
———. 'A House Full of Horrors.' *Household Words*, 4 December 1852, 6: 265–70.
———. 'Justice to Chicory.' *Household Words*, 13 November 1852, 6: 208–10.
———. 'Latest Intelligence from Spirits.' *Household Words*, 30 June 1855, 11: 513–15.
———. 'Looking out of Window.' *Household Words*, 1 March 1856, 13: 166–8.
———. 'Men Made by Machinery.' *Household Words*, 31 January 1857, 15: 97–100.
———. 'Our Phantom Ship: China.' *Household Words*, 28 June 1851, 3: 325–31.
———. 'Our Phantom Ship: Negro Land.' *Household Words*, 18 January 1851, 2: 400–407.
———. 'Poison Sold Here!' *Household Words*, 9 November 1850, 2: 155–7.
———. 'Scholastic.' *Household Words*, 15 January 1853, 6: 409–13.
———. 'Silk from the Punjaub.' *Household Words*, 8 January 1853, 6: 388–90.
———. 'Starvation of an Alderman.' *Household Words*, 31 March 1855, 11: 213–16.
———. 'Use and Abuse of the Dead.' *Household Words*, 3 April 1858, 17: 361–5.
———. 'A Way to Clean Rivers.' *Household Words*, 10 July 1858, 18: 79–82.
———. 'What Is Not Clear About the Crystal Palace.' *Household Words*, 19 July 1851, 3: 400–402.
———. 'Your Very Good Health.' *Household Words*, 28 January 1854, 8: 524–6.
[Morley, Henry, and W.H. Wills]. 'Photography.' *Household Words*, 19 March 1853, 7: 54–61.
[Murray, Grenville]. 'The Roving Englishman: A Few More Hints.' *Household Words*, 25 December 1852, 6: 358–60.
———. 'The Roving Englishman: The Great Do.' *Household Words*, 19 March 1853, 7: 67–72.
[Ollier, Edmund]. 'Left Behind.' *Household Words*, 22 July 1854, 9: 543–6.
[Owen, William]. 'A German Table d'Hôte.' *Household Words*, 15 December 1855, 12: 478–80.
[Payn, James]. 'Among the Tombs.' *Household Words*, 3 April 1858, 17: 372–5.
———. 'Photographees.' *Household Words*, 10 October 1857, 16: 352–4.
———. 'Spirits over the Water.' *Household Words*, 5 June 1858, 17: 580–583.
[Prince, John Critchley]. 'A Voice from the Factory.' *Household Words*, 5 April 1851, 3: 35–6.
[Ross, Thomasina]. 'The "Mouth" of China.' *Household Words*, 5 July 1851, 3: 348–53.
[Russell, William Howard]. 'Yourself at Turin.' *Household Words*, 6 November 1852, 6: 189–92.
[Sala, George A.]. 'Arcadia.' *Household Words*, 18 June 1853, 7: 376–82.
———. 'Beef.' *Household Words*, 2 February 1856, 13: 49–52.
———. 'Cities in Plain Clothes.' *Household Words*, 17 July 1852, 5: 417–22.

———. 'Curiosities of London.' *Household Words*, 23 June 1855, 11: 495–502.
———. 'Down Whitechapel Way.' *Household Words*, 1 November 1851, 4: 126–31.
———. 'Down Whitechapel, Far Away.' *Household Words*, 13 August 1853, 7: 569–73.
———. 'Fashion.' *Household Words*, 29 October 1853, 8: 193–6.
———. 'The Foreign Invasion.' *Household Words*, 11 October 1851, 4: 60–64.
———. 'Further Travels in Search of Beef.' *Household Words*, 12 April 1856, 13: 306–12.
———. 'The Great Hotel Question. In Three Chapters. – Chapter I.' *Household Words*, 16 February 1856, 13: 97–103.
———. 'The Great Hotel Question. In Three Chapters. – Chapter the Third.' *Household Words*, 1 March 1856, 13: 148–54.
———. 'The Great Invasion.' *Household Words*, 10 April 1852, 5: 69–73.
———. 'The Great Red Book.' *Household Words*, 9 December 1854, 10: 404–8.
———. 'Houses to Let.' *Household Words*, 20 March 1852, 5: 5–11.
———. 'A Journey Due North.' *Household Words*, 6 December 1856, 14: 493–8.
———. 'The Key of the Street.' *Household Words*, 6 September 1851, 3: 565–72.
———. 'Leicester Square.' *Household Words*, 19 March 1853, 7: 63–7.
———. 'Mars a La Mode.' *Household Words*, 14 October 1854, 10: 193–6.
———. 'More Places Wanted.' *Household Words*, 15 October 1853, 8: 156–62.
———. 'Music in Paving Stones.' *Household Words*, 26 August 1854, 10: 37–43.
———. 'Old Clothes!' *Household Words*, 17 April 1852, 5: 93–8.
———. 'Our Doubles.' *Household Words*, 10 July 1852, 5: 388–91.
———. 'Perfidious Patmos.' *Household Words*, 12 March 1853, 7: 25–9.
———. 'Play.' *Household Words*, 25 November 1854, 10: 357–60.
———. 'Second-Hand Sovereigns.' *Household Words*, 13 January 1855, 10: 511–16.
———. 'The Secrets of the Gas.' *Household Words*, 4 March 1854, 9: 45–8.
———. 'Things Departed.' *Household Words*, 17 January 1852, 4: 385–408.
———. 'Travels in Cawdor Street.' *Household Words*, 21 February 1852, 4: 517–21.
———. 'Want Places.' *Household Words*, 27 August 1853, 7: 601–8.
———. 'Where Are They?' *Household Words*, 1 April 1854, 9: 152–8.
[Siddons, Joachim Heywood]. 'Christmas in India.' *Household Words*, 21 December 1850, 2: 305–6.
[Sidney, Samuel]. 'Coats and Trousers.' *Household Words*, 3 November 1855, 12: 321–5.
———. 'From Paris to Chelmsford.' *Household Words*, 20 September 1856, 14: 217–23.
———. 'Indian Railroads and British Commerce.' *Household Words*, 15 March 1851, 2: 590–595.
———. 'A Ladies' Warehouse.' *Household Words*, 27 October 1855, 12: 301–5.
[Smith, Albert Richard]. 'Nearly Lost on the Alps.' *Household Words*, 27 February 1858, 17: 241–4.
[Strange, Charles, and W.H. Wills]. 'Death in the Teapot.' *Household Words*, 14 December 1850, 2: 277.
'Summer in Rome.' *Household Words*, 14 May 1853, 7: 257–61.
[Thomas, William Moy]. 'Covent Garden Market.' *Household Words*, 30 July 1853, 7: 505–11.

[White, Rev. James]. 'Long Life under Difficulties.' *Household Words*, 4 April 1857, 15: 325–8.
———. 'Your Life or Your Likeness.' *Household Words*, 25 July 1857, 16: 73–5.
[Wills, W.H., and Christopher Hill]. 'Railway Waifs and Strays.' *Household Words*, 28 February 1850, 2: 319–22.
[Wills, W.H., Grenville Murray, and Thomas Walker]. 'German Advertisements.' *Household Words*, 5 October 1850, 2: 33–5.
[Wills, W.H., and George A. Sala]. 'Fairyland in 'Fifty-Four.' *Household Words*, 3 December 1853, 8: 313–17.
[Wills, W.H., and Charles Strange]. 'Death in the Bread-Basket.' *Household Words*, 28 December 1850, 2: 323.
[Wills, W.H.]. 'The Appetite for News.' *Household Words*, 1 June 1850, 1: 238–40.
———. 'Death in the Sugar Plum.' *Household Words*, 25 January 1851, 2: 426–7.
———. 'The Private History of the Palace of Glass.' *Household Words*, 18 January 1851, 2: 385–91.
[Wood]. 'Departed Beggars.' *Household Words*, 29 May 1852, 5: 244–6.
[Wreford, Henry G.]. 'Vesuvius in Eruption.' *Household Words*, 9 June 1855, 11: 435–9.
[Wynter, Andrew]. 'Saint George and the Dragon.' *Household Words*, 10 April 1852, 5: 77–80.

General Bibliography

A.W. 'Needlemaking.' *Once a Week*, 19 November 1859, 1: 424–5.
Addison, Joseph, Richard Steele and others. *The Spectator* ed. Gregory Smith. 1712; 1714. Everyman's Library. 4 vols. London: Dent, 1945.
'Advertisements of the Times.' *Chambers's Edinburgh Journal* 3 (1845): 199–202.
'Advertising Considered as an Art.' *Chambers's Edinburgh Journal*, 28 December 1844, 2: 401–3.
'The Age of Veneer: The Science of Puffing.' *Fraser's Magazine*, January 1852, 45: 87–93.
Altick, Richard D. *The English Common Reader: A Social History of the Mass Reading Public, 1800–1900*. Second ed. Columbus: Ohio State University Press, 1998.
———. *Punch: The Lively Youth of a British Institution 1841–1851*. Columbus: Ohio State University Press, 1997.
———. *The Shows of London*. Cambridge, Mass.: Harvard University Press, 1978.
Anderson, Amanda. *Tainted Souls and Painted Faces: The Rhetoric of Fallenness in Victorian Culture*. Ithaca: Cornell University Press, 1993.
Anderson, Benedict. *Imagined Communities: Reflections on the Origin and Spread of Nationalism*. Revised ed. London: Verso, 1991.
Appadurai, Arjun. 'Introduction: Commodities and the Politics of Value.' In *The Social Life of Things: Commodities in Cultural Perspective*, edited by Arjun Appadurai, 3–63. New York: Cambridge University Press, 1986.
Arnold, Matthew. *Culture and Anarchy, with Friendship's Garland and Some Literary Essays*, ed. R.H. Super. Complete Prose Works of Matthew Arnold. Reprint edn. Vol. 5. Ann Arbor: University of Michigan Press, 1965.

Auerbach, Jeffrey. *The Great Exhibition of 1851: A Nation on Display*. New Haven: Yale University Press, 1999.

[Bagehot, Walter]. 'Charles Dickens.' In *Dickens: The Critical Heritage*, edited by Philip Collins, 390–401. London: Routledge, 1971.

———. 'The First Edinburgh Reviewers.' *National Review*, 1 (October 1855): 253–84.

Baudrillard, Jean. *The Consumer Society: Myths and Structures*. Translated by Chris Turner. Theory, Culture and Society. London: Sage, 1998.

Beetham, Margaret. 'Towards a Theory of the Periodical as a Publishing Genre.' In *Investigating Victorian Journalism*, edited by Laurel Brake, Aled Jones and Lionel Madden, 19–32. Basingstoke: Macmillan, 1990.

Benjamin, Walter. *The Arcades Project*. Translated by Howard Eiland and Kevin McLaughlin. Cambridge, Mass.: Belknap Press of Harvard University Press, 1999.

———. *Charles Baudelaire: A Lyric Poet in the Era of High Capitalism*. Translated by Harry Zohn. London: Verso, 1983.

———. 'The Work of Art in the Age of Mechanical Reproduction.' In *Illuminations*, edited by Hannah Arendt, translated by Harry Zohn, 217–51. New York: Schocken Books, 1968.

Bennett, Tony. *The Birth of the Museum: History, Theory, Politics*. London: Routledge, 1995.

Bernstein, Carol L. *The Celebration of Scandal: Toward the Sublime in Victorian Urban Fiction*. University Park, Pennsylvania: Pennsylvania State University Press, 1991.

Black, Jeremy. *The English Press in the Eighteenth Century*. London: Croom Helm, 1987.

Bowlby, Rachel. *Just Looking: Consumer Culture in Dreiser, Gissing and Zola*. New York: Methuen, 1985.

Brand, Dana. *The Spectator and the City in Nineteenth-Century American Literature*. New York: Cambridge University Press, 1991.

Breward, Christopher. *Fashioning London: Clothing and the Modern Metropolis*. Oxford: Berg, 2004.

Briggs, Asa. *Victorian Things*. London: Batsford, 1988.

Brown, Lucy. *Victorian News and Newspapers*. Oxford: Clarendon Press, 1985.

Buck-Morss, Susan. *The Dialectics of Seeing: Walter Benjamin and the Arcades Project*. Studies in Contemporary German Social Thought. Cambridge, Mass.: MIT Press, 1989.

———. 'The Flaneur, the Sandwichman and the Whore: The Politics of Loitering.' *New German Critique* 39 (1986): 99–144.

[Burn, James Dawson]. *The Language of the Walls: And a Voice from the Shop Windows. Or, the Mirror of Commercial Roguery*. Manchester: Abel Heywood, 1855.

Burnett, John. *Plenty and Want: A Social History of Food in England from 1815 to the Present Day*. Third ed. London: Routledge, 1989.

Butwin, Joseph. '*Hard Times*: The News and the Novel.' *Nineteenth-Century Fiction* 32 (1977): 166–87.

Buzard, James. *The Beaten Track: European Tourism, Literature, and the Ways to 'Culture' 1800–1918*. Oxford: Clarendon Press, 1993.

Campbell, Kate. 'Journalistic Discourses and Constructions of Modern Knowledge.' In *Nineteenth-Century Media and the Construction of Identities*, edited by Laurel Brake, Bill Bell, and David Finkelstein, 40–53. Houndmills, Basingstoke: Palgrave, 2000.

Carey, John. *The Violent Effigy: A Study of Dickens's Imagination*. London: Faber, 1979.

Carlyle, Thomas. *Past and Present* ed. Ernest Rhys. 1843. Everyman's Library. London: Dent, 1912.

———. *Sartor Resartus* ed. Kerry McSweeney and Peter Sabor. 1833–34. World's Classics. Oxford: Oxford University Press, 1987.

Cavallaro, Dani, and Alexandra Warwick. *Fashioning the Frame: Boundaries, Dress and Body*. Dress, Body, Culture. Oxford: Berg, 1998.

Clemm, Sabine. '"Amidst the Heterogeneous Masses": Charles Dickens's *Household Words* and the Great Exhibition of 1851.' *Nineteenth-Century Contexts* 27 (2005): 207–30.

Cohen, Erik. 'Authenticity and Commoditization in Tourism.' *Annals of Tourism Research* 15 (1988): 371–86.

Collins, Philip, ed. *Dickens: The Critical Heritage*. London: Routledge, 1971.

Conrad, Peter. *The Victorian Treasure-House*. London: Collins, 1978.

Cowling, Mary. *The Artist as Anthropologist: The Representation of Type and Character in Victorian Art*. Cambridge: Cambridge University Press, 1989.

Curtis, Gerard. *Visual Words: Art and the Material Book in Victorian England*. Aldershot: Ashgate, 2002.

Darwin, Bernard. T*he Dickens Advertiser: A Collection of the Advertisements in the Original Parts of the Novels by Charles Dickens*. New York: Haskell House, 1930.

David, Deirdre. 'Imperial Chintz: Domesticity and Empire.' *Victorian Literature and Culture* 27 (1999): 569–77.

Davis, Dorothy. *A History of Shopping*. London: Routledge and Kegan Paul, 1966.

Debord, Guy. *The Society of the Spectacle*. New York: Zone Books, 1994.

Dickens, Charles. *Great Expectations* ed. Margaret Cardwell. 1860. World's Classics. Oxford: Oxford University Press, 1994.

———. *Little Dorrit* ed. Harvey Peter Sucksmith. 1855–57. World's Classics. Oxford: Oxford University Press, 1982.

———. 'Meditations in Monmouth Street.' In *Sketches by Boz and Other Early Papers 1833–39*, edited by Michael Slater. Dent Uniform Edition of Dickens' Journalism. 76–82. London: Dent, 1994.

———. *Nicholas Nickleby*. ed. Paul Schlicke. 1838–39. World's Classics. Oxford: Oxford University Press, 1990.

———, *The Pickwick Papers* ed. James Kinsley. 1836–37. World's Classics. Oxford: Oxford University Press, 1988.

———. 'To Miss Coutts.' In *Letters from Charles Dickens to Angela Burdett-Coutts, 1841–1865*, edited by Edgar Johnson, 106. London: J. Cape, 1953.

———. *'The Uncommercial Traveller' and Other Papers* ed. Michael Slater and John Drew. Dent Uniform Edition of Dickens' Journalism. London: Dent, 2000.

Dodd, George. *Days at the Factories; or the Manufacturing Industry of Great Britain Described, and Illustrated by Numerous Engravings of Machines and Processes*. 1843. Wakefield: EP Publishing, 1975.

Dolin, Tim. '*Cranford* and the Victorian Collection.' *Victorian Studies* 36 (1993): 179–206.

Drew, John M.L. *Dickens the Journalist*. Houndmills, Basingstoke: Palgrave Macmillan, 2003.

Edwards, P.D. *Dickens's 'Young Men': George Augustus Sala, Edmund Yates and the World of Victorian Journalism. The Nineteenth Century*. Aldershot: Ashgate, 1997.

'The English Thugs.' *Chamber's Edinburgh Journal* 23 (1855): 273–6.

Erickson, Lee. *The Economy of Literary Form: English Literature and the Industrialization of Publishing, 1800–1850*. Baltimore: Johns Hopkins University Press, 1996.

Farina, Jonathan V. 'Characterizing the Factory System: Factory Subjectivity in *Household Words*.' *Victorian Literature and Culture* 35 (2007): 41–56.

Fielding, K.J., and Anne Smith. '*Hard Times* and the Factory Controversy.' In *Dickens Centennial Essays*, edited by Ada Nisbet and Blake Nevius, 22–45. Berkeley: University of California Press, 1971.

Finkelstein, David, and Douglas M. Peers. '"A Great System of Circulation": Introducing India into the Nineteenth-Century Media.' In *Negotiating India in the Nineteenth-Century Media*, edited by David Finkelstein and Douglas M. Peers, 1–22. Houndmills, Basingstoke: Macmillan, 2000.

Fitzgerald, Percy. *Memories of Charles Dickens*. Bristol: J.W. Arrowsmith, 1913.

Fitzsimons, Raymund. *The Baron of Piccadilly: The Travels and Entertainments of Albert Smith 1816–1860*. London: Geoffrey Bles, 1967.

Flint, Christopher. 'Speaking Objects: The Circulation of Stories in Eighteenth-Century Prose Fiction.' *PMLA* 113 (1998): 212–26.

Forster, John. *The Life of Charles Dickens* ed. A.J. Hoppé. 1872–74. Everyman's Library. 2 vols. London: Dent, 1966.

Foucault, Michel. 'Different Spaces.' In *Aesthetics, Method, and Epistemology*, edited by James D. Faubion, translated by Robert Hurley and others. Essential Works of Foucault 1954–1984. Vol. 2. 175–85. London: Penguin, 1998.

Fraser, Hilary, and Daniel Brown. *English Prose of the Nineteenth Century*. London: Longman, 1997.

Freedgood, Elaine, ed. *Factory Production in Nineteenth-Century Britain*. New York: Oxford University Press, 2003.

———. '"Fine Fingers": Victorian Handmade Lace and Utopian Consumption.' *Victorian Studies* 45 (2003): 625–47.

———. *The Ideas in Things: Fugitive Meaning in the Victorian Novel*. Chicago: University of Chicago Press, 2006.

———. *Victorian Writing about Risk: Imagining a Safe England in a Dangerous World*. Cambridge Studies in Nineteenth-Century Literature and Culture. Cambridge: Cambridge University Press, 2000.

Freud, Sigmund. 'Instincts and Their Vicissitudes.' In *A General Selection from the Works of Sigmund Freud*, edited by John Rickman, 77–9. New York: Doubleday Anchor, 1957.

Friedberg, Anne. *Window Shopping: Cinema and the Postmodern*. Berkeley: University of California Press, 1993.

Fromer, Julie. '"A Typically English Brew": Tea Drinking, Tourism, and Imperialism in Victorian England.' In *Nineteenth-Century Geographies: The Transformation of Space from the Victorian Age to the American Century*, edited by Helena Michie and Ronald R. Thomas, 99–108. New Brunswick: Rutgers University Press, 2003.

Frow, John. 'A Pebble, a Camera, a Man Who Turns into a Telegraph Pole.' *Critical Inquiry* 28/1, 'Things' (2001): 270–85.

———. *Time and Commodity Culture: Essays in Cultural Theory and Postmodernity*. Oxford: Clarendon Press, 1997.

———. 'Tourism and the Semiotics of Nostalgia.' *October* 57 (1991): 123–51.

'A Funeral after Sir John Moore's (Furnished by an Undertaker).' *Punch* 18 (January–June 1850): 4.

Gagnier, Regenia. *The Insatiability of Human Wants: Economics and Aesthetics in Market Society*. Chicago: University of Chicago Press, 2000.

Garlick, Harry. 'The Staging of Death: Iconography and the State Funeral of the Duke of Wellington.' *Australian Journal of Art* 9 (1992): 59–77.

Ghent, Dorothy Van. *The English Novel: Form and Function*. New York: Harper and Row, 1961.

Gilloch, Graeme. *Myth and Metropolis: Walter Benjamin and the City*. London: Polity Press, 1996.

Goody, Jack. *Cooking, Cuisine and Class: A Study in Comparative Sociology*. Themes in the Social Sciences. Cambridge: Cambridge University Press, 1982.

Greenhalgh, Paul. *Ephemeral Vistas: The Expositions Universelles, Great Exhibitions and World's Fairs, 1851–1939*. Manchester: Manchester University Press, 1988.

Greenwood, James. *The Seven Curses of London*. 1869. Oxford: Blackwell, 1981.

Gregson, Nicky, and Louise Crewe. *Second-Hand Cultures*. Materializing Culture. Oxford: Berg, 2003.

Hack, Daniel. *The Material Interests of the Victorian Novel*. Victorian Literature and Culture Series. Charlottesville: University of Virginia Press, 2005.

Hamilton, Kristie. *America's Sketchbook: The Cultural Life of a Nineteenth-Century Literary Genre*. Athens: Ohio University Press, 1998.

Hansen, Peter H. 'Albert Smith, the Alpine Club, and the Invention of Mountaineering in Mid-Victorian Britain.' *Journal of British Studies* 34 (1995): 300–324.

[Hassall, A.H.]. 'Adulteration, and Its Remedy.' *Cornhill Magazine* 2 (1860): 86–96.

Hemstedt, Geoffrey. 'Dickens's Later Journalism.' In *Journalism, Literature and Modernity*, edited by Kate Campbell, 38–53. Edinburgh: Edinburgh University Press, 2000.

———. 'Inventing Social Identity: *Sketches by Boz*.' In *Victorian Identities: Social and Cultural Formations in Nineteenth-Century Literature*, edited by Ruth Robbins and Julian Wolfreys, 215–29. London: Macmillan, 1996.

Hobhouse, Hermione. *A History of Regent Street*. London: Macdonald and Jane's, 1975.

Hollingshead, John. *My Lifetime*. 2nd ed. 2 vols. London: Sampson Low, Marston and Co., 1895.

———. *Under Bow Bells: A City Book for All Readers*. London: Groombridge and Sons, 1860.

Hollington, Michael. 'Dickens the Flâneur.' *Dickensian* 77 (1981): 71–87.

———. 'Dickens, *Household Words*, and the Paris Boulevards (Part One).' *Dickens Quarterly* 14 (1997): 154–64.

———. 'Dickens, *Household Words*, and the Paris Boulevards (Part Two).' *Dickens Quarterly* 14 (1997): 199–212.

House, Madeline, Graham Storey, and Kathleen Tillotson, eds. *The Letters of Charles Dickens*. 12 vols. Oxford: Clarendon Press, 1965–2002.

Huett, Lorna. 'Among the Unknown Public: *Household Words, All the Year Round* and the Mass-Market Weekly Periodical in the Mid-Nineteenth Century.' *Victorian Periodicals Review* 38 (2005): 61–82.

———. 'Commodity and Collectivity: *Cranford* in the Context of *Household Words*.' *Gaskell Society Journal* 17 (2003): 34–49.

Hyde, Ralph. *Panoramania: The Art and Entertainment of the 'All-Embracing View'*. London: Trefoil, 1988.

'Industrial History of a Straw-Bonnet.' *Chambers's Journal of Popular Literature, Science and Arts*, 26 May 1855, 3: 327–8.

James, Henry. 'The Art of Fiction.' In *The House of Fiction*, edited by Leon Edel, 23–45. London: Rupert Hart-Davis, 1957.

Jerrold, Douglas. *The Story of a Feather*. London: Bradbury, Evans and Co., 1867.

'The Jolly Undertakers.' *Punch* 17 (July-December 1849): 254.

'A Journey Round the Globe.' *Punch* 22 (July-December 1851): 4–5.

Kappel, Andrew J. 'The Gurney Photograph Controversy.' *Dickensian* 74 (1978): 167–72.

Ketabgian, Tamara. 'The Human Prosthesis: Workers and Machines in the Victorian Industrial Scene.' *Critical Matrix* 11 (1997): 4–32.

King, Andrew. *The London Journal 1845–1883: Periodicals, Production and Gender*. The Nineteenth Century. Aldershot: Ashgate, 2004.

Knight, Charles. *London*. London: Henry G. Bohn, 1851.

Kriegel, Lara. 'Narrating the Subcontinent in 1851: India at the Crystal Palace.' In *The Great Exhibition of 1851: New Interdisciplinary Essays*, edited by Louise Purbrick, 146–78. Manchester: Manchester University Press, 2001.

———. 'The Pudding and the Palace: Labour, Print Culture and Imperial Britain in 1851.' In *After the Imperial Turn: Thinking with and through the Nation*, edited by Antoinette Burton, 230–45. Durham, North Carolina, 2003.

Laqueur, Thomas. 'Bodies, Death, and Pauper Funerals.' *Representations* 1 (1983): 109–31.

Lehmann, R.C., ed. *Charles Dickens as Editor, Being Letters Written by Him to William Henry Wills His Sub-Editor*. New York: Haskell House, 1972.

Levell, Nicky. 'Reproducing India: International Exhibitions and Victorian Tourism.' In *Souvenirs: The Material Culture of Tourism*, edited by Michael Hitchcock and Ken Teague, 36–51. Aldershot: Ashgate, 2000.

Lindner, Christoph. *Fictions of Commodity Culture: From the Victorian to the Postmodern*. Aldershot: Ashgate, 2003.

Logan, Thad. *The Victorian Parlour: A Cultural Study*. Cambridge: Cambridge University Press, 2001.

Lohrli, Anne. *'Household Words' A Weekly Journal 1850–1859 Conducted by Charles Dickens, Table of Contents, List of Contributors and Their Contributions Based on The 'Household Words' Office Book*. Toronto: University of Toronto Press, 1973.

Long, William F. 'Dickens and the Adulteration of Food.' *Dickensian* 84 (1988): 160–70.

MacCannell, Dean. *The Tourist: A New Theory of the Leisure Class*. Revised ed. New York: Schocken Books, 1989.

Maidment, Brian. 'Entrepreneurship and the Artisans: John Cassell, the Great Exhibition and the Periodical Idea.' In *The Great Exhibition of 1851: New Interdisciplinary Essays*, edited by Louise Purbrick, 79–113. Manchester: Manchester University Press, 2001.

———. 'Review of Peter W. Sinnema, Dynamics of the Pictured Page – Representing the Nation in the "Illustrated London News."' *Journal of Victorian Culture* 5 (2000): 164–9.

Mandler, Peter. '"The Wand of Fancy": The Historical Imagination of the Victorian Tourist.' In *Material Memories*, edited by Marius Kwint, Christopher Breward, and Jeremy Aynsley. 125–41. Oxford: Berg, 1999.

Martineau, Harriet. *Harriet Martineau's Autobiography*. 1877. 2 vols. Farnborough: Gregg, 1969.

Marx, Karl. *Capital: An Abridged Edition* ed. David McLellan. 1867. World's Classics. Oxford: Oxford University Press, 1995.

Maynard, Margaret. *Fashioned from Penury: Dress as Cultural Practice in Colonial Australia*. Cambridge: Cambridge University Press, 1994.

McClintock, Ann. *Imperial Leather: Race, Gender and Sexuality in the Colonial Context*. London: Routledge, 1995.

McKendrick, Neil. 'The Consumer Revolution of Eighteenth-Century England.' In *The Birth of a Consumer Society: The Commercialization of Eighteenth-Century England*, edited by Neil McKendrick, John Brewer, and J.H. Plumb, 9–33. London: Europa, 1982.

McKenzie, Judy. 'An Edition of the Letters of George Augustus Sala to Edmund Yates, in the Edmund Yates Papers, University of Queensland.' Diss. University of Queensland, 1994.

Miller, Andrew. *Novels Behind Glass: Commodity Culture and Victorian Narrative*. Cambridge: Cambridge University Press, 1995.

Miller, J. Hillis. 'The Fiction of Realism: *Sketches by Boz*, *Oliver Twist*, and Cruikshank's Illustrations.' In *Dickens Centennial Essays*, edited by Ada Nisbet and Blake Nevius, 85–153. Berkeley: University of California Press, 1971.

Mitford, Mary Russell. *Country Stories*, 1896. Short Story Index Reprint Series. Freeport, NY: Books for Libraries Press, 1970.

Moore, Grace. *Dickens and Empire: Discourses of Calss, Race and Colonialism in the Works of Charles Dickens*. The Nineteenth Century. Aldershot: Ashgate, 2004.

Morgan, Marjorie. *National Identities and Travel in Victorian Britain*, Studies in Modern History. Houndmills, Basingstoke: Palgrave, 2001.

'Mr Sala on Life in London.' *Saturday Review*, 3 December 1859, 676–8.

Murray, John Fisher. *The World of London*. 2 vols. London: Blackwood, 1843.
Nead, Lynda. *Myths of Sexuality: Representations of Women in Victorian Britain*. Oxford: Blackwell, 1988.
———. *Victorian Babylon: People, Streets and Images in Nineteenth-Century London*. New Haven: Yale University Press, 2000.
'Needles.' *Chambers's Journal of Popular Literature, Science and Arts*, 17 May 1856, 25: 316–18.
Nord, Deborah Epstein. *Walking the Victorian Streets: Women, Representation, and the City*. Ithaca: Cornell University Press, 1995.
O'Connor, Erin. *Raw Material: Producing Pathology in Victorian Culture*. Body, Commodity, Text. Durham: Duke University Press, 2000.
Oost, Regina B. '"More Like Than Life": Painting, Photography, and Dickens's *Bleak House*.' In *Dickens Studies Annual*, edited by Stanley Friedman, Edward Guiliano, and Michael Timko, 141–58. New York: AMS Press, 2001.
'Panoramas.' *Chambers's Journal of Popular Literature, Science and Arts*, 21 January 1860, 13: 33–5.
Pearsall, Cornelia D.J. 'Burying the Duke: Victorian Mourning and the Funeral of the Duke of Wellington.' *Victorian Literature and Culture* 27 (1999): 365–93.
Pemble, John. *The Mediterranean Passion: Victorians and Edwardians in the South*. Oxford: Clarendon Press, 1987.
'"Performers" after a Respectable Funeral.' *Punch* 18 (January–June 1850): 5.
Perrot, Philippe. *Fashioning the Bourgeoisie: A History of Clothing in the Nineteenth Century*. Translated by Richard Bienvenu. Princeton: Princeton University Press, 1994.
Peters, Laura. '"Double-Dyed Traitors and Infernal Villains": *Illustrated London News*, *Household Words*, Charles Dickens and the Indian Rebellion.' In *Negotiating India in the Nineteenth-Century Media*, edited by David Finkelstein and Douglas M. Peers, 110–134. Houndmills, Basingstoke: Macmillan, 2000.
Pettitt, Clare. *Patent Inventions: Intellectual Property and the Victorian Novel*. Oxford: Oxford University Press, 2004.
'The Philosophy of Advertising.' *Once a Week*, 1 August 1863, 9: 163–5.
Plunkett, John. 'Celebrity and Community: The Poetics of the *Carte-De-Visite*.' *Journal of Victorian Culture* 8 (2003): 55–79.
Pointon, Marcia. 'Materializing Mourning: Hair, Jewellery and the Body.' In *Material Memories*, edited by Marius Kwint, Christopher Breward, and Jeremy Aynsley, 39–57. Oxford: Berg, 1999.
Porter, Roy. *Health for Sale: Quackery in England 1660–1850*. Manchester: Manchester University Press, 1989.
———. *Quacks: Fakers and Charlatans in English Medicine*. Stroud, Gloucestershire: Tempus, 2000.
Purbrick, Louise. 'Introduction.' In *The Great Exhibition of 1851: New Interdisciplinary Essays*, edited by Louise Purbrick, 1–25. Manchester: Manchester University Press, 2001.
Pykett, Lyn. *Charles Dickens*, Critical Issues. Houndmills, Basingstoke: Palgrave, 2002.
Radin, Margaret Jane. *Contested Commodities*. Cambridge, Mass.: Harvard University Press, 1996.

Reidy, Denis V. 'Panizzi, Gladstone, Garibaldi and the Neapolitan Prisoners.' *eBLJ* Article 6 (2005): 1–15.

Rendell, Jane. '"Industrious Females" and "Professional Beauties" or Fine Articles for Sale in the Burlington Arcade.' In *Strangely Familiar: Narratives of Architecture in the City*, edited by Joe Kerr Iain Borden, Alicia Pivaro, and Jane Rendell, 32–5. London: Routledge, 1996.

Richards, Thomas. *The Commodity Culture of Victorian England: Advertising and Spectacle 1851–1914*. Stanford: Stanford University Press, 1990.

Richardson, Ruth. *Death, Dissection and the Destitute*. London: Penguin, 1988.

Roof, Judith. 'Display Cases.' In *Victorian Afterlife: Postmodern Culture Rewrites the Nineteenth Century*, edited by John Kucich and Dianne F. Sadoff, 101–21. Minneapolis: University of Minnesota Press, 2000.

Roston, Murray. *Victorian Contexts: Literature and the Visual Arts*. New York: New York University Press, 1996.

Said, Edward W. *Culture and Imperialism*. London: Chatto and Windus, 1993.

Sala, G.A. 'Charles Dickens.' In *Lives of Victorian Literary Figures I: Charles Dickens*, edited by Corinna Russell, 125–58. London: Pickering and Chatto, 2003.

Sala, George Augustus. *Things I Have Seen and People I Have Known*. 2 vols. London: Cassell and Company, 1894.

Scarry, Elaine. *The Body in Pain: The Making and Unmaking of the World*. New York: Oxford University Press, 1985.

Schivelbusch, Wolfgang. *Disenchanted Night: The Industrialisation of Light in the Nineteenth Century*. Oxford: Berg, 1988.

Schwartz, Vanessa. *Spectacular Realities: Early Mass Culture in Fin-De-Siecle Paris*. Berkeley: University of California Press, 1998.

Searle, G.R. *Morality and the Market in Victorian Britain*. New York: Oxford University Press, 1998.

Seltzer, Mark. *Bodies and Machines*. New York: Routledge, 1992.

Sennett, Richard. *The Fall of Public Man*. Cambridge: Cambridge University Press, 1977.

Sheridan, Richard Brinsley. 'The Critic; or, a Tragedy Rehearsed.' In *Plays*, edited by Ernest Rhys, 308–53. London: Dent, 1906.

'Shop-Windows.' *Chambers's Journal of Popular Literature, Science and Arts*, 11 April 1857, 27: 225–7.

'Shops, Shopkeepers, Shopmen, and Shop Morality.' *Chambers's Edinburgh Journal*, 14 September 1850, 14: 161–3.

'Shops, Shopkeepers, Shopmen, and Shop Morality: Concluding Article.' *Chambers's Edinburgh Journal* 14 (1850): 244–6.

'Shops, Shopkeepers, Shopmen, and Shop Morality: Second Article.' *Chambers's Edinburgh Journal* 14 (1850): 216–18.

Simmel, George. 'The Philosophy of Fashion.' In *Simmel on Culture: Selected Writings*, edited by David Frisby and Mike Featherstone, 187–206. London: Sage, 1997.

Sinnema, Peter. *Dynamics of the Pictured Page: Representing the Nation in the 'Illustrated London News'*. The Nineteenth Century. Aldershot: Ashgate, 1998.

Slater, Michael. *Douglas Jerrold 1803–1857*. London: Duckworth, 2002.
Smith, Charles Manby. *Curiosities of London Life*. London, 1853.
Smith, Graham. *Charles Dickens: A Literary Life*. Houndmills: Macmillan, 1996.
'The Song of the Undertaker.' *Punch* 18 (January–June 1850): 215.
'Speculative Sympathy.' *Punch* 23 (July–December 1852): 167.
Stallybrass, Peter. 'Marx's Coat.' In *Border Fetishisms: Material Objects in Unstable Spaces*, edited by Patricia Spyer, 183–207. London: Routledge, 1998.
———. 'Worn Worlds: Clothes, Mourning, and the Life of Things.' *Yale Review* 81 (1993): 35–50.
'The Starved-out Undertakers.' *Punch* 18 (January-June 1850): 185.
Steinlight, Emily. '"Anti-Bleak House": Advertising and the Victorian Novel.' *Narrative* 14 (2006): 132–62.
Steward, Jill. '"How and Where to Go": The Role of Travel Journalism in Britain and the Evolution of Foreign Tourism, 1840–1914.' In *Histories of Tourism: Representation, Identity and Conflict*, edited by John K. Walton, 39–54. Clevedon: Channel View Publications, 2005.
Stewart, Susan. *On Longing: Narratives of the Miniature, the Gigantic, the Souvenir, the Collection*. Durham: Duke University Press, 1993.
———. 'Prologue: From the Museum of Touch.' In *Material Memories*, edited by Marius Kwint, Christopher Breward and Jeremy Aynsley, 17–36. Oxford: Berg, 1999.
Stone, Harry, ed. *Charles Dickens' Uncollected Writings from Household Words, 1850–59*. 2 vols. Bloomington: Indiana University Press, 1968.
Straus, Ralph. *Sala: The Portrait of an Eminent Victorian*. London: Constable, 1942.
Sussman, Herbert. 'Machine Dreams: The Culture of Technology.' *Victorian Literature and Culture* 28 (2000): 197–204.
Sussman, Herbert, and Gerhard Joseph. 'Prefiguring the Posthuman: Dickens and Prosthesis.' *Victorian Literature and Culture* 32 (2004): 617–28.
Trilling, Lionel. *Sincerity and Authenticity*. London: Oxford University Press, 1972.
Tweedale, Geoffrey. '"Days at the Factories": A Tour of Victorian Industry with *The Penny Magazine*.' *Technology and Culture* 29 (1988): 888–903.
Urry, John. *The Tourist Gaze: Leisure and Travel in Contemporary Societies*. Theory, Culture and Society. London: Sage, 1990.
'Vulcanised Caoutchouc.' *Chambers's Edinburgh Journal*, 3 July 1847, 8: 5–6.
Walton, John K. 'Introduction.' In *Histories of Tourism: Representation, Identity and Conflict*, edited by John K. Walton, 1–18. Clevedon: Channel View, 2005.
Washbrook, David. 'From Comparative Sociology to Global History: Britain and India in the Pre-History of Modernity.' *Journal of the Economic and Social History of the Orient* 40 (1997): 410–43.
Wechsler, Judith. *A Human Comedy: Physiognomy and Caricature in 19th Century Paris*. London: Thames and Hudson, 1982.
Whitlock, Tammy C. *Crime, Gender and Consumer Culture in Nineteenth-Century England*. The History of Retailing and Consumption. Aldershot: Ashgate, 2005.
Wicke, Jennifer. *Advertising Fictions: Literature, Advertisement and Social Reading*. New York: Columbia University Press, 1988.

Williamson, Judith. *Decoding Advertisements: Ideology and Meaning in Advertising.* London: Marion Boyars, 1978.

Wilson, Elizabeth. *Adorned in Dreams: Fashion and Modernity.* Revised ed. London: Tauris, 2003.

Woolf, Virginia, *Orlando* ed. Rachel Bowlby. 1928. World's Classics. Oxford: Oxford University Press, 1992.

Wynne, Deborah. 'Responses to the 1851 Exhibition in *Household Words.*' *Dickensian* 97 (2001): 228–34.

Wynter, Andrew. *Our Social Bees: Pictures of Town and Country Life.* London: David Bogue, 1866.

Young, Paul. 'Economy, Empire, Extermination: The Christmas Pudding, the Crystal Palace and the Narrative of Capitalist Progress.' *Literature and History* 14 (2005): 14–30.

Index

Addison, Joseph, 7–9, 66
advertisements, 19, 24–5, 50, 20n8; see also *Household Words*, advertisement in; Puff
   advertorials, 45
   educational, 28–9
   housing, 23, 28, 30–32
   newspaper, 19, 25–8, 30–34, 50
   paparazzi and celebrity images, 34–7
   personal, 26–33
advertising, 24–5, 28–31
   and commodity culture, 128
   history of, 19, 30
   puffery, 24, 29–30, 131
   and social life of goods, 19, 25, 156
alienation, factory workers, 93
   urban life and, 26–7, 40–41, 68
All the Year Round, 6, 19, 85
Altick, Richard, 13n67, 58n106, 60–61, 70n39, 72n51, 127
America, 46, 72, 90, 116–17
Analytical Sanitary Commission, 47–8
Anatomy Act, 136–40
Anderson, Benedict, 1, 27
animation, 8–9, 16
animism, 3–4
anonymity, 26–7
anthropomorphism, 87n27, 96, 104, 107, 109, 156
antiques, 42–4; see also art
anxiety of consumer class, 40–41, 46, 48–50, 54, 93, 143
   Household Words and, 64
Appadurai, Arjun, 5–6, 114, 116
arcades, 76–8
Arnold, Matthew, 13, 40
art, 42, 72–3, 79, 97
   shamming of, 42–4
artificial eyes, 97
'Ascent of Mont Blanc'(multi-media show) (Smith), 58–61, 59, 59n114
Athenaeum, 85, 85n14

Auerbach, Jeffrey, 103n11, 119
Australia, 26, 128, 149
authenticity, 39, 40–44, 43n19, 53, 59, 64
autobiography, 26, 104

Bagehot, Walter, 9, 12, 20
ballooning, 70–72
bargain and bargaining, 40, 53, 114
bargain hunter, 52–3
Baudrillard, Jean, 31, 32
bazaars, 75, 113–14
begging, 44
begging letters, 45
Benjamin, Walter, 27, 77, 151n53, 156
   Arcades Project, The, 10, 65, 68, 70, 96, 105, 144
   Charles Baudelaire, 9–10, 70, 146n26
   'Work of Art in the Age of Mechanical Reproduction, The,' 42, 43
biography, 13, 31–3, 116, 154–5; see also *Household Words*, process articles
bird's-eye view, 70–73
Blanchard, Sidney Laman, contributor to *Household Words*, 13–15
Bleak House (Dickens), 20, 20n82, 34n82, 50, 126
bodies, commerce in, 134, 136–40
bodysnatching, 126, 134, 137
book trade, 13–14
boots, 22–3, 131, 141, 151
boundaries, 90–92, 143
Brand, Dana, 8–9
branding and brand names, 21–2, 23
broadcloth, 149–50
Brown, Daniel, 7, 9
Buck-Morss, Susan, 65, 65n3, 77n75, 144, 151n53
Burn, James Dawson, 50
Burnett, John, 47
Burns, Robert, 131–2
butcher shops, 47, 75–6
buttons, 99

Buzard, James, 54, 61
Capital (Marx), 4–5, 85, 89
capitalism, 2–3, 49–50, 63, 103, 116
　　consumer, 64, 78
　　industrial, 103, 107
Capper, John, contributor to *Household Words*, 113–16
　　essays, *see under Household Words*, essays
Carey, John, 140
caricature, 31–2
Carlyle, Thomas, 40, 141, 150; *see also Sartor Resartus*
carpets, 99n88
celebrities, 34–6, 79
cemeteries, 126, 134–36, 135n52, 137
Ceylon, 116–18
Chambers's Edinburgh Journal, 2, 24, 25, 26, 40, 52, 86, 102–3
　　continued as *Chambers's Journal of Popular Literature, Science and Arts* 72, 74–5, 86
charity subscriptions, 33–4
charlatans, 45, 50
cheap goods, 52, 91, 105, 113
cheap shops, 53
Chimes, The (Dickens), 14
China, 118–19
Christmas, 39, 107–9
city, the, 8–10, 12, 16, 68–70, 72, 80–81, 143, 149–50; *see also* flâneur; London; Paris; journalism, metropolitan sketch writing
clairvoyants, 45–6
class, 3, 9–11, 41, 67, 84, 104, 132–3
Clemm, Sabine, 104
clothing, fashion, 78, 142, 144–5, 149–50
　　function of, 141–4; *see also* boots; second-hand clothing
　　and identity, 90, 105, 141, 149–51
　　merchandizing of, 90, 110–12
　　and people and things, 146
　　sign-value of, 145–6
coffee, 48
Collins, Wilkie, contributor to *Household Words*, 7, 131
colonialism, 90, 113, 119, 123–4, 145
　　Household Words and, 102
comedy, 32–3, 88–9
commodification, 80–81, 110, 132, 154, 184
　　ethics of, 132

commodities, 25–6, 50, 53, 126–7, 132, 145; *see also* recycled goods; souvenirs
　　contested, 126
　　exchange value and trajectory, 4–6, 17, 156
　　fetishism of, 4, 75, 77, 142, 156
　　Household Words on, 95, 97, 87, 87n27; *see also* process articles
　　imperial transformation of, 101–3, 108, 112, 114–16
commodity culture, 2–5, 129, 145
　　Dickens on, 142
　　global commodity culture, 101–3
　　people and things, of, 4–5, 16, 142
　　　　Dickens on, 3, 87n27
　　　　of production, 103, 87, 87n27, 93, 121
　　　　second-hand trade, 17, 144, 146, 156
　　　　social life of goods, 19, 25, 156
commodity spectacles, *see* spectacle
Conrad, Peter, 61–2
consumer as new middle-class, 1, 7, 41–2, 84–6, 91, 101–3, 105, 145; *see also* food adulteration
　　and authenticity, 37, 40–41, 64
　　cheated and cheating, 44, 50, 50n51, 53
　　moral choices, 116–17
consumer capitalism, 64, 78; *see also* capitalism
cosmopolitanism, 79, 101–2
Costello, Dudley, contributor to *Household Words*, 10, 26, 151
　　essays, *see under Household Words*, essays
cotton, 90, 112, 116–17
counterfeit wares, 40
Coutts, Angela Burdett, 151
Cowling, Mary, 10–11, 67
Cranford (Gaskell), *see under Household Words*, serialized novels
Crewe, Louise, 17, 155
Crystal Palace, 103–7; *see also* Great Exhibition
Curtis, Gerald, 19, 36

Daily Advertiser, 19
Daily Courant, 30, 30n66
Darwin, Bernard, 50
David, Deirdre, 112, 114
death; *see also* cemeteries; funerals; funerary reform
　　and class, 132–3

Index

and clothing, 143
commodification of, 139–40
in Dickens's fiction, 135n52, 140, 143
by machine, 94
marketability of, 46, 126–32
defamiliarization, 13–14
dialogism, 7, 88–9, 107–8, 119
Dickens, Charles, 19, 24n31, 22, 37, 80; *see also under Household Words*, essays; and under separate works
on advertising, 23–4
on the city, 65
criticism of, 22, 37, 140
death fascination, 135n52, 136, 140
fiction of, 3–4, 140, 142
on government, 50n51
on the Great Exhibition, 103
Household Words control, 2, 22
journalism style, 6
and process articles, 85, 97
on second-hand clothing, 142–3
on the *Spectator*, 7–8
on spirits, 39
on tourism, 56–7
Urania Cottage project, 151–2
dioramas, 73, 127
Dixon, Edmund Saul, contributor to *Household Words*, 154
Doctor Dulcamara, 45
Dodd, George, contributor to *Household Words*, 35, 86, 103, 119–20, 130
essays, *see under Household Words*, essays
at *The Penny Magazine*, 85–6, 103
dollhouses, 77–8
dolls, 121–2
dress-lodging, 152–3
Drew, John, 6, 65n7

East India Company, 116–17, 119
economy (England), 3, 7, 84, 101–3
emporium, 75
entertainment, optical entertainments, 73
entertainments; *see also* exhibitions; panoramas; tourism, virtual
entrepreneurs, 34, 50–51, 126, 139–40
essay and essayists, eighteenth-century, 7–9, 66
European markets, 101–3
Evening Intelligencer, 30, 30n66
Examiner, 7

exhibitions, 109–10, 147; *see also* Crystal Palace; Great Exhibition
exhibitionism, 129
exports, 102, 123, 145
eye-witness reporting, 11–12, 86–7

factories, 85, 97–8; *see also* manufacturing
factory accidents, 84, 94–6
Factory Act of 1844, 94
factory tourism, 87n27
factory workers, 93–5
Farina, Jonathan, 87n27
fashion, 78, 142, 144–5, 149–50; *see also* clothing; second-hand clothing
'fashion in undress', 17, 146, 156
military, 150–51
fetishism, 4, 75, 77, 144, 156
first-person narratives, 60, 88–9
Fitzgerald, Percy, contributor to *Household Words*, 2, 22
essays, *see under Household Words*, essays
flâneur, 1, 9–11, 12, 65–66, 65n3, 81, 141
gender and, 10–12
second-hand clothes and, 148, 155
in 'The Key of the Street' (Sala), 68
see also journalism, metropolitan sketch writing
Flint, Christopher, 13–14
food adulteration, 39, 47, 49–50
food markets, 47, 49–50, 102, 126
Forster, John, 2, 8
Foucault, Michel, 113
France, 109–10; *see also* Paris
Fraser, Hilary, 7, 9
Fraser's Magazine, 24, 28, 29, 31
fraud, 39, 44–6, 53
Freedgood, Elaine, 4–5, 60, 86n21, 101n5, 111, 115
free trade, 107–9
Freud, Sigmund, 129
Friedberg, Anne, 66, 106
Frow, John, 5, 54
funerals, 126, 130, 133–6; *see also* Wellington, Duke of, funeral
funerary reform, 126, 132–34
General Interment Bill, 132–4
Gaskell, Elizabeth, contributor to *Household Words*, 15, 101, 114–15, 118, 141; *see also Household Words*, serialized novels

gold refineries, 86–7, 95–6
graveyards, *see* cemeteries
Great Exhibition (1851), 103–7, 119
    importance of, 2–3, 84, 103–5
    Jury reports, 84, 104, 119–20
    nationalism and competition, 102
    satire on, 41
Great Expectations (Dickens), 4, 143
Greenhalgh, Paul, 103n10
Greenwood, James, 152
Gregson, Nicky, 17, 155

hair, 76, 96–7, 130
hair-cutting, 76
Hannay, James, contributor to *Household Words*, 48, 65, 135–6
    essays, *see under Household Words*, essays
Hard Times (Dickens), 16, 47, 83–4, 94, 102
Hassall, Arthur, 48–9
health issues, 47–53, 133–5
Hemstedt, Geoffrey, 45, 154
Hollingshead, John, as contributor to *Household Words*, 15, 17, 22, 35–7, 53, 71–2
    on Dickens, 15, 22
    essays, *see under Household Words*, essays
Hollington, Michael, 65–6
home, the, 3, 69–70
    Victorian, 63, 101–2, 114–15
Horne, Richard, contributor to *Household Words*, 47, 71, 103–4
    essays, *see under Household Words*, essays
horse meat, 47
hotels, 57–8
Household Narrative of Current Events (supplement to *Household Words*), 19
Household Words, 6–8, 10–14, 16–20, 24–5, 41, 64, 66, 84–5
    advertisements in, 16, 19–27, 30, 33–4, 50–51
    business and appearance of, 1–2, 6, 16, 19–22, 65, 87, 98
    contributors, 2, 7, 12–13, 65, 98
    criticism of, 15
    Dickens's role, 2, 6–7, 15, 21–2, 85, 104
    essays, 65, 65n7, 22, 98, 136
        'All Night on the Monument' (Hollingshead), 71

'Amusements of the People, The' (Dickens), 23
'Arcadia' (Sala), 76
'Begging-Letter Writer, The' (Dickens), 45
'Bill-Sticking' (Dickens), 16, 23–4, 24n31
'Biography of a Bad Shilling' (Blanchard), 13–15
'Burns. Viewed as a Hat-Peg' (Collins), 131–2
'Buying in the Cheapest Market' (Hollingshead), 53
'Catalogue's Account of Itself, The' (Morley), 104
'Cattle-Road to Ruin, The' (Horne), 47
'Christmas Pudding, A' (Knight), 107–8
'Christmas Tree, A' (Dickens), 109, 109n43
'Cinnamon Garden, A' (Capper), 116
'Cities in Plain Clothes' (Sala), 54–5, 67
'City of Sudden Death, The' (Lewis), 61
'Coats and Trousers' (Sidney), 110
'Cocoa-Nut Palm, The' (Capper), 116
'Constitutional Trials' (Morley), 47–8
'Cornwall's Gift to Staffordshire' (Dodd), 115
'Counterfeit Presentment, A' (Hollingshead), 35–7
'Country News' (Morley), 33
'Cow with the Iron Tail, The' (Horne), 48
'Curiosities of London' (Sala), 81
'Deadly Lively' (Jerrold), 135
'Death in the Bread-Basket' (Wills and Strange), 48
'Death in the Sugar Plum' (Wills and Strange), 48
'Death in the Teapot' (Wills and Strange), 48
'Departed Beggars' (Wood), 44
'Dirty Cleanliness' (Dixon), 22, 154
'Down Among the Dutchmen' (Fitzgerald), 56

Index

'Down Whitechapel, Far Away' (Sala), 45
'Down Whitechapel Way' (Sala), 67, 75
'Dust or Ugliness Redeemed' (Horne), 154
'Enemy's Charge, An' (Morley), 134–5
'Epsom' (Dickens), 23
'Eyes Made to Order' (Jerrold), 97
'Fairyland in 'Fifty-Four'' (Wills), 107
'Fashion' (Sala), 16, 144–6
'Fencing with Humanity' (Morley), 94–5
'Flower Shows in a Birmingham Hot-House' (Martineau), 122–3
'Food for the Factory' (Jerrold), 90
'Foreign Invasion, The' (Sala), 104–5
'From Paris to Chelmsford' (Sidney), 109–10
'From the Raven in the Happy Family' (Dickens), 133
'Funerals in Paris' (Morley and Wills), 132
'German Advertisements' (Murray and Walker), 25–6
'German Table d' Hôte, A' (Owen), 57
'Ghost of the Cock Lane Ghost, The' (Morley), 46
'Globe in a Square, A' (Morley), 73–4
'Gold and Gems' (Martineau), 86–7, 92, 95
'Golden Newspaper, A' (Keene and Wills), 26
'Good Brushing, A' (Dodd), 121
'Graves and Epitaphs' (Hannay), 135–6
'Great Coffee Question, The' (Hannay), 48
'Great Exhibition and the Little One, The' (Dickens and Horne), 118
'Great Hotel, The' (Sala), 57–8
'Great Invasion, The' (Sala), 71
'Great Red Book, The' (Sala), 80–81
'Ground in the Mill' (Morley), 94
'Home for Homeless Women' (Dickens), 151–2

'House Full of Horrors, A' (Morley), 41
'Houses to Let' (Sala), 23, 31
'House that Jack Built, The' (Dodd), 122
'H.W.' (Dickens and Morley), 90, 98
'Important Rubbish' (Dodd), 153–4
'Indian Wedding, An' (Capper), 123–24
'India-Rubber' (Dodd), 121
'Iron Seamstress, The' (Jerrold), 96
'Jean Raisin' (Dixon), 109
'Journey Due North, A' (Sala), 67
'Kendal Weavers and Weaving' (Martineau), 99n88
'Key of the Street, The' (Sala), 65, 67–9
'Ladies Warehouse, A' (Sidney), 111
'Latest Intelligence from Spirits' (Morley), 45
'Leicester Square' (Sala), 80
'Lively Turtle' (Dickens), 49
'Long Life under Difficulties' (White), 51
'Looking Out of Window' (Morley), 69–70
'Lying Awake' (Dickens), 143
'Manchester Warehouse, A' (Lowe), 112
'Mars a la Mode' (Sala), 151
'Men Made by Machinery' (Morley), 83–4
'Methusaleh Pill, The' (Jerrold), 50–51
'Modern Robbers of the Rhine', (Hunt), 54
'More Places Wanted' (Sala), 32–3
'"Mouth" of China, The' (Ross), 119
'Music in Paving Stones' (Sala), 79
'Nearly Lost on the Alps' (Smith), 60
'Needles' (Martineau), 86, 92, 95, 98, 101
'Nightly Scene in London, A' (Dickens), 68–9
'Nothing Like Leather' (Dodd), 122
'Number Forty-Two' (Capper), 113–14
'Old Clothes!' (Sala), 146–8, 155
'Oranges and Lemons (Capper), 116
'Our Commission' (Dickens), 50n51

'Our Doubles' (Sala), 150
'Our French Watering-Place' (Dickens), 56–7
'Our Phantom Ship: China' (Morley), 119
'Our Phantom Ship: Negro Land' (Morley), 151
'Paper Mill, A' (Dickens and Lemon), 16, 90
'Pasha's New Boat, The' (Horne), 122
'Passing Faces" (Lynn), 10–12
'Peasants of British India, The' (Capper), 123–4
'Penny Wisdom' (Dodd), 91, 153
'Perfidious Patmos' (Sala), 102
'Photographers' (Payn), 37n92
'Photography' (Morley and Wills), 34–5
'Picture Advertising in South America' (Costello), 26
'Pill-Box, A' (Dodd), 35
'Plate Glass' (Dickens and Wills), 87–9, 96
'Play' (Sala), 66
'Poisons Sold Here!' (Morley), 48
'Preliminary Word, A' (Dickens), 21
'Preservation in Destruction' (Lewis), 62
'Private History of the Palace of Glass, The' (Wills), 106
'Rabbit-Skins' (Jerrold), 154
'Railway Dreaming' (Dickens), 143
'Railway Waifs and Strays' (Wills and Hill), 148
'Rainbow Making' (Martineau), 98
'Roving Englishman: The Great Do, The' (Murray), 54
'Ruins with Silver Keys' (Jerrold), 63
'Russian Stranger, A' (Dodd), 122
'Scholastic' (Morley), 28–9
'Second-Hand Sovereigns' (Sala), 147
'Secrets of the Gas, The' (Sala), 67
'Several Heads of Hair' (Dodd), 96–7, 130
'Shawls' (Martineau), 93–4
'Some Account of an Extraordinary Traveller' (Dickens), 73–4, 107
'Spirit Business, The' (Dickens), 46

'Spirits over the Water' (Payn), 46
'Starvation of an Alderman' (Morley), 48–9
'Subscription List, The' (Jerrold and Wills), 33–4
'Things Departed' (Sala), 22–3
'Trading in Death' (Dickens), 126–31
'Travels in Cawdor Street' (Sala), 42–4
'Unsettled Neighbourhood, An' (Dickens), 80–81
'Use and Abuse of the Dead' (Morley), 136–7, 137n63
'Vesuvius in Eruption' (Wreford), 61
'Walking-Sticks' (Dodd), 120–21
'Wanderings in India' (Lang), 114
'Want Places' (Sala), 32–3
'Waste' (Capper), 153
'Way to Clean Rivers, A' (Morley), 154
'Well-Authenticated Rappings' (Dickens), 39, 48
'What There Is in a Button' (Martineau), 99
'Where Are They?' (Sala), 26–7, 149
'Why People Let Lodgings" (Jerrold), 28
'Wonders of Nails and Screws, The' (Martineau), 90, 98
'Your Life or Your Likeness' (White), 34–5
'Yourself at Turin' (Russell), 57
on factory accidents, 94–6
on food adulteration, 39, 48–50
on funerary reform, 126–31, 134–35, 139–40
on the Great Exhibition, 41, 103, 106
on imperialism, 114, 116–17
on manufacturing, 83–5, 83–9, 96–7
Office Book, 2
poetry
'Smithfield Bull to His cousin of Nineveh, The' (Horne), 118
'Voice from the Factory, A' (Prince), 93
process articles, 15, 84–7, 87n27, 97
glass-making, 87–9
on reform, 41, 50n51, 64
serialized novels
    Cranford (Gaskell), 101, 118, 123, 141

Hard Times (Dickens), 16, 47, 83–4, 94, 102
North and South (Gaskell), 76, 102, 114–15
style, 3–4, 11–13, 15–16, 24–5, 87–90, 92, 116
supplements of, 19
on tourism, 54–62
Household Words Almanac, 19
Huett, Lorna, 21, 118
Hunt, Frederick Knight, contributor to *Household Words*, 54

identity, 3–4, 41–2, 44–5, 132–33, 138, 141, 149–50, 156; *see also* alienation, urban life and
clothing as expression of, 141, 153, 156
male, 60, 77, 131, 141, 151
metropolitan, 26, 141
middle-class, 41–2, 53–4, 60
national, 1, 79, 102
Illustrated London News, 79, 103
imperialism and empire, 101–3, 110–119, 123
commodity exchange and exploitation, 123–24, 145
exports, 113–14, 123–24, 144–45
free trade, 107–8
imports, 111–113, 99, 99n88, 117–20, 145, 149
impostors, 45
India, 116–17
industrial disease, 95–6
industrialism, 19, 47, 49–50, 63, 87, 126
industrialization, 42, 94–5
representation in journals, 87–90
industrial tourist tale, 85, 86, 87n27; *see also Household Words*, process articles
inventorying, 8–15, 75–7
it-narratives, 13–15; *see also Household Words*, process articles

Jerrold, Douglas, 14, 22
Jerrold, William Blanchard, contributor to *Household Words*, 10, 14, 22, 28, 33–4, 48, 51–2, 63, 65, 90, 96–7, 135–36, 154
essays, *see under Household Words*, essays
jewellery, 78
Joseph, Gerhard, 4, 83n1
journalism, 6–8, 12, 19–21 *see also* essay

and essayists, eighteenth-century criticism of, 6–7, 9
investigative, 17, 66, 68
metropolitan sketch writing, 8–12, 20, 65–7, 81
news and newspapers, 1, 6, 7, 19, 26, 27, 50
penny press, 2, 21
spiritualist press, 45–6

Kappel, Andrew, 37
Keene, John, contributor to *Household Words*, 26
essays, *see under Household Words*, essays
Ketabgian, Tamara, 84–5, 92
Knight, Charles, as contributor to *Household Words*, 7, 26, 86, 90–91, 105, 115
editor of *The Penny Magazine*, 7, 85
essays, *see under Household Words*, essays

labour, commodification of, 84, 89–90, 107–8, 142
Marx on, 89, 94, 142
production of commodities, 4, 7, 17, 84, 87, 145
second-hand commodities and, 17, 144
universal exchange of, 107–8
lace, 111–12
Lancet, 47–8, 50
Lang, John, contributor to *Household Words*, 114
Language of the Walls: And a Voice from the Shop Windows. Or, The Mirror of Commercial Roguery, The (Burns), 25, 25n39, 50
Last Days of Pompeii, The (Bulwer Lytton), 61
Leigh, Percival, contributor to *Household Words*, 133–4
Lemon, Mark, contributor to *Household Words*, 90
Logan, Thad, 3, 133–4
Lohrli, Anne, 2
London, 8, 10, 20, 65–6, 70–71, 81
London Magazine, 7
London Monument, 71
Lucifer matches, 91–2
Lynn, Eliza, 10, 10n53, 11–12

182 Commodity Culture in Dickens's Household Words

MacCannell, Dean, 40, 59
machines, anthropomorphic properties, 90–91, 93, 95–6
  and cheap production, 111–12
  prostheses, 83–4, 89–90, 92, 96–7
Maidment, Brian, 6, 85
malachite, 122
Mandler, Peter, 61–2
manufacturing, 91, 97–8, 111, 121, 145; *see also* raw materials
  and labor, 91–3, 96
  warehouses, 105, 110–13
Martineau, Harriet, contributor to *Household Words*, 7, 86, 87n27, 93–5, 98, 99, 116–17, 122–23
  essays, *see under Household Words*, essays
  personal life, 95
Marx, Karl, 4–5, 85, 89, 94, 96, 142–3, 150, 155
mass-produced goods, 3, 41, 91
mass-production, 3, 15, 91, 96, 98
medicine, 48, 137–38; *see also* quackery
  patent, 23, 33, 45, 50–51
  and science, 137–39
mendicancy, 44
merchandizing, 53, 74–6, 113
metamorphosis, 69, 80–81
metropolis, *see* city, the
metropolitan travel writing, *see* journalism, metropolitan sketch writing
Miller, Andrew, 2–3, 84, 145
Miller, J. Hillis, 3–4
miniaturization, 73, 77–8
Mitford, Mary Russell, 131
morality in the marketplace, 39–40, 44, 52–3, 116–17
Morison's Pill, 20, 23, 40, 50, 106
Morley, Henry, (contributor to *Household Words*), 17, 29, 33–4, 41, 45–6, 48, 65, 83–4, 90, 94–5, 98, 104, 106, 116–17, 132, 134–9, 151, 154
  campaign against factory accidents, 94–5
  medical background, 48, 136n63, 139
  essays, *see under Household Words*, essays
Murray, Grenville, contributor to *Household Words*, 54
Murray, John Fisher, 21
Murray's Guidebook, 57, 59, 60
Musée des Souverains, 147

museums, 62, 64, 151

nationalism, 103–4, 127–8
Nead, Lynda, 10n53, 65, 75, 138–9
Neapolitan prisoners, 56
'Needlemaking' (A.W.), 95
needles, 86, 92, 95, 98, 101, 112
New Monthly Magazine, 7
New Poor Law, 137–8
New York Herald, 37
North and South (Gaskell), *see under Household Words*, serialized novels
novel, Victorian, 3–6, 19, 101–2, 114–15, 142

object narratives, *see* it-narratives; *Household Words*, process articles
Oost, Regina, 34n82
orientalism, 50, 55, 75, 89
Owen, William, contributor to *Household Words*, 57

panoramas, 57, 58, 59, 66, 70, 72–5, 128n19, 129n23
paparazzi, 34–7
papier mâché, 122–23
Paris, cemetery and morgues, 132, 135–6, 143
  flâneur and, 12, 65
  metropolitan life, 9–10, 68, 79
parody, 31–2, 125
Parr's Life Pill, 51
patents, 40, 51
Payn, James, contributor to *Household Words*, 37n92, 46, 136n57
Penny Magazine, 85–90
periodical press, *see* journalism; and under separate titles
Perrott, Phillipe, 151–2
Pettitt, Clare, 84, 86
Pfeiffer, Ida, 119
photography, 34–37, 37n92
  Mayall's Portrait Gallery, 34, 34n82
physiognomy, 10, 11, 40, 67, 69, 76, 81
physiologies, 9–10, 20, 65
Pickwick Papers, The (Dickens), 68, 139
plate glass, 96, 128–9
Plunkett, John, 35
Poerio, Carlo, 56
Pointon, Marcia, 130
politics, *Household Words* and, 56, 56n96
Pompeii, 61–2

Porter, Roy, 50, 51–2
Prince, John Critchley, contributor to *Household Words*, 93
process articles, *see under Household Words*
prostheses, *see under* machines
prostitution, 76–7, 138–9, 152–3
 reform, Urania Cottage project, 151–3
provenance, 8–9, 130, 130n31
Public Ledger, 30, 30n66
puff, 24, 36, 50, 130
Puff (in Sheridan's *The Critic*) 30
Punch, 14, 36, 55, 70, 72–3, 74, 125–6
Pykett, Lyn, 11

quackery, 40, 45, 50–52; *see also* medicine, patent

Radin, Margaret Jane, 126, 132
railways, 80, 148
raw materials, 89–91, 97, 99, 102, 119–20
readers, Victorian, 1, 7, 12–13, 27
realism, 4, 73, 101, 142
recycled goods, 17, 90–91, 142, 153–6; *see also* second-hand clothing
relics, 62, 63, 130–32, 147, 155
resurrectionism; *see under* bodies, commerce in; bodysnatching
Richards, Thomas, 2–3, 25n39, 105, 127n15, 145
Richardson, Ruth, 136–8
Risorgimento, 56
Roof, Judith, 128
Ross, Thomasina, contributor to *Household Words*, 119
Roston, Murray, 4, 142
rubber, 121
ruins, 62–4
Russell, William Howard, contributor to *Household Words*, 57
 essays, *see under Household Words*, essays

Said, Edward, 101
Sala, George Augustus, as contributor to *Household Words*, 7, 9–10, 13, 15, 26–7, 29, 31–3, 42–5, 54–5, 57–60, 65–9, 71, 75, 81, 102, 129n23
 and clothing, 104–5, 142–51, 153, 155
 on Dickens, 22, 22n19, 24n31
 essays, *see under Household Words*, essays
 as flâneur, 9, 12, 65, 67–9, 78–81
 satirized by Arnold, 13

style of writing, 15, 30, 42
Sartor Resartus (Carlyle), 141, 146–7
Saturday Review, 15, 140
Saville House, 80
Schwartz, Vanessa, 135n52
science, 40, 49, 91, 134, 137–39, 153
 Chemistry, 91
second-hand clothing, defined, 14, 17, 146–9, 152–6
 Dickens's interest in, 142–3
 and dress-lodging, 152–3
 and former owners, 143–4, 148
 and issues of labor, 144
 people and things and, 16–17, 156
second-hand cultures, 17, 155
second-hand shops, 148; *see also* commodities
 descriptions, *Sketches by Boz* (Dickens), 142–3
 and use of the senses, 155, 155n70
 versus window-shopping, 155
Sennett, Richard, 66, 141, 144, 149–50
Seven Curses of London, The (Greenwood), 152
sewage waste, 154
sewing machines, 96
shamming, 40, 42, 43–4, 78, 87
shawls, 93–4
Sheridan, Richard Brinsley, 30
shops, 78–80
'Shops, Shopkeepers, Shopmen, and Shop Morality', 40, 53, 102–3
shop windows, 74–5, 128–29
Sidney, Samuel, contributor to *Household Words*, 110
Simmel, Georg, 9, 10, 70, 156
Sinnema, Peter, 6n31, n32, 127
Sketches by Boz (Dickens), 12, 20, 142–3, 154
Slater, Michael, 6, 14, 22n17
slavery, 116–17, 151
Smith, Albert, 57–9; *see also* 'Ascent of Mont Blanc'
Smith, Charles Manby, 24
Smith, Graham, 7–8
Smith, Thomas Southwood, 136n63
Society for the Diffusion of Useful Knowledge, 7, 86
souvenirs, 41, 43, 63, 129–30; *see also* relics
speaking objects, *see* it-narratives; *also Household Words*, process articles

spectacle, 81, 127; *see also* Great Exhibition; panoramas; Wellington, Duke of, funeral
Spectator, 7–9, 66
spectators, 8–9, 70, 128–9; *see also* flâneur; journalism, metropolitan travel writing; tourists
spiritualism, 39, 45–6
Spiritual Telegraph, The, 46
Stallybass, Peter, 142, 156n74
steam-engines, 54, 84–5, 96
Steele, Richard, 7–8, 66
Stephen, James Fitzjames, 140, 140n79
Stewart, Susan, 41, 43, 78, 130n26, 130n31, 155n70,
Strange, Charles, contributor to *Household Words*, 48
    essays, *see under Household Words*, essays
Sussman, Herbert, 4, 83
Sydney Morning Herald, 26

tea, 15, 21
tea trays, 123
testimonials, 28–9, 51
thing culture, 4–5
Times, The, 23, 25, 26, 26n46, 28–9, 29n58, 32, 127
Tipping, 39, 46
tourism, 53–63
    authenticity and, 40–41, 53, 56, 64
    continental travel, 57, 61–2
    importance of, 63–4
    origins, 53–4, 61–2
    virtual, 58, 72–4, 107
tourists, 40–41, 54–7, 61–3
toys, 77–8
trade, European markets, 101–2
traveller, versus the tourist, 63
Trilling, Lionel, 40, 44
Tweedale, Geoffrey, 88

undertakers, 132–3, 137–8
uniforms, 110–11, 150–53
Urania Cottage project, 151–3
urban experience, 26–7, 80–81, 141, 143–4; *see also* city, the; London; Paris
urban sketch writers, *see under* flâneur; *also* journalism, metropolitan sketch writing

vagrancy, in 'The Key of the Street' (Sala), 68–9
value, use-value and exchange-value, 142, 154–5
Van Ghent, Dorothy, 3
Vesuvius eruption, 60–61
Victorian Contexts (Roston), 4n18, 142
visual culture, 73–5
voyeurism, 66, 69–70, 129, 141

Wakley, Thomas, 47–8, 50
walking-sticks, 120
waste, 153–56
waste traders, 154
weaving, 117, 93, 99n88
Wechsler, Judith, 10, 11, 20n6, 70
Wellington, Duke of, diorama of life, 127
    and exhibition of uniforms, in 'Mars a la Mode' (Sala), 151
    funeral, 126–31, 127n7
    souvenirs, 35, 129–31
White, James, contributor to *Household Words*, 34–5, 51n59
Whitlock, Tammy, 53, 64
Wicke, Jennifer, 19, 20, 22
Williamson, Judith, 25, 29, 30
Wills, W.H., contributor to *Household Words*, 1, 6, 25–6, 27, 34–5, 37, 48, 87–9, 96, 104, 106–7, 132, 148
    sub-editor of *Household Words*, 12, 13, 16
    essays, *see under Household Words*, essays
Wilson, Elizabeth, 142–3
Adorned in Dreams, 143
windows, 69–70, 128–29
window-shopping, 74–5, 155
women, commodities and, 111
    as factory workers, 89–90, 92
    and the flâneur, 10–12, 10n53
    personal advertisements, 32–3
    poverty and, 138–9
    prostitution and, 76–7, 138–9
Woolf, Virginia, 146
workhouse, 137–8
Wyld, James, 73–4
Wynne, Deborah, 103, 104
Wynter, Andrew, contributor to *Household Words*, 10, 95n67
Our Social Bees, 25, 26,

Young, Paul, 107–8